D1242524

Ruth and Esther:
Women of Faith

Other Books by the Author

Thru the Bible with J. Vernon McGee, Vols. I–V
The Best of J. Vernon McGee

RUTH AND ESTHER:
Women of Faith

J. VERNON McGEE

THOMAS NELSON PUBLISHERS
Nashville

Published in Nashville, Tennessee, by Thomas Nelson, Inc. and distributed
in Canada by Lawson Falle, Ltd., Cambridge, Ontario.

Printed in the United States of America.

Scripture quotations are from the King James Version.

Ruth: the Romance of Redemption was first published in 1943. The Thomas
Nelson edition was first published in 1981. *Esther: the Romance of Providence*
was first published by Thomas Nelson Publishers in 1982.

ISBN 0-8407-3119-1

To My Wife

RUTH

*who worthily wears
the name of the maid from Moab,
and who bears many traits of character
which make her an ideal namesake.
Her presence in the home
made a rich contribution to
the life of a minister of
the Lord Jesus Christ,
for she has been able to say
with Ruth the Moabitess,
"Thy God my God."*

• CONTENTS •

BOOK ONE: *Ruth*

BOOK TWO: *Esther*

• PREFACE •

The subject of redemption has been studied and interpreted continuously since the days of Paul. It is not possible to make a startling new contribution to so rich a theme as this, for theories of redemption have sprung up like mushrooms in every age. Another word on this subject will only increase the babel of voices. However, there is one aspect of the topic that has been almost entirely neglected. That is the Kinsman-Redeemer feature. As the Book of Ruth is the only historical illustration in the Bible of the Hebrew *goel*, the Book of Ruth makes a true contribution to this already crowded field. The conflicting theories of redemption would have been delivered from extreme and radical positions if this little brochure had been given the place it rightly deserves. The law of Moses excluded the Moabitess, and the theories of men have excluded the book that bears her name.

I have made no attempt to exhaust the subject of redemption, but rather to highlight the relationship of the Book of Ruth to redemption. Here, redemption is

told in the language of romance. The terms of the marketplace, the clink of silver on the counter, and the
shoptalk of buying and selling are entirely omitted
from its simple pages. The language of life, love, and
light is spoken, the language understood by simple,
sinful folk.

As for the Book of Esther, it is my prayer that these
simple studies may encourage the pilgrim who has lost
his way in the dark mountains of life. Many have
adopted the attitude that luck and chance control the
destiny of this world. They sit gambling at the table of
time. Others have taken a fatalistic attitude toward the
future. There is nothing to do but sit in sloth and
gloom, waiting until their number comes up.

But as you will learn from the study of Esther, God is
the coach sitting on the bench on the sidelines of time.
You can listen to his voice: "You can so run that you
may obtain." At any rate the game of life is thrilling.
The whistle has blown. Now listen to the coach!

• BOOK ONE •

Ruth

· 1 ·

A Story of Love and Grace

The Book of Ruth has been recognized as a literary gem in most unexpected quarters. It is reported that Dr. Samuel Johnson, the literary giant of the eighteenth century, made a copy of the Book of Ruth and read it before a London club as a production he had recently read.[1] The club, thinking it was a modern composition, was loud and unanimous in its praises of the book. Then Dr. Johnson informed them that it was taken from a book which they all rejected—the Bible.

The beauty and excellence of this story cannot escape the most casual reader. This little brochure records the love story of the maid from Moab. It reveals the power of passionate, pure love. It tells, first of all, the strong attachment of Ruth to her mother-in-law, "for love is strong as death." It records how a romance triumphed over racial and religious barriers and how two hearts were joined together "with bands of love." The Book of Ruth is a laborato-

---

[1]Robert Lee, *The Outlined Bible* (Glasgow: Pickering and Inglis, n.d.), Analysis No. 8.

ry demonstration that "the greatest of these is love" (1 Cor. 13:13).

The most remarkable feature of the entire book is that the word *love* is entirely omitted from the narrative. It does not occur even once. This is altogether amazing when it is recognized that our modern age uses the term *love* frequently in all of its literature. Every novel, every song, and every play abounds with a superfluity *ad nauseam* of this word. It is certainly overworked in an age that boasts of sophisticated genius. Perhaps the literary lights today might learn from this love story that the most ardent passion and the deepest devotion do not require the raven-like repetition of this much abused word. The most precious object will become soiled by much handling, and the word *love* becomes commonplace by constant use.

What beautiful restraint is exercised in this simple story; yet what soul-stirring passion of a noble and strong man and a beautiful and queenly woman is portrayed for us. On the human plane, this book tells of the sanctity of domestic life and the holiness of marital love. It lifts marriage to a very high position. It exalts true manhood and virtuous womanhood. It gives the lie to the modern triangle, and it condemns the evil of divorce. The Book of Ruth blesses the marriage vow. It sets before the reader the high ideals of wedlock in the time of Samson.

The Bible has been libeled by some critics as a man's book, in which woman is neglected or ignored. Like most criticism, this caricature of the Bible is built upon a false assumption. The Book of Ruth contributes to the destruction of this false notion. There are two books in the Bible that bear the names of women. They tell the heart-story of two noble women. These are the Books of Ruth and Esther. Ruth tells the story of a gentile girl who married an Israelite; Esther tells the story of a Jewish maiden who married a Gentile. In the New Testament there is one book written to a woman: The second epistle of John is addressed "unto the elect lady and her children" (2 John 1:1). Woman's place is prominent in the Bible; she is not ignored. The Book of Ruth tells the life story of a gentile girl who "did build the house of Israel" and of one who was "famous in Bethlehem." The Book of Ruth is essentially a woman's story, and God has set His seal of approval upon it by its inclusion in the divine library.

The Jews ascribed an unusual importance to this book. In the national life of Israel it figured prominently. During the Feast of Pentecost it was read. Dr. Gaebelein placed it with four other books that were read during the five great feasts of the Jews. He wrote:

> Five books are called by the Jews "Megilloth" and are read by them at different feasts commemorating past events. The Song of Solomon is read during Passover; Ruth at Pentecost; Lamentations on the ninth day of the month Ab in memory of the destruction of Jerusalem; Ecclesiastes is read during the Feast of Tabernacles and Esther they read when they celebrate Purim.[2]

This seemingly uneventful story of an insignificant family during the days of national decline in Israel was given a place of unusual importance. It would

[2]A.C. Gaebelein, *The Annotated Bible* (New York: "Our Hope" Publication, 1915), Vol. II, p. 117.

appear on first examination that its position was out
of all proportion to the merits of the story. On more
careful consideration, this book looms on the sky-
line of Scripture as a book of skyscraper significance. The very fact that it was read on the Day of
Pentecost should be thought-provoking to the Christian. Pentecost suggests the first birthday of the church.
Pentecost marks the Bethlehem of the Holy Spirit, for
He came on that day to be made flesh; "Know ye not
that your body is the temple of the Holy Ghost which
is in you?" (1 Cor. 6:19).

Pentecost is the line of demarcation between law
and grace. It marks the ending of the age of law and
the beginning of the age of grace. The Book of Ruth
tells the story of grace. It tells the story of how a
gentile girl, whom the law condemned, was brought
under the wings of the Lord God of Israel. How could
she enter when the law said, "An Ammonite or Moabite
shall not enter the congregation of the LORD" (Deut.
23:3)? Ruth was brought all the way in and every step
of the way by grace. She believed Boaz, and he
brought her into his heart and home. By grace was
she saved through faith.

This story comes from the period of the judges, a
time of political decay, moral degradation, and spiritual degeneration which began after the death of
Joshua and continued to the time of Samuel. This
decadent era extended over a period of about four
hundred years. In many respects these were the darkest
days in the history of Israel. The Israelites had been
redeemed from Egypt by blood, brought safely through
the wilderness by power, and delivered to the Land
of Promise personally by God. It would appear that

with such a propitious background, they were on the
threshold of great blessing and much prosperity. Certainly such an auspicious entrance afforded high ex-
pectations of the future. Their tragic failure makes the
gloom all the more impressive. The story of Ruth
stands in bright contrast to the dark ages of the
judges.

The Book of Ruth is unique in that it reveals the
only example in the Bible of the kinsman-redeemer at
work. Herein is a detailed account of the Hebrew *goel*
functioning in his full capacity. There could be no
redemption for either property or the individual without the person and presence of a kinsman-redeemer.
Unless the work of the kinsman-redeemer is adequately apprehended, there cannot be a comprehension of the work of redemption. Redemption requires
a kinsman-redeemer.

Boaz furnishes us with a miniature figure of the
Lord Jesus Christ as the Redeemer. Boaz is the type,
the Christ is the archetype. A full treatment of the
theme of redemption necessitates a careful consideration of the Book of Ruth. This, however, has been
neglected by many of the reputable writers on the
theme of redemption. Jonathan Edwards in the *History of Redemption*, Stuart Robinson in the *Discourse of
Redemption*, and Sir Robert Anderson in *For Us Men*
entirely omitted any reference to the Book of Ruth.
This seems all the more remarkable as each one of
these writers traced the history of redemption through
the Old Testament, paying particular attention to the
figures and types.

As a result of this method of writing, redemption
has come to mean a cold business transaction, devoid

of the personal element. God did not buy man in the slave market of sin as a chattel is bought and sold. Redemption is not the story of a sharp trader who made a profitable investment in the markets of trade. No, a thousand times no! Redemption is the love story of a Kinsman who neither counted the cost nor figured up the profit and loss, but for joy paid an exorbitant price for one that He loved. The Book of Ruth declares that redemption is not a business transaction but a love affair. The personal element must not be withdrawn from the doctrine of redemption or the most vital part will be sacrificed.

The presence of the Book of Ruth in the Old Testament is justified by a fourfold purpose. Any one of these purposes furnishes a worthy motive for including it in the canon of Scripture. They are given in the reverse order of their importance: (1) the historical purpose; (2) the dispensational purpose; (3) the genealogical purpose; and (4) the doctrinal purpose.

·2·

The Historical Purpose

The record of one small family is contained in the Book of Ruth, and certainly their story is not spectacular. However, it does throw a most important sidelight upon the times of the judges. The period of the judges, as has been stated previously, was a day of decline and decay. *Ichabod* was written over this phase of the history of Israel. There is a proverb that identifies this time of the judges. It is: "Righteousness exalteth a nation: but sin is a reproach to any people" (Prov. 14:34).

That proverb furnishes a philosophy of history for all nations. The silent ruins and dead ashes of destroyed civilizations bear silent but eloquent testimony to this profound truth. Every nation in antiquity has demonstrated the truth of that statement. The time of the judges is but a mere page out of a long list. Every nation that has followed righteousness has been exalted. Every nation that has taken the well-beaten path of sin has finally gone down into the dust of oblivion, fit only for the spade of the archaeologist.

Israel took the familiar path of sin and reproach, and the ignominy came upon them like an avalanche. War and long periods of servitude punctuated this period indelibly. Faithlessness to God and immorality characterized this age. However, there were rare instances of those in the nation who remained true to the God of Abraham, Isaac, and Jacob. These were fit vessels with which He worked.

The incidents in Ruth deal with some who remained true to God. Here we have recorded life at its best during that evil day. MacNaughton considered Ruth "a kind of appendix to the book of Judges."[1] The Book of Ruth does furnish us with very important clues to the times of the judges by way of contrast, but this does not necessitate considering it as a part of the Book of Judges. The Book of Ruth stands on its own foundation. It shows that in the darkest days God was working out His purposes in the lives of individuals who were rightly related to Him. God is always interested in the private affairs of humble folk, and this book tells how He moves in their lives. God touched the simple lives of these unknown village folk and made them sublime. The Book of Ruth is a pearl in the swine pen of the judges. When God touched the lives of these pastoral people, He brought them into the light of His program for eternity.

We are accustomed to making a distinction between the sacred and profane. That is a false delineation. We automatically classify some things as sacred and some as secular. Before God all life is sacred. Even the monotonous duties of the day are not profane. Wash-

---

[1]G.D. MacNaughton, *Two Hebrew Idylls* (Edinburgh: Oliphant, Anderson, and Ferrier, 1901), p. 11.

ing dishes, gleaning wheat, standing at the work bench, sitting in the office, and digging a ditch are all sacred when lived in the presence of God. The Christian is called upon to live his entire life unto the Lord: "Whether therefore ye eat, or drink, or whatsoever ye do, do all to the glory of God" (1 Cor. 10:31).

The historical significance of Ruth is apparent when considered in relation to the little town of Bethlehem. The story lifts Bethlehem out of "the thousands of Judah" and identifies it as the city of David. It rescues Bethlehem from oblivion. The story of the birth of Christ in Bethlehem loses much of its meaning unless it is seen in light of the Book of Ruth.

The question is sometimes asked: Why was Bethlehem chosen as the birthplace of Jesus? The Book of Ruth answers that question. The first time that the mention of Bethlehem occurs in Scripture is in connection with an incident that took place before Israel became a nation in Egypt. In giving birth to Benjamin, Rachel sacrificed her life and was buried there: "And Rachel died, and was buried in the way to Ephrath, which is Bethlehem" (Gen. 35:19). It was not the birth of Benjamin that gave prominence to this place, but the birth of Another.

Jacob never forgot Bethlehem out of all the places that he had visited. When he was an old man and about to die in Egypt, he remembered Bethlehem as the place where he had buried his beautiful Rachel.

And as for me, when I came from Padan, Rachel died by me in the land of Canaan in the way, when yet there was but a little way to come unto Ephrath: and I buried her there in the way of Ephrath; the same is Bethlehem. (Gen. 48:7.)

Jacob remembered Bethlehem because of a death, but the world remembers Bethlehem because of a birth.

There is not another important reference to Bethlehem until we come to the Book of Ruth. Ibzan, one of the judges, was born there, but only casual mention is made of the fact. All the events of importance in the Book of Ruth center around Bethlehem. The family of Elimelech came from Bethlehem. Naomi returned with Ruth to Bethlehem. Boaz lived at Bethlehem. Ruth was redeemed at Bethlehem. She was wed to Boaz at Bethlehem. Her son, Obed, was born at Bethlehem. Ruth lived the remainder of her life at Bethlehem, and we are to infer that she died and was buried at Bethlehem. It is the story in the Book of Ruth that brought Bethlehem into the family of David. Had not the events of this story taken place, David would never have been born in Bethlehem, and likewise Christ would never have been born there. In other words, it was the coming of Ruth from Moab that made possible the coming of Christ to Bethlehem. When the Bible record is examined as a whole, then the Book of Ruth is seen as one of the most important cogs in the wheel of God's plan.

Three hundred years after David, the prophet of God announced that Bethlehem would be the birthplace of the Messiah, which forever established this place as the most famous spot in the world, with the exception of Jerusalem.

But thou, Bethlehem Ephratah, though thou be little among the thousands of Judah, yet out of thee shall he come forth unto me that is to be ruler in Israel; whose goings forth have been from of old, from everlasting (Mic. 5:2).

The amazing thing about this prophecy is not that Bethlehem was chosen as the place of birth, but how the prophecy came to be fulfilled. This prophecy was uttered over seven hundred years before the event actually took place. During that time the house of David was taken from the throne, the city of Jerusalem was demolished, and the nation was carried away captive to a strange land. In the face of these circumstances, it made the fulfillment of this prophecy unlikely. "When the fulness of the time was come, God sent forth his Son..." (Gal. 4:4), but the mother of the Child dwelt in Nazareth. There was no earthly reason why she should go to Bethlehem. The Davidic family were now peasants, and Bethlehem was no longer the place of refuge for them. How could Jesus be born in Bethlehem?

God was moving. When Caesar Augustus affixed his seal to a tax bill, calling upon the Roman world for a new assessment to keep its legions marching upon the Roman roads to the far-flung corners of its great empire, little did he realize that he was but a puppet in the hands of an omnipotent God. He was carrying out the decree of a power greater than he. Luke, with an historian's pen, wrote, "And it came to pass in those days, that there went out a decree from Caesar Augustus, that all the world should be taxed" (Luke 2:1). This taxing had repercussions throughout the empire. Out in the hinterlands of a small country in the out-of-the-way village of Nazareth, some descendants of Boaz and Ruth started on a long trek toward

Bethlehem that the Word of God might be literally
fulfilled. Luke also wrote:

> And Joseph also went up from Galilee, out of the city
> of Nazareth, into Judea, unto the city of David, which
> is called Bethlehem; (because he was of the house and
> lineage of David:) to be taxed with Mary his espoused
> wife, being great with child. And so it was, that, while
> they were there, the days were accomplished that she
> should be delivered. And she brought forth her firstborn
> son, and wrapped him in swaddling clothes, and laid
> him in a manger; because there was no room for them
> in the inn (Luke 2:4–7).

The ancestral home of David was not there to
receive them. The redeemed property of Boaz was no
longer theirs. They sought refuge with the beasts of
the field, but God's Word was carried out to the letter,
and the Book of Ruth was justified and found its
proper place in the program of God.

> O little town of Bethlehem,
>   How still we see thee lie!
> Above thy deep and dreamless sleep
>   The silent stars go by;
> Yet in thy dark streets shineth.
>   The everlasting Light;
> The hopes and fears of all the years
>   Are met in thee tonight.
> —Phillips Brooks

· 3 ·

The Dispensational Purpose

The dispensational aspect of the Book of Ruth looms significant to many Bible students.[1] In fact, some see this as the supreme objective. In the departure of the family of Elimelech from the land of Israel to the land of Moab, many see a picture of Israel today. Despite the restoration of Israel, many of the Jews are absent from the land of Canaan and are scattered throughout the world. Ruth, the gentile girl, was brought into the place of blessing during that interval. The church today occupies the place of blessing and corresponds to Ruth. Someday the church will be perfectly united to One who is greater than Boaz. In that day all of the Jews will return to the Land of Promise, and blessing will ensue.

The position of the book in the Old Testament canon has been noticed by some Bible teachers. It is not accidental that the Book of Ruth appears after

---

[1]Henry Moorhouse, *Ruth, The Moabitess* (Chicago: Fleming H. Revell Co., 1881), p. 5.

Judges and before First Samuel. Judges tells the story
of the failure of the theocracy under the Mosaic
system, and First Samuel tells of the setting up of the
monarchy. Between the failure and rejection and the
kingdom there occurs Ruth, the gentile bride. Between the rejection of the nation of Israel and the
setting up of Christ's kingdom on the earth there is
found the church, the bride of the Lamb.

Here we find God's salvation going forth to the
Gentiles in spite of the failure of Israel. Dispensationally,
this little book sets forth the age of grace. It tells how
the lowly foreigner, ostracized by the law of Moses,
found redemptive rest in Boaz. He exercised grace in
her behalf and thereby brought her under the protection of his name and home. Ruth is thought by many
to be a type of the church and Boaz a type of Christ.[2]
There is a beautiful analogy here that is worthy of
much thought, but there is a real danger of over-
emphasizing this interpretation.

There are seven marriage types in the Old Testament that depict some phase of the relationship that
exists between Christ and the church.[3] These are:
Adam and Eve, Isaac and Rebekah, Joseph and
Asenath, Moses and Zipporah, Ruth and Boaz, David
and Abigail, and Solomon and the shepherdess in the
Song of Solomon. Ruth and Boaz set before us the
grace that exists between Christ and His church.
There is no lovelier figure used to describe the relationship between Christ and the church than that of

---

[2]F.W. Grant, *The Numerical Bible* (New York: Loizeaux Brothers, 1892), Vol. II,
pp. 268–283.
[3]Lewis S. Chafer, *Systematic Theology* (Grand Rapids, Mich.: Zondervan,
1947), p. 8.

bridegroom and bride. There is no more beautiful type in the Old Testament than Boaz and Ruth as they represent grace. We hesitate to develop this purpose of the Book of Ruth for fear of wandering off into the field of speculation. This is a fruitful study, pregnant with deep spiritual meaning, but we shall leave it for wiser heads and deeper hearts to develop.

· 4 ·

The Genealogical Purpose

The inadequacy of a brief definition as to the purpose of the Bible is self-evident, but these brief statements sometimes contain pertinent facts. This is true in the following summary: The purpose of the Old Testament is to furnish a reliable genealogy of the Lord Jesus Christ. Certainly there needs to be no insistence on the fact that the line which leads to Christ from Adam is the one which is persistently followed in Scripture. The story of that family is recorded in detail, while mere mention is made of more prominent personalities of the day.

The Book of Genesis has as its primary purpose the listing of the generations of a family.[1] Eleven generations are enumerated. The method adopted by the Divine Author is to record all the offspring of the chosen line and then to omit a detailed account of the rejected line and give a brief summary of the reasons for the omission. The record of the chosen line is

[1]M.R. Turnbull, *Studying the Book of Genesis* (Richmond: Presbyterian Committee of Publication, 1924), p. 15.

resumed, and the elect offspring is described and his story given in detail, e.g., Abraham had other children besides Isaac, but only the line of Isaac is followed through the Bible. Isaac had another son besides Jacob, but only Jacob's line is given. The story of the chosen line is the theme of Scripture. Israel was in fact an elect nation.

This being true, the Book of Ruth furnishes the most important link in the Old Testament. It connects David with the tribe of Judah. By so doing, it produces a homogeneous character to the Old Testament. In this respect the Book of Ruth is one of the most essential to the Old Testament canon. The older theologians called attention to this. However, there are those who not only minimize this but actually reject it. MacNaughton said:

> Their [the older theologians] most specious contention was that the Holy Spirit had so ordered it should be there, in order that we might have some account of an ancestress of the Messiah.[2]

The Book of Ruth supplies data that is essential to the genealogy of the chosen line. This cannot be discounted, and a casual perusal shows that the presentation of a genealogy is the evident intent of the writer. Keil and Delitzsch recognized this and called particular attention to it:

> In this conclusion the meaning and tendency of the whole narrative is brought clearly to light. The genealogical proof of the descent of David from Pharez through Boaz and the Moabitess Ruth (chap. 4:18-22)

---

[2]G.D. MacNaughton, *Two Hebrew Idylls* (Edinburgh: Oliphant, Anderson, and Ferrier, 1901), p. 16.

forms not only the end, but the starting point, of the
history contained in the book.[3]

Auberlen expressed the importance of the genealogical purpose of Ruth in even stronger terms.

> The book of Ruth contains, as it were, the inner side,
> the spiritually moral background of the genealogies
> which play so significant a part even in the Israelitish
> antiquity.[4]

James Morison was alarmed that there were many
who not only considered the genealogical purpose to be the primary one but actually thought it
the only purpose for the existence of the book in
the Scripture. He wrote:

> Many have supposed that the *raison d'être* of the book
> is a matter of genealogy... Yet it seems preposterous
> to assume that the whole graphic story of Ruth was
> composed simply in consequence of this genealogical
> interest.[5]

I will not assume here that the only purpose of the
Book of Ruth is to furnish a genealogy, but I also will
not take the position that the purpose is not to give
us a genealogy. There is overwhelming evidence that
this was one of the major motives. Keil and Delitzsch
said:

> The last words of verse 17, 'he is the father of Jesse,
> the father of David,' show the object which the author
> had in view in writing down these events, or compos-
> ing the book itself. This conjecture is raised into a

---

[3]Keil and Delitzsch, *Biblical Commentary on the Old Testament* (Edinburgh: T.
and T. Clark, 1865), Vol. IV, p. 466.
[4]*Ibid.*
[5]James Morison, *The Pulpit Commentary* (London: Kegan Paul, Trench,
Trubner and Company, 1897), Vol. VIII, p. 6.

certainty by the genealogy which follows, and with which the book closes.[6]

The genealogy at the conclusion of the book is a valuable contribution to the biblical narrative. In many respects, it is the most important document in the Old Testament.

> Now these are the generations of Pharez: Pharez begat Hezron,
> And Hezron begat Ram, and Ram begat Amminadab,
> And Amminadab begat Nahshon, and Nahshon begat Salmon,
> And Salmon begat Boaz, and Boaz begat Obed,
> And Obed begat Jesse, and Jesse begat David (Ruth 4:18-22).

There are several observations that need to be made concerning this document. It is only a partial genealogy. It begins with Pharez and ends with David. Pharez was the son of Judah, according to the story in Genesis 38. This genealogy gives the vital link between Judah and David. The fact that the genealogy stops with David suggests that the Book of Ruth was written during the reign of David.

The Companion Bible calls attention to the fact that there are but fourteen generations given in the Bible.[7] Eleven are listed in the Book of Genesis. The generations of Aaron and Moses are recorded in Numbers 3. The last one given in the Old Testament is this account in Ruth. The fourteenth is found in Matthew 1. Between David and Christ there is no genealogy

---

[6]Keil and Delitzsch, p. 492.
[7]Humphrey Milford, *The Companion Bible* (London: Oxford University Press, n.d.), Part I, p. 1.

given in the Old Testament. The Books of Ezra and
Nehemiah contain several genealogical tables, but
they are those of the priests and others. David's line,
the kingly seed, is not given, but the record of the
kings who followed David up to Babylonian captivity
is given in detail in the historical accounts of the
kings.

There are two genealogical tables given in the Gospels of Jesus Christ. The record in Matthew starts
with Abraham and follows the line down through
Solomon, the son of David. This is evidently Joseph's
line, which gave the Lord Jesus Christ the legal title to
the throne of David. The record in Luke is given in
reverse order from all other genealogies in the Bible.
This should arrest the attention of any student of Scripture. Luke traces Mary's genealogy, the line through
Nathan, the son of David (see Luke 3:31). From Mary,
Christ received the bloodline that led through David.
These facts are highly significant when considered in
the light of a prophecy made concerning Jeconiah,
king of Judah, who was in the line that led to Joseph.

> As I live, saith the LORD, though Coniah the son of
> Jehoiakim king of Judah were the signet upon my right
> hand, yet would I pluck thee thence; . . . Thus saith the
> LORD, Write ye this man childless, a man that shall not
> prosper in his days: for no man of his seed shall
> prosper, sitting upon the throne of David, and ruling
> any more in Judah (Jer. 22:24,30).

Compare this prophecy with Matthew 1:11 and a
difficulty presents itself. It would have been impossible for Christ to have been a natural son of Joseph
and at the same time be the one chosen of God to sit
upon the throne of David. There was a curse pro-

nounced upon the legal line. Christ came from a prince of the house of David through His mother, Mary.

The genealogical table in Ruth is brought over into both of the tables in the Gospels. The table in Ruth is essential to both Matthew's and Luke's tables. In Luke's account, it is found in verses 32 and 33 of chapter 3. Matthew's Gospel, which opens the New Testament, likewise begins with the genealogy. The New Testament rests upon the accuracy of that genealogy. The table from Ruth is included in the first chapter of Matthew from verse 3 to 6. This genealogy from Ruth is the most vital link in the chain from Abraham to Christ. The table in Matthew is a duplication of the one in Ruth from Pharez to David, with a few details added to the one in Matthew. Four names are added, and they are not the names of men that are left out of the table in Ruth.

(There is an omission of some names from the pedigree in Ruth as has been pointed out by Keil and Delitzsch:

> ... some of the intermediate links must have been left out even here. But the omission of unimportant members becomes still more apparent in the statement which follows, viz., that Nahshon begat Salmon, and Salmon Boaz, in which only two generations are given for a space of more than 250 years, which intervened between the death of Moses and the time of Gideon.[8]

The writer of Ruth was deliberately giving ten generations; therefore, the omissions are explained. Matthew's Gospel does not attempt to fill in these gaps.)

---

[8]Keil and Delitzsch, p. 493.

These names are those of women. That fact seems altogether strange because women were omitted according to the commonly accepted practice of that day. Yet, we find four women mentioned in Matthew; they are not only women but *gentile* women.

Why are they included in Matthew's genealogy? Several writers have called attention to this unusual fact, drawing beautiful lessons from it. Dr. Gaebelein has called particular attention to these four women.[9] Keil and Delitzsch earlier had drawn attention to three of these women:

> As Judah begat Pharez from Tamar the Canaanitish woman (Gen. 38), and as Rahab was adopted into the congregation of Israel (Josh. 6:25), and according to ancient tradition was married to Salmon (Matt. 1:5), so the Moabitess Ruth was taken by Boaz as his wife, and incorporated in the family of Judah, from which Christ was to spring according to the flesh (see Matt. 1:3,5, where these three women are distinctly mentioned by name in the genealogy of Jesus).[10]

A consideration of these four women will enable us to acquaint ourselves with the pedigree in Ruth. Thamar is the first one mentioned in Matthew: "And Judas begat Phares and Zara of Thamar" (Matt. 1:3). The story of Judah and Tamar, told in Genesis 38, is a base story of fornication. Tamar was a Canaanitish woman who married Er, a son of Judah. Er was evil, and the record says that God slew him. Onan, the next son of Judah, was forced by his father to take Tamar, but he disobeyed, and the Lord likewise slew

---

[9]A.C. Gaebelein, *Gospel of Matthew* (New York: "Our Hope" Publication, n.d.), pp. 25–27.
[10]Keil and Delitzsch, p. 466.

him. Judah told Tamar to wait until his youngest son was grown, and he would give him to her for a husband. Years passed and Judah did not keep his promise. So Tamar laid aside her widow's garments, and having clothed herself as a harlot, she went to Judah. Although he did not recognize her, he had no excuse: he committed a double sin. There were twins born to Tamar, Zarah and Pharez. Only the line of Pharez is followed in Scripture. The list of Ruth opens with the statement, "These are the generations of Pharez" (Ruth 4:18).

In these four women's names, we have an outline of the plan of salvation. Tamar entered the genealogy of Christ because she was a sinner. God's plan of salvation rests upon the statement: "All have sinned, and come short of the glory of God" (Rom. 3:23). Salvation rests upon the foundation that sin is a reality. A Savior is for sinners. The Great Physician sought the sick, for well people do not need a doctor. The first step in obtaining salvation is for the sinner to come to God as a sinner. As the famous hymn says so well:

> Just as I am, without one plea,
>   But that Thy blood was shed for me,
> And that Thou bidd'st me come to Thee,
>   O Lamb of God, I come! I come!

God places all men on the same level. They are all listed at par value. All are sinners. He does this that He might save some. Otherwise, all would be lost.

The second gentile woman in the genealogy of Christ is Rahab: "And Salmon begat Boaz of Rachab" (Matt. 1:5). Rahab is usually identified in Scripture by her profession, "Rahab, the harlot." She lived in the city of Jericho, and when Joshua sent spies into the city, she received them. She believed in the God of Israel and believed that He was going to give the land to them. That was more than some of Israel believed. Rahab made this interesting confession to the spies:

> And she said unto the men, I know that the LORD hath given you the land, and that your terror is fallen upon us, and that all the inhabitants of the land faint because of you. For we have heard how the LORD dried up the water of the Red sea for you (Josh. 2:9,10).

She heard and believed, and God honored her faith, for He had not found so great a faith in Israel. She obeyed the spies and placed the scarlet thread on the outside. Rahab was included in the genealogy of Christ because of her faith, and she is given a niche in the memorial gallery of faith. "By faith the harlot Rahab perished not with them that believed not, when she had received the spies with peace" (Heb. 11:31).

Man has nothing to present to God in respect to works except the fruit of a cursed ground. The works of a sinner are not acceptable to God; yet God requires good works of men. The "good works" are faith. "Jesus answered and said unto them, This is the work of God, that ye believe on him whom he hath sent" (John 6:29).

The only thing that a lost sinner can offer God is the feeble hand of faith. Faith is the means that God places in reach of man to obtain salvation. "For by grace are ye saved through faith; and that not of yourselves: it is the gift of God" (Eph. 2:8).

The third gentile woman in the genealogy is Ruth.

Although her name is omitted from the genealogy at the end, her story is told in the book, and that is evidently the reason why Matthew included her name. The other two women were great sinners, but that is not true of Ruth. Among the others, she is like a flower among weeds. She possessed a fine character, and there was not one flaw found in her story; but the law kept her out of Israel. A Moabite was forbidden to enter the congregation of the Lord (see Deut. 23:3). She had to have a redeemer who would put over her his cloak of righteousness and right to the blessings of God. He had to extend grace to her. This Boaz did, as we have mentioned and will deal with fully when we come to the story proper. Attention must be called here to grace as the way by which she entered the genealogy of Christ.

When a sinner reaches forth the feeble, empty hand of faith to God, God clasps it with the hand of grace which He has outstretched to a lost world. "By grace are ye saved" is the testimony of every sinner. The law condemns every sinner and drives him from the presence of the Lord like Cain: "Therefore by the deeds of the law there shall no flesh be justified in his sight: for by the law is the knowledge of sin" (Rom. 3:20). The law not only excommunicated the sinner but was unable to redeem him. Law cannot redeem without imperiling its own inheritance. Law cannot lower its standard to man's level and still be law. But One greater than Boaz has come, and He not only endangered His inheritance but gave His own life as a ransom for many. Now the vilest sinner can be saved by grace, "being justified freely by his grace through the redemption that is in Christ Jesus" (Rom. 3:24).

The fourth woman in the genealogy of Christ is not mentioned by name: "and David the king begat Solomon of her that had been the wife of Urias" (Matt. 1:6). Although her name is not given, her identity is not difficult to ascertain. She was Bathsheba, the wife of Uriah the Hittite. Her name is concealed by the Holy Spirit, for the sin was David's and not hers. David committed adultery with her, and then to cover his sinful act, he deliberately had Uriah murdered. This is the one black spot on the life of David.

David was God's man and the man of whom God had said, "The Lord hath sought him a man after his own heart" (1 Sam. 13:14). This statement was made before David committed this crime, but God never took His hand off David. After committing the crime, David apparently thought he had escaped detection. It was the custom for kings to commit horrible crimes and for no one to call them to account. But this was not true of God's king, for he could not act like the rulers of the nations round about him. God sent Nathan the prophet unto David, and he pointed his finger at David before the interview was over and said, "Thou art the man" (2 Sam. 12:7). David repented of his sin when he could have had Nathan killed for accusing the king. David did not want anything to separate his soul from God. He had cried, "As the hart panteth after the water brooks, so panteth my soul after thee, O God" (Ps. 42:1). David was willing to take the consequences of his sin, but he learned as he wrote, "Blessed is he whose transgression is forgiven, whose sin is covered" (Ps. 32:1). Trouble followed David all the remaining days of his life. The child of Bathsheba died; his own daughter was ruined; and

his son Absalom led a cruel rebellion against him
when he was an old man. Finally, Absalom was
murdered, which broke old David's heart. He never
whimpered under the hand of God nor complained,
for David knew he had sinned and he wanted fellowship maintained between his soul and God.

After a sinner is saved by grace, he never reaches
the plane of perfection in this life. He commits sins,
but they do not destroy his salvation. They do destroy his fellowship, and these sins must be dealt
with before fellowship can be restored. Another bore
the penalty of these sins, and the Christian is
commanded, "If we confess our sins, he is faithful
and just to forgive us our sins, and to cleanse us from
all unrighteousness" (1 John 1:9). Confession is the
way by which the prodigal son returns to the Father's
house. A genuine Christian never reaches the exalted
plane where he does not commit sin, and he does not
reach the place where he will not confess it. Although
David acknowledged his sin, trouble dogged his steps
till his dying day. There is a law of God that is not
abrogated even for the Christian: "Whatsoever a man
soweth, that shall he also reap" (Gal. 6:7). This law is
especially for Christians. God completely forgives the
sinner and cleanses him from sin, but nevertheless
this law operates in the physical world in which we
live. A man may live a life of sin and wreck his body
with drink. While confession of the sin will bring
forgiveness, it will not remove the marks of transgression from the body. He will reap a harvest of pain and
a wrecked body just the same.

There is a fine example of this in the New Testament. Saul stood and gave his consent to the stoning

of Stephen. Then, after Saul's conversion, on his first missionary journey, he was taken outside of the city of Lystra, was stoned and left for dead. (Apparently, Paul was dead, but God raised him up from the dead. That, evidently, was the occasion when he was caught up into the third heaven.) He learned that there must always be a harvest after seed-sowing in this world.

This chapter may well be concluded with a diagram of the genealogy that concludes the book of Ruth.[11] This is the genealogy of Pharez.

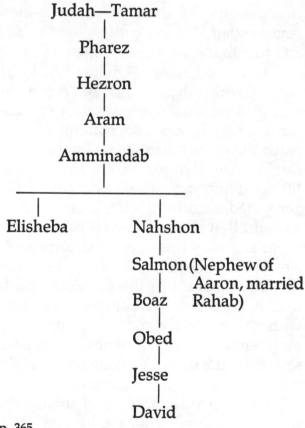

Judah—Tamar
|
Pharez
|
Hezron
|
Aram
|
Amminadab
|

Elisheba   Nahshon
|
Salmon (Nephew of
| Aaron, married
Boaz   Rahab)
|
Obed
|
Jesse
|
David

----

[11]Milford, Part II, p. 365.

· 5 ·

The Doctrinal Purpose

If the foregoing purposes for the Book of Ruth were not adequate to justify its inclusion in the Scripture, there would still be ample justification in its doctrinal purpose. This book presents in pictorial form one of the greatest doctrines of the Bible. A phase of the doctrine of redemption is presented in this book that is not found elsewhere in Scripture. Redemption by a Kinsman-Redeemer is essential to a complete understanding of the doctrine of redemption.

Redemption is possible only through a Kinsman-Redeemer. God could not redeem apart from a Mediator, and since only God could redeem, it was necessary for Him to become that Person. Under the subject, "Redemption for Lost Man to be Sought in Christ," Calvin recognized that God cannot redeem unless He "appears as a Redeemer in the Person of His only begotten Son."[1] Again he affirmed, "I only assert,

---

[1]John Calvin, *The Institutes of the Christian Religion* (Philadelphia: Presbyterian Board of Publication, 1813), p. 305.

that the happiness of the Church has always been founded on the Person of Christ."[2] A.H. Strong, in contemplating Christology, made it synonymous with "The Redemption Wrought By Christ."[3]

Not only is man shut up to salvation by grace, which is the real "offense of the Cross," but also God is shut up—by His own choice—to a redemption wrought by Himself and made available to man only through the avenue of grace. Two alternatives confronted God. Either He could let man bear the penalty of his own sin and be eternally lost, or He could redeem man by paying the penalty Himself. There was no middle ground on which He could stand. The Kinsman-Redeemer is the only symbol in the Bible that gives an adequate understanding of God as the Redeemer.

Moses as the deliverer of the nation of Israel from Egypt furnishes a figure of Christ as the Great Deliverer from sin, but he in no way foreshadows Christ as the Kinsman-Redeemer. The writer to the Hebrews makes the distinction between Moses and Christ: "Moses verily was faithful in all his house, as a servant," but "Christ as a son over his own house" (Heb. 3:5,6). God was the Redeemer of Israel out of Egypt; Moses was functioning in the capacity of a servant. A servant could never be a full figure of our Great Redeemer. Christ was the Son of God, acting in that capacity; therefore, it is written, "God was in Christ, reconciling the world unto himself" (2 Cor. 5:19). Redemption requires a figure that gives us to understand why Christ became a man in order to redeem

---

[2]*Ibid.*, p. 307.
[3]A.H. Strong, *Systematic Theology* (Philadelphia: The Judson Press, 1907), pp. 665–776.

us. Moses in no way illustrates this. Moses shows
that God used a man but does not reveal that God
became a man. Redemption cannot be properly com-
prehended until some figure is found to illustrate the
Person and work of Christ. The Book of Ruth supplies
one aspect to this doctrine that is found nowhere
else.

Moses was not an adequate figure of a redeemer
because he had neither the power nor price of redemption. Boaz was a kinsman who had both the
price and power to function as a redeemer in the
capacity to which he was called. Therefore, Boaz
furnishes the only figure for the Kinsman-Redeemer
aspect of redemption which is so essential for any
proper theory of the Atonement. The commercial
theory of the Atonement would have been delivered
from the unsavory reputation of a cold business transaction if it had been presented with the proper per-
spective of the Kinsman-Redeemer. It was, therefore,
a serious omission on the part of Jonathan Edwards,
Calvin, Robinson, Anderson, Strong, *et al.*, to ignore
the Book of Ruth in a history of redemption. Paul was
careful to guard the doctrine of redemption from
becoming a heartless transaction of buying and selling
when he wrote:

> But when the fulness of the time was come, God sent
> forth his Son, made of a woman, made under the law,
> to redeem them that were under the law, that we
> might receive the adoption of sons (Gal. 4:4,5).

Christ became our Kinsman according to the flesh.
He was included in our genealogy; He intruded into
the history of man; He became one of us; He came

close to us. Someone has framed this picture beauti-
fully: "He came a little baby thing that made a woman cry." But Christ was not involved in our fall. He
was free from our slavery. Boaz was a kinsman of
Elimelech, but he was not involved in the bankruptcy
of Elimelech's estate. He was not a poverty-stricken
relative who could offer nothing but helpless sympa-
thy. He was well able to redeem it from all claims.
Even so, Christ was able to redeem us. He became a
man but not bankrupt humanity, for He "was in all
points tempted like as we are, yet without sin" (Heb.
4:15). He became like us but not one of us. He was
not a poverty-stricken relative, but He was "holy,
harmless, undefiled, separate from sinners, and made
higher than the heavens" (Heb. 7:26).

Boaz not only redeemed the estate of Elimelech,
but he performed another work that only a kinsman-
redeemer could do. The duty of the next of kin was to
marry the wife of the dead, that he might raise up
seed to the dead. In other words, the kinsman-
redeemer preserved the name of the dead man and
furnished an heir to the estate. Boaz married the
foreigner from Moab, the widow of Mahlon, the son
of Elimelech, and he raised up that line once more.
Christ has not only freed us from the slavery of sin,
but He has brought us into the place where we are
able to receive "the adoption of sons." This is personal, intimate, and vital. Little wonder that Paul could
utter this paean of praise regarding the redemptive
work of Christ:

> I am crucified with Christ: nevertheless I live; yet not I,
> but Christ liveth in me: and the life which I now live in

the flesh I live by the faith of the Son of God, who
loved me, and gave himself for me (Gal. 2:20).

This is not a cold business deal but a love affair. It
tells about One who came where we were and became one of us that He might redeem us.

Another reason why God had to become our Kinsman in order to redeem us is found in the price that
was paid for our redemption. Although Boaz was not
compelled to redeem the estate of Elimelech and the
maid from Moab, according to the Mosaic law, if he
did choose to act in that capacity, he had to be a
kinsman. The law did not force the kinsman to act,
but it did say that he must be a kinsman before he
could act. He never could have been the redeemer
and not be a kinsman. God could never have redeemed
man, and we say this reverently, had He not become
our Kinsman. If Christ had been unwilling to leave
heaven, then man would have had to go to hell. God
did not have to redeem us, but if He did involve
Himself in that work, He had to become a man. The
Incarnation, therefore, begins quite properly the work
of redemption. The Virgin Birth of Christ is essential
to any satisfactory plan of salvation. He was made of
a woman for purposes of redemption. Little wonder
that Bethlehem—the earthly lineage of Christ—is
conspicuous in the Book of Ruth; the Kinsman-
Redeemer must be virgin born. The angelic salutation
at His birth was not a meaningless statement: "For
unto you is born this day in the city of David a
Saviour, which is Christ the Lord" (Luke 2:11). Love
was the law that compelled Boaz to act. It was love
that sent Christ from heaven to Bethlehem: "For God

so loved the world, that he gave his only begotten Son..." (John 3:16).

Blood was the price of man's freedom from sin, but not the blood of bulls and goats. Human blood was required. It would have been the rankest sort of heathenism for any son of Adam to have shed his blood for sin. It would have been valueless and vile. The sacrifice of human blood has been, and is, degrading for the natural man in sin. But God took upon Himself flesh, and the blood of that body could be the only satisfactory price. It signified His kinship to us, but it also was not under the curse of sin.

The precious blood of Christ was the only legal tender that could redeem man. God paid this exorbitant price for the redemption of man because nothing less would do. The justice of God demanded the pound of flesh, and the pound of flesh was taken, but it required the bloodletting of Christ. Man had lost his life through sin—and his right to life. Man forfeited all claims to life when he disobeyed God in the Garden. "Thou shalt surely die" (Gen 2:17) is the inexorable law of God. Christ paid in the coin of life the penalty of man's sin. It was His blood. Therefore, "we have redemption through his blood, the forgiveness of sins, according to the riches of his grace" (Eph. 1:7). The blood speaks not only of the heinousness of sin, but tells us that the One who made such a sacrifice was kin to us. The blood was the price of our redemption, but it was not a cold business deal. That blood came from the warm heart of God, and it was made available for every man.

There is a fountain filled with blood
Drawn from Immanuel's veins;
And sinners, plunged beneath that flood,
Lose all their guilty stains.
                              —*William Cowper*

· 6 ·

In the Land of Moab

And not many days after the younger son gathered all together, and took his journey into a far country, and there wasted his substance with riotous living (Luke 15:13).

The story is never delightful when a member of the chosen seed leaves the Land of Promise and goes into the far country. It makes no difference whether he is Abraham going into Egypt to escape the famine or the prodigal son going to the far country and into the face of a famine there; the results are negative and the ending tragic. Elimelech should not have gone into the land of Moab, regardless of the conditions in the Land of Promise. Chapter 1 of the Book of Ruth tells the tragic story of a prodigal family, a story which has been duplicated many times in the course of human events by individuals, by families, and by nations. The tragic story of Elimelech will engage our attention in this chapter.

During the deep declension of the period of the judges, God instituted judgment after judgment as a warning to bring the people back to Himself. The times of the judges were black enough, but these seasons of judgment were especially black. Famine was the stick of His correction and His customary method of judgment. Several times in the history of His people He called for a famine as a means of judgment. Some of the most notable passages are 2 Kin. 8:1; Jer. 16:3–13; Ezek. 5:11–17.[1] This famine enables us to form some opinion as to the approximate time during which the incidents recorded in the Book of Ruth occurred. Robert Lee suggested that this famine is referred to in Judges 6:3,4[2]—a famine caused by siege. If that inference is correct, and there is no reasonable objection to it, the incidents recorded in the Book of Ruth occurred during the time of Gideon. This harmonizes with the viewpoint of Keil and Delitzsch: "The incidents described in the book fall within the times of the judges (chap. 1:1), and most probably in the time of Gideon."[3]

Gideon was the sixth judge and was one of the more outstanding ones, but the condition of the people nullified much that he had done. It is stimulating to think that in all likelihood Gideon and Boaz were acquaintances. If that is true, then they would have held a mutual admiration for each other. Regardless of the time during the period of the judges to which we attempt to assign the happenings of Ruth, the hour was a dark one, made doubly so by the presence

[1]Henry Moorhouse, *Ruth, The Moabitess* (Chicago: Fleming H. Revell, Co. 1881), p. 6.
[2]Robert Lee, *The Outlined Bible* (Glasgow: Pickering and Inglis, n.d.), Analysis 8.
[3]Keil and Delitzch, *Biblical Commentary on the Old Testament* (Edinburgh: T. and T. Clark, 1865), Vol. IV, p. 466.

of a famine, the telltale mark of flagrant sin incurring the displeasure of God.

In the first few verses of Ruth we have the story of another prodigal son. He left the Father's house of bread and went into the far country of Moab. All this was in disobedience to the will of the Father. This man lived as a member of the tribe of Judah in Bethlehem-judah. Bethlehem-judah means "house of bread and praise." How evocative this is of the wonderful house of the Father! It speaks of plenty and peace. There probably was no famine in the land of Moab, for the judgment was restricted to the chosen people. Their privilege, as the chosen people, increased the measure of their responsibility. God was judging them but not Moab. Moab was not called to the high place afforded Israel. However, God could have provided for His own in the place of blessing, and He would have made ample provision if they had but trusted Him. The famine struck terror in their hearts but did not inspire trust of the heart. We know that at least one family migrated immediately to the land of Moab.

There is trouble always for the prodigal son in the far country. He receives his whipping in the far country, not when he returns in repentance and confession to his own hearth. The hickory stick is applied in the far country; new shoes and a robe await his return home. He gets kicks in the far country; he is showered with kisses at home. Tears of sorrow are shed in Moab, but tears of joy fall at Bethlehem.

Elimelech and his family are but one example of many prodigal sons in the Bible. Abraham was called out of Ur of the Chaldees and instructed to dwell in the land of Canaan. In his day there was a famine, the first of thirteen famines mentioned in the Bible: "And there was a famine in the land: and Abram went down into Egypt to sojourn there" (Gen. 12:10). Now, God had given no instructions to Abraham to leave the Land of Promise, but the constant trek of multitudes before his tent door, migrating to the land of Egypt, was too much for Abraham. He silently folded his tent and joined the parade. In the land of Egypt Abraham acquired potentially all his future trouble. He amassed a fortune and procured the Egyptian maid Hagar. These contributed to his undoing. While he abode in Egypt, God did not appear to him, and this is all the more striking in view of the fact that when he returned, God communicated immediately with him.

Elimelech, following the example of his father, Abraham, took his wife and two sons and left the land of Israel in the time of a severe famine. This was contrary to the will of God, and trouble was the inevitable outcome. Elimelech emigrated to the land of Moab. Significantly the record contains this statement: "And they came into the country of Moab, and continued there" (1:2). It was bad enough to leave the town of Bethlehem, the place of bread and a place which was to have future significance, but to go to the land of Moab was doubly bad. To seek temporary relief in the land of Moab was doubly bad, but to take up residence there was a tragedy.

Some prodigals do not stay in the far country and the pigsty is only a momentary experience. Here is the sad story of a prodigal son who stayed in the far country. He seemed to enjoy the swill of the sty more than the house of bread. The house of bread in a famine is better than the land of Moab in time of plenty. Elimelech and his two sons died in the land of Moab. When someone inquired concerning the fate of the prodigal son had he died in the pigsty, Dr. Harry Rimmer is reported to have answered in this splendid way: "Well, he would be a dead son and not a dead pig." The prodigal son, Elimelech, did die in the pig pen, but certainly we are bold enough to add that although he was an Israelite out of the will of God he was still nonetheless one of the children of the covenant.

The family of Elimelech settled at first rather comfortably in the land of Moab. The two sons married daughters of Moab (named Ruth and Orpah), which was contrary to the Mosaic law.

> Neither shalt thou make marriages with them (Hittites, Girgashites, Amorites, Canaanites, Perizzites, Hivites and Jebusites); thy daughter thou shalt not give unto his son, nor his daughter shalt thou take unto thy son (Deut 7:3).

The Companion Bible took the position that this passage only refers to the Canaanites but not to other Gentiles.[4] This is too narrow a restriction of the law, and certainly in practice the nation of Israel applied this law to all Gentiles. At the time of the return from the Babylonian captivity, this law included the Moabites specifically (Ezra 9:12). Nehemiah called attention to those who had made illegal marriages in his day: "In those days also saw I Jews that had married wives of

---

[4]Henry Milford, *The Companion Bible* (London: Oxford University Press, n.d.), Part II, p. 361.

Ashdod, of Ammon, and of Moab" (Neh. 13:23). Nehemiah used very extreme measures with them:

> And I contended with them, and cursed them, and smote certain of them, and plucked off their hair, and made them swear by God, saying, Ye shall not give your daughters unto their sons, nor take their daughters unto your sons, or for yourselves (Neh. 13:25).

In the light of this, the position of *The Companion Bible* is untenable. Let it be said for the justification of Elimelech, the marriages were made after his death, according to the record. However, there was apparently no objection raised by Naomi, the widow of Elimelech. Jewish writers from early times have contended that the early deaths of Naomi's sons were divine judgments because of their unlawful relationships.[5] The story before us concerns primarily one of these wives from Moab. She is Ruth the Moabitess, who married Mahlon.

The meaning of names in Scripture contributes oftentimes to a proper understanding of the passage in which they occur. This is definitely true in the Book of Ruth, and it will be profitable at this juncture to examine the names that occur in the first chapter of our story. Names in Bible times were not given to distinguish a person from Tom, Dick, and Harry. A name was given to a person not only to identify that person among others but to suggest something regarding the character of the individual. (For example, Jacob's name was changed to Israel because the one who had been a "supplanter" became a "prince with

---

[5]Jamieson, Fausset, and Brown, *Commentary on the Old and New Testaments* (Chicago: National Publishing Co., 1871), p. 173.

God." Christ changed the name of Simon to Peter, for Peter means "rock" and this quality was to character-ize him henceforth.)

Ruth means "beauty" and "appearance," according to Gesenius. The root word means "to feed a flock." Brown, Driver, and Briggs gave "friendship" as a meaning of Ruth. All these meanings are significant. Ruth was beautiful, as we shall have occasion to mention subsequently. A pastoral picture of loveliness is suggested by the root word. The meaning that follows more closely the theme of the story is that of friendship. The friendship extended to her mother-in-law has become a proverb of that which is best. She came as a stranger and foreigner into the land of Israel, but she found one there in the person of Boaz who was more than a friend. She was a stranger to the God of Israel, but she came to know Him and to trust Him. This friendship He honored in a most singular way, as we shall see.

Elimelech means "the God of the king." This man bore a royal name, but he apparently did not measure up to its intention. Naomi means "pleasant." This woman found life bitter in the land of Moab, but when she returned to the land of Israel, the fra-grance of the meaning of her name appeared again in her life.

The two sons of Elimelech and Naomi are virtually unknown. Nothing is said concerning them, but their names convey a wealth of suggestion. The meaning of the names must have applied to their lives. Mahlon means "sick," and Chilion means "pining."[6] Certain-

---

[6]Milford, p. 361.

ly neither one of them could have been a robust picture of health. Their untimely demise confirms the meaning of their names. The death of the two sons left two widows in the family. Now there were three widows.

There is another name here that needs to be considered: the name of the country to which this Jewish family fled in time of famine. Moab was the terminus of their trek from Bethlehem, a name ominous in the ears of the children of Israel. There was a distant blood relationship between Israel and Moab. Moab appears first in Scripture in connection with the flight of Lot from the city of Sodom: "And the firstborn bare a son, and called his name Moab: the same is the father of the Moabites unto this day" (Gen. 19:37).

This verse completes a story that is one of the most sordid on the pages of Scripture, revealing the depths of iniquity. Moab was the son of Lot by an incestuous union with his eldest daughter. Lot was the nephew of Abraham. The Moabite people, who constituted the country of Moab, sprang from this offspring of Lot. No mention is made on the pages of Scripture of the growth of the son of Lot to the nation of Moab, for Scripture is concerned with that nation only as it touches the chosen nation of Israel. The next reference to Moab occurs in the song of redemption in Exodus after the children of Israel crossed the Red Sea. In Exodus 15:15 mention is made of the mighty men of Moab. In the interval during which Israel was becoming a strong nation in the brickyards of Egypt, Moab was likewise becoming a strong nation. Moab occupied a place to the southeast of the Promised Land. They stood on the route of Israel from Egypt,

blocking the way. Moab became a thorn in the side of
Israel after they turned back at Kadesh-barnea. The
wilderness experience of Israel is concerned to a great
extent with Moab and the land of Moab. It appears
that about this time the Amorites had subjugated the
land of Moab. When the children of Israel overcame
the Amorites in battle at Jahaz, the victory struck
terror into the hearts of the Moabites.

Balak, king of Moab, became frightened and sent
for Balaam to come and curse Israel. Balaam's inability to conform to the desires of Balak is recorded in the
Book of Numbers. It is not in our sphere to examine
the different prophecies of Balaam, but there is one
phrase in the fourth and last one that concerns Moab.

> I shall see him, but not now: I shall behold him, but
> not nigh: there shall come a Star out of Jacob, and a
> Sceptre shall rise out of Israel, and shall smite the
> corners of Moab, and destroy all the children of Sheth
> (Num. 24:17).

This is probably the prophecy that the magi had in
their possession to help bring them to Jerusalem in
their search for the king of the Jews.

This strange prophecy contains some unique statements which might bear inspection, but we wish to
call attention to the one where it is indicated that
there would be enmity and strife between Israel and
Moab. The Star out of Jacob will smite the country of
Moab. Not the fulfillment of this prophecy, but the
revelation of enmity between these two concerns us.
Balaam was not able to curse Israel, but he did
accomplish a far more subtle thing, for he taught
Balak to cast a stumbling block before Israel. Israel
began to mix with the Moabites; the people indulged

in the most grievous sins and worshiped their foreign idols. In spite of all this, Moab did not exhibit a friendly spirit toward Israel. This formed the basis for their exclusion from the nation:

> Because they met you not with bread and water in the way, when ye came forth out of Egypt; and because they hired against thee Balaam the son of Beor of Pethor of Mesopotamia, to curse thee (Deut. 23:4).

The unfriendly conduct of Moab was not forgotten by Israel during the period of the judges, which is contemporaneous with the story of Ruth. Jephthah sent the following message in his day to the king of Ammon:

> Then Israel sent messengers unto the king of Edom, saying, Let me, I pray thee, pass through thy land: but the king of Edom would not hearken thereto. And in like manner they sent unto the king of Moab: but he would not consent: and Israel abode in Kadesh (Judg. 11:17).

In spite of the enmity that existed between Israel and Moab, God forbade Israel to fight with Moab for possession of their land:

> And the LORD said unto me, Distress not the Moabites, neither contend with them in battle: for I will not give thee of their land for a possession; because I have given Ar unto the children of Lot for a possession (Deut. 2:9).

The land of Moab had, however, an attraction for Israel because there Moses died and was buried by the Lord. Moses, in some respects, was a prodigal son on the way to the Promised Land, but he died en route and was buried in the far country. Elimelech,

Mahlon, and Chilion were not the first Israelites to die and be buried in the far country.

The Moabites became the natural enemies of the children of Israel after the Israelites entered the Land of Promise. During the early days of the judges, immediately preceding the events of our story, Moab had enslaved the children of Israel (see Judg. 3:12–14).

David subjugated the land of Moab during his reign (2 Sam. 8:2–12). David uttered a very strange but revealing statement concerning Moab: "Moab is my washpot" (Ps. 60:8). The prophets denounced Moab as the enemy of God (see Is. 15). The famous Moabite Stone contains a record of the bitterness that existed between Israel and Moab.[7]

When Nebuchadnezzar captured the Moabites, they disappeared from history as a nation but not as a race. During the time of Israel's return under Nehemiah, the Moabites were still identified as a race. Even at this late date, the Moabite retained his proverbial position as an enemy of Israel.

It is strange that Elimelech would have gone to Moab in the first place, considering that Moab was not a name to call upon for help, as far as the Jews were concerned. Stranger than this is the story of how Ruth came into the congregation of Israel and entered into the plan of God in a very intimate way. She is called Ruth the Moabitess in the record and she was a member of that hated and hating race. Little wonder that the Chaldee Targum puts it in this plain language: "And they transgressed the edict of the

---

[7]John D. Davis, *Dictionary of the Bible* (Grand Rapids, Mich.: Baker Book House, 1954), p. 508.

word of the Lord, and took to themselves alien wives of the daughters of Moab."[8]

Naomi, after the death of her husband and two sons, was no longer content to abide in the land of Moab. Reports emanating from the Land of Promise brought assurance that the famine had ended and that there was bread in abundance in the house of bread. She had had enough of tragedy in the land of Moab; so she determined to set out for home and Bethlehem. Apparently, both of her daughters-in-law were of the same mind and fully intended to make the return trip with her. Both would have continued in the journey with her had not Naomi asked them to return to their own homes. She pronounced a blessing on each and commended both for their kindly treatment in dealing with their husbands, her sons, and also with her. The affection of Ruth and Orpah for their mother-in-law abolishes the shopworn bromide regarding mothers-in-law. Here is a mother whose sons' wives evidently pleased her immensely. Here also are two women of Moab who do not bear the marks of their race.

The parting of these three is a typically feminine scene, marked by much weeping. There was much waving of damp handkerchiefs, and passionate embraces made the scene exceedingly touching. Ruth and Orpah were loathe to leave and finally avowed that they would continue with Naomi: "We will return with thee unto thy people" (1:10). Then Naomi gave them a sensible talk from the woman's view-

---

[8]James Morison, *The Pulpit Commentary* (London: Kegan Paul, Trench, Trubner and Co., 1897), Vol. VIII, p. 3.

point (1:11–13). The two young women needed a home and a husband. These could not be readily procured if they followed her, and anyway she did not want them to come on some false hope. She had no more sons, and she had no notion of taking another husband.

This bit of information prepared the way for some near kinsman to become the kinsman-redeemer for Ruth. If Naomi had been blessed with another son, it would have been incumbent upon him, under the Sinaitic code, to have married one of the daughters-in-law:

> If brethren dwell together, and one of them die, and have no child, the wife of the dead shall not marry without unto a stranger: her husband's brother shall go in unto her, and take her to him to wife and perform the duty of an husband's brother unto her (Deut. 25:5).

If there was no brother, the legal obligation fell on some relative outside the immediate family. This information coming from Naomi is but preparation for Boaz to act as the kinsman-redeemer. This was good advice from an older woman to younger women. She revealed to them how preposterous it would be for them to follow her, and at the same time expect to have a home and children. This bit of advice for the young women occasioned more weeping, and the thought of parting forever produced a fresh flood of tears. This scene depicts the real affection that bound these three women together and is worthy of favorable comment.

The crisis brought out the real character of these two young women and revealed the underlying difference between Ruth and Orpah. The record brings it out in this striking manner: "And Orpah kissed her mother in law; but Ruth clave unto her" (1:14). Orpah was emotional and ready to shower kisses upon Naomi, but the advice of Naomi had chilled her desire to follow, and she demonstrated her love through feelings. Not so with Ruth. Ruth possessed real faith and love. She exhibited the stamina of one who not only ran well but who was not hindered in obeying the truth. Ruth did not fall from grace in the climactic event of her career. She was willing to undergo the consequences of following Naomi, whatever they might be. This expression of faith on the part of Ruth was acknowledged of God and rewarded by Him later an hundredfold.

Ruth and Orpah demonstrate the two kinds of members in the church—the professors and the possessors. Orpah made only a profession of faith and failed at the climactic moment; Ruth possessed genuine faith, which produced fruit and works. Paul says, "All men have not faith" (2 Thess. 3:2). Orpah was in that class. As the remainder of the story demonstrates, Ruth possessed a faith that could only come from God: "By grace are ye saved through faith; and that not of yourselves: it is the gift of God" (Eph. 2:8).

Naomi, realizing the firm decision of Ruth to accompany her, made a final but futile attempt to persuade Ruth to return to her own people and to her own religion, "unto her gods" (1:15). Oddly enough, one of the inducements held out by Naomi to Ruth was the heathen idolatry of Moab. In the days of the judges, it had reached a new low in the depths of degradation. It seems strange that Naomi should have insisted upon Ruth's return to idol worship. One explanation in support of Naomi's conduct is that she was testing the mettle of the faith of Ruth. If Ruth's faith was genuine, she could not be driven back to idolatry. If it were not, there would be no reason for her to continue with Naomi.

The very mention of the gods of the Moabites reveals that these young Moabite women were called upon to make a decision regarding their religion. A return to Moab meant a return to idolatry. Evidently they had become worshipers of the God of Israel. Their departure from Naomi would mean, for all practical purposes, the sacrifice of their newfound faith. The test went deeper than human affection; the test was the heart's relation to the true God. This was a momentous decision in the lives of these young widows. This was the crucial test and the line of demarcation that was to separate them for eternity. This was the turning point in the lives of these two: They chose that day whom they would serve.

Orpah went back to idolatry. Nothing more is said of her. No word of commendation or condemnation is spoken. Like Judas, she went to her place. The very silence of Scripture is sufficiently eloquent to tell of a life of tragedy. When Ruth chose to follow Naomi, she made a momentous decision for Jehovah and the true worship of Him. Ruth chose God, and He chose her in the greatest plan of the ages: namely the bringing of Jesus Christ into the world. Ruth made a choice for God when she elected to go with Naomi. She never stood again at the crossroads of life to make a decision for eternity. After that moment, she had only to walk the ordinary path of His leading.

Ruth chose the God of Israel and took her place of trust under His wings. Orpah went backward to darkness, paganism, superstition, and gloom. Ruth went onward to the light of glory, truth, and the light of life.

> One ship sails East
> And another West,
>   By the selfsame winds that blow;
> 'Tis the set of the sails,
> And not the gales,
>   That tells them the way to go!
>
> Like the winds of the sea
> Are the waves of Time,
>   As we voyage along through life;
>   'Tis the set of the soul
> That determines the goal,
> And not the calm or the strife!

Ruth's answer to the urging of Naomi could have been given only by a character of the highest caliber— one who had decided for God. If a monument had been reared to Ruth, this certainly would have been the inscription, chiseled in marble:

> And Ruth said, Entreat me not to leave thee, or to return from following after thee: for whither thou goest, I will go; and where thou lodgest, I will lodge: thy people shall be my people, and thy God my God: where thou diest, will I die, and there will I be buried: The LORD do so to me, and more also, if aught but death part thee and me" (1:16,17).

Robert Lee said, "There is nothing in human literature more beautiful than Ruth's address to her mother-in-law (1:16–17)—it is sublime."[9] Ruth's speech is not only a literary gem, but it is the decision of a noble character at a dramatic moment, expressed in the language of pathos, passion, and poetry.

Ruth made seven statements which constituted a vow that she never broke. These seven statements reveal definite progress in the development of her decisions. First, Ruth asked Naomi to desist in requesting her to leave her, for she was determined to follow Naomi. This was not merely a halfhearted decision but extended into all the ramifications of life. In the second place, she was determined to go wherever Naomi went. In the third place, Ruth intended to live with her mother-in-law in whatever place Naomi resided. She would share the same privations under the same roof. She locked her life intimately into that of Naomi. In the fourth place, she was leaving her people for good, and she was choosing Naomi's people forever. Ruth was willing to break down the agelong barrier of enmity and hatred and become one of the people of Israel. That was a tremendous decision for a member of the nation of Moab.

In the fifth place, Ruth was making a decision for God. She was leaving the idolatry of Moab permanently and was putting her trust in Jehovah forever. This was the supreme decision for Ruth. This was the highest affirmation of the seven statements that Ruth made. In the sixth place, this was a decision for life that extended through to death. But even in death she did not want to be separated from Naomi, and this constituted the seventh affirmation. She would be

---

[9]Lee, Analysis No. 8.

buried with her. She confirmed all this with an oath. The last statement is in the form of an oath that occurs frequently in the historical books of First and Second Samuel (see 1 Sam. 3:17).[10]

Naomi was thoroughly convinced that Ruth intended to go with her, and she refrained from further attempts to persuade her to abide in Moab. These two widows began the weary journey back to Bethlehem. They must have made a sad spectacle as they trudged along the road. The prodigal daughter was returning home, and it must have been a sad experience in the life of Naomi, filled with mingled feelings. How good home must have looked after years of absence! Her return and plight moved the city of Bethlehem to compassion. They were dazed to see the prodigal daughter return in the rags of poverty, and their only comment was, "Is this Naomi?" But there is always "joy in heaven" over the return of the prodigal. Naomi had left Bethlehem with a husband and two sons, but she returned with only a gentile girl. She was given one stranger for three loved ones. This was not nearly so tragic as it appeared on the surface, however, as subsequent events proved. The women of Bethlehem were right when they said to Naomi at the birth of Obed, "Thy daughter in law, which loveth thee, which is better to thee than seven sons, hath born him". (4:15)

Evidently Elimelech had been well-to-do when he left the city of Bethlehem. Ten years in the land of Moab, with its accompanying misfortunes, had re-

---

[10]Walter Baxendale, *The Preacher's Homiletic Commentary* (New York: Funk and Wagnalls Co., 1892), Vol. VIII, p. 66.

duced the family fortune to nil. This radical change of fortune, which was very evident when Naomi returned, touched the heart of the little town of Bethlehem. Then Naomi related her sad story with a complaining note. She requested that they no longer call her Naomi, but *Mara*, which meant that she no longer wanted to be called "Pleasant," but "Bitter," because the latter name conformed more closely to her appearance.

Naomi committed the grievous error of placing the blame for all her trouble upon God by charging, "The Almighty hath dealt very bitterly with me." This has been symptomatic of the Adamic nature from the very beginning. Adam inferred that the woman whom God had given him was responsible for the presence of sin. He thereby threw the blame back into the lap of God, suggesting that if God had not given her to him, the tragedy of the Fall would have been averted. The children of Adam have been making that and similar charges against God ever since. God had not dealt bitterly with her; she was reaping the fruit of the sin of disobedience. Naomi was but gleaning in the fields of a far country, away from the presence of God. God was not responsible for her misfortune, but He was responsible for the voice that had wooed her back home. The grace of God was responsible for the blessing that was to come to her now that she had listened to the voice and returned. Glorious things awaited her, but she was blinded to all that at this time.

She described the sad experience through which she had passed in these striking words, "I went out full, and the Lord hath brought me home again empty" (1:21). Quite evidently, the contrast between her former economic condition and her poverty when she returned was great. It was a long way on the economic scale from "full" to "empty." A family of four prosperous Bethlehemites had emigrated to Moab. The three males had died, and after ten years of adversity, the lone female of the family returned with a lone daughter-in-law, and she was a member of the hated nation of Moab. The prodigal son mentioned in Luke 15 had no more bitter experience. Job had passed through no more excruciating time of adversity. Fuller has described the plight of Naomi in this very picturesque style:

> Of the two sexes, the woman is the weaker; of women, old women are the feeblest; of old women, widows most woeful; of widows, those that are poor, their plight most pitiful; of poor widows, those who want children, their case most doleful; of widows that want children, those that once had them, and after lost them, their estate most desolate; of widows that have had children, those that are strangers in a foreign country, their condition most comfortless. Yet all these met together in Naomi, as in the center of sorrow, to make the measure of her misery pressed down, shaken together, running over. I conclude, therefore, many men have had affliction—none like Job; many women have had tribulation—none like Naomi.[11]

Naomi's insistence for a name that would be more in keeping with her plight was not complied with by the writer of this book, for in the very next verse it is asserted, "So Naomi returned" (1:22). There was a blessing awaiting her back in Bethlehem that would

----

[11]Morison, p. 4.

have made the name Mara as unsuitable for her as she now supposed Naomi to be. Pleasant things were in store for her henceforth, and bitter experiences belonged back in the land of Moab. As the time of her journeying was over, she would settle down in contentment in the house of bread, even though straitened circumstances were to continue for a short period.

Naomi and Ruth returned at a most propitious time: the season of the barley harvest. Dr. Davis said that the barley harvest was in April and began with the celebration of the Feast of Firstfruits.[12] The barley was the firstfruits of that land and day, according to Exodus 9:31,32, and came at the conclusion of the rainy season while the river Jordan was overflowing (see Josh. 3:15). The time was spring, the season of firstfruits. To the church this season and the Feast of Firstfruits speak of the resurrection of Christ, for He is "the firstfruits" in resurrection. Certainly, it is not without significance that the gentile stranger was brought into the blessings of God at the season which speaks of the resurrection of Christ. It was the death and resurrection of Christ that brought the Gentiles into the place of blessing in the church.

> Wherefore remember, that ye being in time past Gentiles in the flesh, who are called Uncircumcision by that which is called the Circumcision in the flesh made by hands; that at that time ye were without Christ, being aliens from the commonwealth of Israel, and strangers from the covenants of promise, having no hope, and without God in the world: but now in Christ Jesus ye who sometimes were far off are made nigh by the blood of Christ. . . . Now therefore ye are

---

[12]Davis, p. 290.

no more strangers and foreigners, but fellowcitizens with the saints, and of the household of God" (Eph. 2:11–13,19).

Too much stress cannot be placed upon the entrance of Ruth into Bethlehem. It is not only a beautiful picture of the church, but it marks the moment that was to bring fame to Bethlehem. Likewise, God was going to take this event which was marked with simplicity and pathos and crown it with glory and honor. In the eternal counsel of an omnipotent God, this forlorn gentile girl, the insignificant village of Bethlehem, and the apparently nonessential circumstances that brought them together were to be lifted out of the commonplace and made to shine with divine light. Thus God was moving in that out-of-the-way village in the far-off yonder time with a down-and-out individual.

· 7 ·

In the Field of Boaz

The fragrant sheaves of the wheat
Made the air above them sweet;
Sweeter and more divine
Was the scent of the scattered grain,
That the reaper's hand let fall
To be gathered again
By the hand of the gleaner:
Sweetest, divinest of all,
Was the humble deed of thine,
And the meekness of thy demeanor.
—*Longfellow*

The second chapter of the Book of Ruth introduces the last principal character in this story. He is Boaz, a kinsman of Naomi and the hero of our story. His name means "in whom is strength." Delitzsch rejected this meaning but gave "alacrity" as the correct meaning.[1] Both meanings could readily apply to the character of the one who possessed this name in our

---

[1]Keil and Delitzsch, *Biblical Commentary on the Old Testament* (Edinburgh: T. and T. Clark, 1865), p. 477.

story. He is called a "mighty man of wealth." The Chaldee gave the phrase "mighty in the law" as a third possible rendering for this expression which describes Boaz. The same phrase occurs in the Book of Judges for the deliverers,[2] and the same expression was used by the angel to address Gideon (Judg. 6:12). Certainly the expression as used with reference to Gideon did not connote wealth. There is a Jewish tradition that associates Ibzan, one of the judges (Judg. 12:8) with Boaz.[3] Ibzan was from Bethlehem, and the tradition does have some support. From the foregoing, it is quite permissible to conjecture that Boaz was an outstanding man of his day, a man of character and strength. What a contrast he must have been to Mahlon, the first husband of Ruth, whose name and life speak of weakness and frailty! All three of the suggested meanings reveal an aspect of the character of this great soul whom we are now studying. Each one presents some aspect of his life that the Spirit purposed to reveal.

On the canvas of God's Word, Boaz is drawn with noble features. He fulfilled in his life all that the Latin suggests in the great word *virtus*. Boaz was a man of virtue in the literal sense of that word. There is not a more winsome character presented in the Old Testament than Boaz, and there is not a more lovely woman in the Bible than Ruth. She compares favorably with her descendant Mary, the mother of Jesus. These two, Ruth and Boaz, stand out like stars on the black

---

[2]Grant, *The Numerical Bible* (New York: Loizeaux Brothers, 1894), Vol. II, p. 274.
[3]Walter Baxendale, *Preacher's Homiletic Commentary* (New York: Funk and Wagnalls Co., 1892), Vol. VIII, p. 89.

background of that corrupt day. Boaz was a wealthy
kinsman of Naomi. The first verse uses a word that
does not convey that strong meaning, but a word
used later, which we will consider, does so. We shall
reserve for a succeeding chapter the consideration of
Boaz as the kinsman-redeemer. His position of wealth
made it possible for him to redeem the estate of
Elimelech.

In the suggestion that Boaz was a man of valor
there is found an explanation why he had not met
Ruth when the two widows first returned. He was
probably away at the time on some military expedition, which prevented him from meeting the comely
Moabitess. As a man who was mighty in the law, he
is revealed as one who was acquainted with the
Mosaic law. He possessed a knowledge of the Word
of God. The implications in the remainder of the story
support this interpretation of the text.

Boaz as the kinsman-redeemer is a figure of the
Lord Jesus Christ, our Kinsman-Redeemer. There is
not a finer and truer type of the Lord Jesus Christ in
the Bible than Boaz. There was no ugly blot on his life
that marred him as a type of Christ. That is not true
of the other outstanding types of Scripture: e.g.,
Moses sinned and David sinned grievously. Ruth, as
the Gentile redeemed by grace, is a glorious picture of
the church as the bride of Christ to be presented to
Him "without spot or blemish."

Ruth accepted her poverty in humbleness and
quietness, and she sought to make the best of an
unfortunate situation. She did not rebel against the
pinch of penury but requested permission from her
mother-in-law to glean in the fields. These two must

have been in danger of starving. Her request revealed that she was acquainted with the Mosaic law. Otherwise, how would she have known that it was possible for her, a stranger, to glean in the fields? The Moabites possessed no such just law. God's wonderful arrangement for taking care of the poor among His people reveals His great concern for them. There was an expressed law, which was given that the poor might have adequate provisions made for their needs:

> And when ye reap the harvest of your land, thou shalt not wholly reap the corners of thy field, neither shalt thou gather the gleanings of thy harvest (Lev. 19:9).
>
> And when ye reap the harvest of your land, thou shalt not make clean riddance of the corners of thy field when thou reapest, neither shalt thou gather any gleaning of thy harvest: thou shalt leave them unto the poor, and to the stranger: I am the LORD your God (Lev. 23:22).
>
> When thou cuttest down thine harvest in thy field, and hast forgot a sheaf in the field, thou shalt not go again to fetch it: it shall be for the stranger, for the fatherless, and for the widow: that the LORD thy God may bless thee in all the work of thine hands" (Deut. 24:19).

Poverty is in no way a blessing. On the contrary, it was part of the curse that Christ bore. It was no proud confession but a sad admission that He made to the scribe who sought to follow Him, "The foxes have holes, and the birds of the air have nests; but the Son of man hath not where to lay his head" (Matt. 8:20). It is possible to become so involved in the question raised by the Pharisees when His disciples were gathering corn on the Sabbath, that the raw fact of the hunger of His disciples is completely ignored. Following Him meant hunger to them. "He became poor" in material things, for poverty is one of the results of sin. One of the most marvelous things prophesied concerning our Lord in the kingdom is: "But with righteousness shall he judge the poor" (Is. 11:4). The poor will some day enter a new era, and then poverty will be removed from this earth. Man's utopias cannot remove poverty; only the coming of the King can do that.

Riches in and of themselves constitute no evil. God is rich, and He makes that claim concerning Himself: "For every beast of the forest is mine, and the cattle upon a thousand hills" (Ps. 50:10). One of the promises made concerning those who enter the Father's house is that they will inherit riches. I care not whether this be considered literally or spiritually; the children of the Father shall lack no good thing and shall inherit some day with Christ. Christ is wealthy beyond the dreams of Croesus: "He was rich. . . ." God's intention is to abolish poverty in His universe by making wealthy all those who enjoy being wealthy. Under the theocracy of Israel, God made adequate provision for the poor.

Ruth was but exercising her prerogative under the theocracy of Israel. Strangers were permitted to go into the fields of those who were harvesting grain and gather what the reapers left in the field. Ruth qualified in a twofold way: she was a stranger and a widow. Many wealthy and miserly farmers disobeyed this law as they did all the other laws. Therefore, the poor probably had to search diligently sometimes before they could find a field in which they could glean. A farmer who permitted the poor to glean in his fields was a keeper of the Mosaic law in this respect. It spoke well of any who did this.

Evidently, when Ruth went out of the city of Bethlehem into the surrounding fields to glean, she had no definite destination in mind. She chanced to enter the field of Boaz. The Authorized Version has it: "and her hap was to light on a part of the field belonging unto Boaz" (2:3). Keil and Delitzsch gave this literal translation: "her chance chanced to hit upon the field. . . ."[4] For Ruth it was the barest kind of a coincidence. On the human side, it was the fortuitous concurrence of circumstances. At this time Ruth had not even so much as heard of Boaz. Not until she returned at the conclusion of that day did she learn from the lips of Naomi, "The man is near of kin unto us, one of our next kinsmen" (2:20).

There are multitudes who would interpret the episode of that day as fate. In the program of God there is no such thing as fate, chance, or accident. As the remainder of the story well illustrates, this was not chance but the leading of the unseen hand of God. All this happened according to His direction. This was one instance out of millions of the providential dealings of God in the everyday affairs of man. Cromwell said:

> Let us look into providences; surely they mean somewhat. They hang so together; have been so constant, so clear, so unclouded.[5]

God was moving all events in the life of this for-

---

[4]Keil and Delitzsch, p. 477.
[5]Baxendale, p. 149.

eigner that she might occupy a strategic position and be an important link in the scarlet chain running through Scripture.

In the final analysis, no accident can happen to a child of God. He may be in a car wreck, or he may be killed instantly, but for the child of God that cannot be finally defined as an accident. Nothing can come to a Christian that does not first receive the permission of God. Chance is removed from the child of God, for he is like Job of whom Satan said, "Hast not thou made an hedge about him?" (Job 1:10). The Christian can arise amidst the alarming vicissitudes of life and affirm, "And we know that all things work together for good to them that love God, to them who are the called according to his purpose" (Rom. 8:28).

Ruth found herself unwittingly in the field of Boaz, unaware of the great events which were presently to ensue in her life. Boaz had been absent from the harvest field, probably attending to some urgent business in Bethlehem which detained him in the early part of the morning. As he entered the harvest field, he addressed the laborers with a most unusual greeting, "The LORD be with you" (2:4). Virtually every commentator calls special attention to the form of greeting. First of all, it reveals the close relationship that existed between Boaz and the reapers. There was no labor problem in his field. Management and labor were on speaking terms, and these were of the friendliest sort. The most remarkable part is the inclusion of the Lord's name and a gracious recognition of Him in all relationships of life. To his "The LORD be with you," they responded with the cheery and gracious greeting, "The LORD bless thee" (2:4). God was reverently recognized in the harvest field by both the owner and the laborers. This all transpired in the days of the judges when there was decline, decay, and disintegration. The remainder of Israel might forget God and turn to idols, but there was one man who did not forget Him but remembered Him even in the extension of a morning greeting.

Observing the presence of an attractive stranger, Boaz inquired of the servant, who was acting as an overseer of the reapers, concerning her identity. "Whose damsel is this?" (2:5) betrays more than a passing interest on the part of Boaz. It was love at first sight. The fact that Boaz had fallen desperately in love with Ruth is not concealed in the Book of Ruth. The love of man and woman is an arrangement of God and is never wrong except when perverted by sin.

There are those who see in Boaz an old man well past the meridian of life.[6] This is based on an extreme but general interpretation of Ruth 3:10 where Boaz commended Ruth in this manner: "And he said, Blessed be thou of the LORD, my daughter: for thou hast shewed more kindness in the latter end than at the beginning, inasmuch as thou followedst not young men, whether poor or rich."

There is no positive statement here that Boaz was an old man, nor does the passage imply that Boaz was making a contrast between the young men and himself in respect to their ages. Ruth, as a young widow, had not attached herself to the young set of her day in order to make a marriage for herself. Boaz called

---

[6]James Morison, *The Pulpit Commentary* (London: Kegan Paul, Trench, Trubner and Co., 1897), Vol. VIII, p. 49.

attention to the fact that she had followed neither poor nor rich. Ruth was not attempting to get married, and therefore had not followed the younger men who were eager to get married. The normal inference from this passage is that Boaz was not a boy but a man of middle age. Quite evidently, he was in the full vigor of manhood and not a dyspeptic man approaching senility. The tenor of the story contradicts any such notion. The meeting of Ruth and Boaz involved a man who could in no sense be an old man.

The servant of Boaz identified Ruth as "the Moabitish damsel that came back with Naomi out of the country of Moab" (2:6). Then the overseer explained Ruth's presence in the field of Boaz. With that bit of information, Boaz addressed Ruth with more than common courtesy. He insisted that she abide in his field and avail herself of the provision and protection which he had established for his maidens who were workers in the harvest. In the time of the judges, it was very likely unsafe for a young woman to go unchaperoned into the harvest fields to enjoy the benefits granted by the Mosaic law to the poor and to strangers. Boaz realized that Ruth's attractiveness would jeopardize her womanly position, and some unscrupulous person might take advantage of her because of her straitened circumstances. Boaz offered to place the mantle of his protection about her. Boaz urged her to "go not to glean in another field" (2:8).

Moorhouse calls attention to a beautiful comparison here with Christ and the church.[7] The field belonged

---

[7]Henry Moorhouse, *Ruth, The Moabitess* (Chicago: Fleming H. Revell Co., 1881), p. 26.

to Boaz. The fields of Boaz stretched over the entire landscape. It was not necessary for Ruth to go into another field, for there was plenty in the field of Boaz. The fields of Boaz were ample to supply more than the needs of Ruth. Christ has said to His church, "Love not the world, neither the things that are in the world" (1 John 2:15). There is enough for the Christian in Christ; therefore, it is not necessary for the Christian to glean in the fields of the world.

Ruth realized that Boaz had passed the bounds of ordinary courtesy, and she demonstrated an admirable humility in response to this gracious provision. "Then she fell on her face, and bowed herself to the ground, and said unto him, Why have I found grace in thine eyes, that thou shouldest take knowledge of me, seeing I am a stranger?" (2:10).

Ruth recognized that she was the recipient of grace, and she knew that she had done nothing to merit it: "Surely he scorneth the scorners: but he giveth grace unto the lowly" (Prov. 3:34). In thankfulness she fell on her face according to the Eastern custom, and as the text indicates, she bowed down to the ground. What thankful humility on her part was manifested by this act! As we have previously shown, Ruth was included in the genealogy of Christ because of the grace of Boaz extended to her in this time of need.

Although Boaz had not met the Moabitish maiden, he had heard much concerning her. The report was good and revealed that Ruth, a stranger, had won her way into the hearts of the natives of Bethlehem simply by her noble character and sterling worth exemplified in her dealings with her mother-in-law. It was common knowledge in Bethlehem that Ruth was exceptionally good to her husband's mother, and this conduct had ingratiated her to the Bethlehemites. She had chosen to forsake her native land to make a home with her adopted mother. Likewise, it was known that she had made a decision in favor of the "LORD God of Israel, under whose wings thou art come to trust" (2:12) against the idols of Moab. Ruth's decision was for God, and by it she had found grace. All of this favorable comment had come to the ears of Boaz. It is comforting to note, in this connection, that Christ knows our hearts and understands thoroughly those little things that we do for Him which go unnoticed by an indifferent world.

Ruth accepted the gracious hospitality extended to her and acknowledged that the act of Boaz had brought comfort to her heart. She recognized and called attention to the fact that she was a stranger and "not like unto one of thine handmaidens" (2:13). Wittingly or unwittingly, she called attention to the very fact that had directed the attention of Boaz to her. Boaz had come to maturity without marrying simply because there was a monotonous similarity among the women of his people. We might say, adopting the common colloquialism, "Ruth was *different*." Her unlikeness to the other maidens drew from the heart of Boaz the interested inquiry, "Whose damsel is this?" (2:5). These facts confirm the suggestion that the meaning of the name Ruth is "beauty." The physical beauty of the gentile girl, together with her beautiful character, found a responsive chord in the heart of Boaz.

There is a modern but false notion that beauty is something that God cannot use. This pseudo-piety is encouraged by the prevailing custom of prostituting beauty on the altar of mammon. But beauty, like any other gift of God (e.g., a good voice), can be dedicated to the service of God. Modern youth needs to be reminded of this. A very noteworthy feature of this entire episode is the silence of the record as to the physical appearance of Ruth. The beauty of her character, however, assumes great prominence in the account.

Boaz continued to make ample provision for the comely stranger who had wandered into his field through the direct providence of God. At noontime, Boaz invited her to partake of the midday meal with him and his workers. This portion of the story bears all the earmarks of a very modern story. He met her sometime during the late morning and invited her to lunch with him the same day. The rapidity with which these events occurred compares favorably with the acceleration of the Machine Age. Perhaps this decadent age, in spite of its vaunted improvement, is not far removed from the similar period in the days of our story.

Boaz granted her full liberty to glean where she pleased in the afternoon. He went so far as to instruct his reapers to leave some grain in her path. "And let fall also some of the handfuls of purpose for her, and leave them, that she may glean them, and rebuke her not" (2:16). Boaz, by this conduct, was showing marked attention to Ruth, a fact that could not escape the observation of the workmen and maidens in the field. Ruth herself could not have been oblivious to his magnanimous gesture on her behalf. Due to this generous consideration, Ruth gleaned that day "about an ephah" (2:17). This was about one bushel and three pints.[8] She returned to Naomi with the fruit of her labor at the end of that first day.

Not only had Boaz made it possible for her to glean this great amount, but Ruth had been diligent in the task. "She continued even from the morning," all through the day, "until even" (2:7, 17). This is a virtue that commends itself to every Christian and receives the full sanction of Scripture: "Not slothful in business; fervent in spirit; serving the Lord" (Rom. 12:11). Ruth wàs a woman of faith, but she was likewise found faithful in every task. True faith produces faithfulness: "Faith without works is dead" (James 2:20). Although Boaz extended to her extraordinary privileges, she did not fail to avail herself of them and to apply herself to the task all that day. She never would have filled her bushel basket if she had not labored.

We sometimes sing rather lustily, "We shall come rejoicing, bringing in the sheaves," and then we go out and do nothing. Two acts are essential if we are to harvest "precious seed" (Ps. 126:6). One is praying, and the other is going into the fields to glean. Christ gave these as the essential requirements.

> Then saith he unto his disciples, The harvest truly is plenteous, but the labourers are few; Pray ye therefore the Lord of the harvest, that he will send forth labourers into his harvest (Matt. 9:37,38).

In the first place, the disciples were to pray that laborers might be sent forth into the harvest. That did not terminate their task. In the very next chapter, Christ called His disciples to Himself, and then He

---

[8]*Scofield Reference Bible*, p. 316.

commanded them to "go rather to the lost sheep of
the house of Israel" (Matt. 10:6). After His crucifixion
and resurrection, He enlarged the commission to include the world: "Go ye into all the world, and
preach the gospel to every creature" (Mark 16:15).
The normal and logical order is "pray" and "go." The
Christian who is not out in the harvest field somewhere is somehow failing in the very first essential of
Christian living. A living faith is a going faith; a vital
faith is an evangelizing faith. Calvin's comment is
apropos: "Faith alone saves, but the faith that saves is
not alone." Every Christian ought to be in the field of
the One who is greater than Boaz. If he goes into the
field to glean, he will find that some "handfuls of
purpose" have been left by Christ, which will enable
him to do more than glean. He will reap a bountiful
harvest in white fields.

The full basket of Ruth caused Naomi to exclaim,
"Blessed be he that did take knowledge of thee"
(2:19). This bountiful supply could not have been the
fruits of gleaning. Ruth related the incidents of that
day, which furnished an explanation for the full grain
sack. Naomi probably hoped that Boaz had fallen in
love with Ruth, and her woman's heart suspected, in
view of the circumstances, that her hopes were fulfilled. Naomi, in turn, informed her concerning Boaz
and his kinship to them. Naomi calls him "one of our
next kinsmen." The word used here for kinsman is
the Hebrew word *goel*. This is not the same word
used in the first verse of this chapter. Here it means
all that the word *kinsman-redeemer* implies. It indicated
that Boaz was in the position, by blood relationship,
to redeem the estate of Elimelech and to fulfill the

duty of a kinsman by marrying Ruth. The word *goel* indicated more than merely a relation, and our story demonstrates the truth of that. We shall reserve for a subsequent chapter a full discussion of the word *goel*.

Naomi confirmed the action of Boaz by encouraging Ruth to follow him in his suggestions. "And Naomi said unto Ruth her daughter in law, It is good, my daughter, that thou go out with his maidens, that they meet thee not in any other field" (2:22).

The concluding verse of this second chapter shows that the first day's experience was only a precursor of many that followed. "So she kept fast by the maidens of Boaz to glean unto the end of barley harvest and of wheat harvest; and dwelt with her mother in law" (2:23).

Ruth went daily into the field of Boaz until barley harvest was ended. It is natural to infer that the first meeting of Boaz with Ruth was not the last, and the record of this first day was but typical of many that followed. To recognize this is sufficient preparation for the incidents in the next chapters. It is not an interpolation of this verse to add that the love of Boaz was deepened by constant contact and that their friendship blossomed into mutual admiration and adoration for each other. Ruth continued to hold Boaz in high regard and esteem, and he, in turn, respected her nobility of character, which was studded with many virtues.

We may be sure that by the end of barley harvest, Boaz, the rich kinsman, and Ruth, the stranger from Moab, were in love. The entire town of Bethlehem must have smiled when they saw that the town's most eligible bachelor had fallen in love with a girl from Moab, whom they, too, had taken into their hearts. The beauty of this story, which occurred during the time of men like Gideon, of whom it is written "he had many wives," and Samson, whose affairs with the opposite sex were notorious, would touch the hardest heart with profound wonder of the love of a great man for a noble woman. The honest love of a great man and a good woman is born in the heart of God, and this kind of love is noble and ennobling, and is described in the poetry of the Holy Spirit:

... for love is strong as death ... Many waters cannot quench love, neither can the floods drown it: if a man would give all the substance of his house for love, it would utterly be contemned (Song 8:6,7).

· 8 ·

On the Threshingfloor of Boaz

Whatever hypocrites austerely talk
Of purity, and place, and innocence,
Defaming as impure what God declares
Pure, and commands to some, leaves free to all,
Our Maker bids increase.

—*John Milton*

"Then Naomi her mother in law said unto her, My daughter, shall I not seek rest for thee, that it may be well with thee?" (3:1).

The harvest season was ending, and Ruth and Boaz's love had blossomed full.

It is most likely that the "rest" referred to in this first verse is marriage. This has been the generally accepted interpretation, and it is a sound one. Ruth's marriage into the family of Naomi had brought travail to her heart. She had tasted the bitter fruits of disappointment and felt the keen pangs of sorrow. She had come in contact with the seamy side of life and had learned of the relentless struggle for a livelihood that raw poverty brings.

Life in the presence of penury could not have been pleasant for the maid from Moab, but there is not a scintilla of suggestion that she ever complained. She had cast her lot with Naomi on the side of God, and she abode with fortitude in her decision. The mother heart of Naomi went out to her daughter-in-law, and she sought for her a place of rest. This could only be attained in the quiet shelter of a godly home, where some strong man protected Ruth from the stormy winds of a harsh world. The injunction of Paul in this connection has always been the mind of God: "I will therefore that the younger women marry" (1 Tim. 5:14).

This suggests the heart cry of Christ for those who know the sting of sin and have borne the burdens of life: "Come unto me, all ye that labour and are heavy laden, and I will give you rest" (Matt. 11:28). The soul of the sinner needs to find rest. There is no rest in the world, but "there remaineth therefore a rest to the people of God" (Heb. 4:9). This rest is found only in Christ. If we have found rest for our souls in Christ, we should seek, like Naomi, rest for some other storm-tossed sinner.

Naomi suggested the possibility of marriage. This was the evident tenor of her question when she asked, "Shall I not seek rest for thee, that it may be well with thee?" (3:1). She appointed herself to the role of matchmaker. This should not be cause for criticism of Naomi, for she was engaged in a worthy cause that had the sanction of God. Naomi's proposal was discreet and in no way transgressed the bounds of propriety. She was accepting the role of mediator in marriage. She not only suggested marriage but named the one whom Ruth should marry.

This was not a groundless proposal, as the events of the barley harvest bore mute but eloquent witness. Boaz had made all proper overtures, and Naomi's suggestion to Ruth was to make it possible for Boaz to know of her willingness and to encourage further negotiations. According to the Mosaic system, it was incumbent upon Ruth to make a definite move, especially after the events of barley harvest had occurred. If Ruth had remained taciturn after Boaz had shown his interest in her during the harvest season, it would have constituted a rejection of him as a suitor for her hand. This was made necessarily so, as we indicated earlier, by the very strange custom instituted by the Mosaic system.

Boaz was a *goel*, and as such, his duty was to marry the widow of a kinsman, provided he was next of kin. The widow's duty was to claim this provision for her interest if she so desired. Only a false modesty or weakness would keep her silent. She was fulfilling God's intention for her if she asserted her rights, as given in God's law. Here is the very strange law:

> If brethren dwell together, and one of them die, and have no child, the wife of the dead shall not marry without unto a stranger: her husband's brother shall go in unto her, and take her to him to wife, and perform the duty of an husband's brother unto her.... And if the man like not to take his brother's wife, then let his brother's wife go up to the gate unto the elders, and say, My husband's brother refuseth to raise up unto his brother a name in Israel, he will not perform the duty of my husband's brother. Then the elders of his city shall call him, and speak unto him: and if he stand to it, and say, I like not to take her;

then shall his brother's wife come unto him in the presence of the elders, and loose his shoe from off his foot, and spit in his face, and shall answer and say, So shall it be done unto that man that will not build up his brother's house. And his name shall be called in Israel, The house of him that hath his shoe loosed (Deut. 25:5,7–10).

According to this law, Ruth was the one to take the initiative and prosecute her case. Her condition was not the same as that of an unmarried woman. In that case, the man was to take the initiative. As a widow, it was incumbent upon her to let her intention be known to the kinsman. If the kinsman refused her proposal, she could hale him into court and bring disgrace upon him. Only ignorance could lead one to maintain that the Mosaic law was in favor of the man and that woman had no rights under it. Here is but one case out of many where women were protected by the Law.

The evident interest of Boaz furnished Naomi with confidence and Ruth with assurance. His conduct opened up the way for Ruth to request with boldness that he act as kinsman-redeemer for her. Boaz had gone as far as he could, under the Law, toward making a marriage with the Moabitess. Quite frankly, it was her move. The step that Naomi proposed to Ruth must be examined, therefore, in the light of the Mosaic law and the events of the barley and wheat harvest that year. When so viewed, any thought of presumption on the part of Naomi or of immodesty or brazenness on the part of Ruth must be dismissed as utterly ridiculous. Only a prudish mind can find anything improper in the incident of chapter 3 after all the facts are considered fairly. Kitto said that there was "nothing in these directions which was considered improper under the special and peculiar circumstance of the case."[1]

"Wash thyself therefore, and anoint thee, and put thy raiment upon thee, and get thee down to the floor: but make not thyself known unto the man, until he shall have done eating and drinking. And it shall be, when he lieth down, that thou shalt mark the place where he shall lie, and thou shalt go in, and uncover his feet, and lay thee down; and he will tell thee what thou shalt do" (3:3,4).

Until the events in this chapter, Ruth evidently had been attired in widow's weeds. She had worn the badge of mourning out of respect for the dead. Time had elapsed sufficiently now for the wounds to be healed, and her heart was occupied with another. Naomi, the mother of the deceased husband of Ruth, was the one who suggested that she substitute for her garments of mourning a raiment that was more in harmony with her bright beauty. For Ruth, this meant breaking the last thread that tied her to an unhappy past in the land of Moab. The garments of mourning were fit symbols of her past, but now the future loomed before her, blazing with light and joy. For Ruth, ". . . old things are passed away; behold, all things are become new" (2 Cor. 5:17).

The barley harvest was over, and the time for threshing and winnowing had come. An understanding of the harvest season of that day furnishes a

---

[1]*Scofield Reference Bible*, p. 144.

background on which the proceedings of this chapter were enacted. James A. Patch outlined the following description of the threshing process in that day:

> The threshing-floors are constructed in the fields, preferably in an exposed position in order to get the full benefit of the winds. If there is a danger of marauders they are clustered together close to the village. The floor is a level, circular area twenty-five to forty feet in diameter, prepared by first picking out the stones, and then wetting the ground, tamping or rolling it, and finally sweeping it. A border of stones usually surrounds the floor to keep in the grain. The sheaves of grain which have been brought on the backs of men, donkeys, camels, or oxen, are heaped on this area, and the process of tramping out begins. In some localities several animals, commonly oxen or donkeys, are tied abreast and driven round and round the floor. . . . Until the wheat is transferred to bags some one sleeps by the pile on the threshingfloor.[2]

Boaz had joined his laborers in the work of threshing the grain. A multitude had gathered there, some even bringing their families. It was a time of celebrating with profuse expressions of joy, when man made vocal his gratitude to God for His gracious provision in a bountiful harvest and expressed his appreciation for God's abundance; it was a season with a definite religious meaning. Boaz, though a rich man, joined his workmen in this happy occasion. It is not pure speculation to suggest that on the threshingfloor of Boaz the religious significance was kept in the foreground. The activity was truly a festival unto Jehovah.

---

[2]James Orr, ed. *International Standard Bible Encyclopedia*, rev. ed. (Grand Rapids, Mich.: Wm. B. Eerdmans, 1930), Vol. I, p. 77.

They winnowed the grain at night to take advantage of the night wind of that country, which was ideal for the process. Winnowing consisted of picking up the grain with some instrument after the grain had been tramped out, then pitching it into the wind that the chaff might be blown away. After the workmen had labored into the night and the wind had abated, they ate a midnight meal and retired for the night, sleeping on the threshingfloor to guard the winnowed grain.

Naomi instructed Ruth how to proceed according to the threshingfloor technique. Ruth was to go down to the threshingfloor in the evening, but she was not to make herself known. The great crowd, the excitement, the cover of darkness, and her change in the manner of dress would all contribute toward accomplishing this. She was to observe Boaz when he finished the late repast and lay down for the night on the threshingfloor. Note that the threshingfloor was a public place and that these incidents all took place in the open. Both men and women were lying about the threshingfloor. Entire families were gathered there. There was not much privacy connected with such circumstances, but it was the custom of the day and was not considered immodest or even questionable. This was a happy family gathering in the spirit of a religious festival. Naomi never would have suggested anything that would have compromised her daughter-in-law. Ruth was merely following the instructions of Naomi in all this. We may be sure that neither Naomi nor Ruth was doing anything indiscreet, and if they had it would not have received the approbation of Boaz. His wholehearted approval and complimentary

speech to Ruth for her behavior removes any appearance of evil from the whole affair.

Ruth was instructed to go to the place where Boaz
had retired and to take her place at his feet. There she
was to pull his long mantle, the *Chudda*, over her that
he might know that she sought shelter and protection. This was a symbolic and modest way of telling
Boaz that she would be willing to accept him as the
goel to take Mahlon's place in a leviritic marriage.
Ruth could have gone before the elders of the city and
demanded that he do it, and she would have been
within her legal rights. But the method adopted by
her, at the suggestion of Naomi, was a quiet and
reticent manner of procedure. It was so interpreted
by Boaz, as we shall see.

If there is any criticism of this rather audacious
method, certainly Naomi must bear the brunt of it, as
it was entirely her plan. Many see no good in this
plan at all. Trapp said, "It was a bold expedient but
not necessarily the worse because of that.[3] Thomson
censured Naomi for not "abstaining from all appearance of evil."[4] Others look upon it as forcing providence upon a too-perilous artifice. However, others
look upon this plan in a favorable way, as we have
suggested beforehand. The circumstances and the
period of time must be taken into consideration in
judging the plan.

Ruth was obedient to Naomi in this matter, and she
fulfilled every direction. In the middle of the night,
Boaz became restless and turned upon his pallet. As

---

[3]Walter Baxendale, *Preacher's Homiletic Commentary* (New York: Funk and
Wagnalls Co., 1892), Vol. VIII, p. 146.
[4]*Ibid*.

he did, he discovered someone at his feet, and upon closer investigation, he found that it was a woman. In the darkness, he made inquiry as to her identity. The answer of Ruth to his question is notable: "I am Ruth thine handmaid: spread therefore thy skirt over thine handmaid; for thou art a near kinsman" (3:9). Instead of bringing him before the public eye and forcing him to perform the part of a *goel*, she was giving him the opportunity of rejecting or accepting the office of *goel* quietly. We may be sure that Naomi and Ruth would not have prosecuted the case further. They would not have embarrassed him publicly or forced him legally to do that which he had no mind and heart to perform. But Naomi and Ruth had every provocation to believe that he was waiting to seize the opportunity to act as *goel* when the opportunity presented itself. Instead of being indecorous in this plan, they were adopting the utmost discretion and consideration. Ruth called upon Boaz to perform the duty of a *goel*. She was entirely within her rights according to the Mosaic injunction, and in all this she had not removed herself from the bounds of propriety. Boaz was a *goel*, and as such he had a duty to perform.

In the chapter on "The Kinsman-Redeemer," we shall consider three meanings of the Hebrew word *goel*. There is a fourth meaning that Gesenius gave for *goel* that has a bearing on the action of this chapter. When a man died, it was the office of the next of kin to marry his widow. We have quoted this law previously as given in Deuteronomy 25. When Ruth called Boaz a near kinsman, she was asking him frankly to perform the duty of a *goel*. Ruth was not approaching a stranger in this way, nor was she forcing this claim upon a kinsman who had manifested no interest. She was revealing her willingness to a kinsman who had given every token of evidence that he was desirous of performing the office of a *goel*. When she asked Boaz to spread his skirt over her, and when she called him a near kinsman, she was using a figure of speech that was tantamount to the acceptance of a marriage proposal. It was the Eastern way in that day of saying, "Yes, I will marry you." This is accentuated by one of the prophets:

> Now when I passed by thee, and looked upon thee, behold, thy time was the time of love; and I spread my skirt over thee, and covered thy nakedness: yea, I sware unto thee, and entered into a covenant with thee, saith the Lord GOD, and thou becamest mine (Ezek. 16:8).

The response of Boaz to Ruth revealed that he so interpreted her language. He complimented her for the expeditious and sagacious manner in which she had conducted herself. He blessed her—not blamed her—for the method of procedure.

"And he said, Blessed be thou of the LORD, my daughter: for thou has shewed more kindness in the latter end than at the beginning, inasmuch as thou followedst not young men, whether poor or rich. And now, my daughter, fear not; I will do to thee all that thou requirest: for all the city of my people doth know that thou art a virtuous woman. And now it is true that I am thy near kinsman: howbeit there is a kinsman nearer than I. Tarry this night, and it shall be in the morning, that if he will perform unto thee the part of a kinsman, well; let him do the kinsman's part: but if he will not do the part of a kinsman to thee, then will I do the part of a kinsman to thee, as the LORD liveth: lie down until the morning" (3:10–13).

This speech of Boaz is noteworthy. It shows that he, too, had been thinking along these lines. He had observed that she was not interested in the young men who wanted to marry. He probably had wondered many times if she had thought of marriage again, but her widow's weeds must have repelled any action on his part. He rejoiced to learn that she was willing for him to become the kinsman-redeemer. He recognized his duty under the Mosaic ordinance and eagerly sought to fulfill it to its last jot and tittle.

Boaz had given this matter much careful consideration beforehand, for he immediately mentioned another kinsman who exercised a prior claim under the law. Boaz, doubtless, had thought many times of pressing his claim, but he knew of the other kinsman, and that brought trepidation to his heart and hesitation to his action. As he could not be sure about Ruth and the other kinsman, Boaz remained patiently in the background for a propitious time to move. Now that time had come. The willingness of Ruth made him resolve to push this case with all the energy and influence that he could muster. He would now attempt to remove this legal obstacle which stood in his way.

Throughout the remainder of this book there is evidenced the eloquent fact that Boaz possessed a knowledge of this case which no one could have had unless he had spent much time considering its legal implications. He not only pointed out to Ruth the presence of another kinsman, but later he also pointed out to the other kinsman the legal difficulty that would confront him if he married Ruth. He knew more about the other kinsman's legal status in the case than the kinsman did himself. That night was the turning point in the life of Ruth, and it was the decisive moment in the life of Boaz.

Boaz asserted himself fully and without delay to Ruth and promised that the very next morning he would begin action on her behalf. The threshingfloor was the scene of the turning point of Boaz's life, but in the next few weeks it lost its glamor and the place of first importance for him. Instead of winnowing wheat, he would be winnowing out the other kinsman and gathering into his garner someone more precious than grain. It was praiseworthy, on the part of Boaz, to recognize the right of the other kinsman who was legally before him. Boaz had no intention of acting illegally in order to gain his heart's desire. This was commendable, but it is evident from the text that Boaz did everything that was honorable to discourage the kinsman from asserting his preferred claim.

Boaz bade Ruth tarry until the morning but to return home before daylight so that she might not be recognized. Evidently, if Boaz had rejected the overture of Ruth, either he or she would have been disgraced. She would have acted in presumption. She could have brought him before the elders of the city. If the other kinsman insisted on his prior claim, Boaz did not wish to cast any dark shadow over the character of Ruth. He exercised the utmost caution on her behalf. Bertheau paid this fine compliment to Boaz:

> The modest man even in the middle of the night did
> not hesitate for a moment what it was his duty to do

with regard to the young maiden (or rather woman) towards whom he felt already so strongly attached; he made his own personal inclinations subordinate to the traditional custom, and only when this permitted him to marry Ruth was he ready to do so. And not knowing whether she might not have to become the wife of the nearer *goel*, he was careful for her and her reputation, in order that he might hand her over unblemished to the man who had the undoubted right to claim her as his wife.[5]

In verse 14, Boaz evidently was addressing his laborers when he said, "Let it not be known that a woman came into the floor." This was a prudent step on his part. Before Ruth left the next morning, he filled her veil with six measures of barley. This man was not only generous in the harvest field, but he was generous on the threshingfloor. In the field Ruth had to glean, but on the threshingfloor she received a generous portion of winnowed grain for which she had expended no labor. The veil was the large mantle worn by the poorer classes, and it was large enough to cover the entire body. It would have held a great deal of grain, but certainly Boaz did not fill it. The size of the measure used is not given. If it were as large as some suggest, then Ruth could not have lifted the load. The Targum stated that it was over two bushels.[6] Although we are forbidden to speculate, we may be sure that it was a generous portion.

The Authorized Version, in following the Vulgate, translated the final clause of verse 15 "and she went

---

[5]Keil and Delitzsch, *Biblical Commentary on the Old Testament* (Edinburgh: T. and T. Clark, 1865), Vol. IV, p. 483.
[6]Morison, p. 51.

into the city." Coverdale also used this translation, and in reading the passage, it seems the normal and easy method. However, the American Standard Version changed this quite properly to "and *he* went into the city." Ruth returned with the grain to her mother-in-law, and Boaz went into the city to prosecute his case on behalf of the fair damsel. Both went into the city with full hearts, quickened stride, and hastening steps. This slight change in the gender of the pronoun brings to our attention, by way of confirmation, the suggestion previously made, namely that Boaz lost no time in expediting matters that would clear the way for him to marry Ruth. The eagerness of the man is clearly detected and must be carefully considered as we shall make further reference to this feature.

Ruth returned to her mother-in-law before it was yet light. Naomi did not recognize her as she approached and called out, "Who art thou, my daughter?" (3:16). Dr. James Morison saw in this question of Naomi no suggestion that Naomi did not distinguish the identity of Ruth but rather that Naomi asked knowingly, "Art thou Boaz' betrothed?"[7] If the question of Naomi is treated as an idiom, then this evidently is the implication.

Ruth related all her experiences of that night to an interested mother-in-law. As a token of her reception by Boaz, Ruth called attention to the amount of grain she had brought back. It was evidently more than she had brought back the first day when she gleaned in the fields of Boaz, although handfuls of purpose had

---

[7]*Ibid.*

made it possible for her to bring back more than could otherwise be expected. Naomi was confirmed in her thinking that her womanly intuition had been right. The outcome demonstrated that Naomi had been correct at the outset.

Chapter 3 opened with Naomi seeking rest for Ruth, and it closes with that rest attained. We read in this last verse that Naomi did not send Ruth out on another mission to gain rest but advised her to remain at home and enjoy the rest which another had provided. "Then said she, Sit still, my daughter, until thou know how the matter will fall: for the man will not be in rest, until he have finished the thing this day" (3:18).

Naomi told Ruth to remove all thought of restless anxiety from her heart, as another had become restless on her behalf. Boaz could not rest until he had found rest for Ruth, and she could rely absolutely upon him.

This is a rest that only a godly redeemer can provide. It is the rest of redemption. After God created the heavens and the earth, Scripture instructs us that He rested. That was a creation rest. All was good and complete, and nothing needed to be done to improve it. Then man sinned, and God broke His creation rest. "His ox was in the ditch," and God began to move to get man out of the ditch of sin. From that day on, God has not rested. Christ said, "My Father worketh hitherto, and I work" (John 5:17). God will not rest until redemption is finished and sin is destroyed. Christ, as our Boaz, came down and redeemed us that we might have a redemption rest from the penalty of sin. He lives today and is busy that we might rest in His power.

The redemption rest that is provided today for a lost sinner is to cease from his own works and trust his Redeemer-Kinsman to provide his rest. Hebrews 4:9,10 tells us, "There remaineth therefore a rest to the people of God. For he that is entered into his rest, he also hath ceased from his own works, as God did from his." This is the rest that comes when we no longer trust our works but receive His work of redemption on the Cross as the penalty for our sins. Furthermore, we are instructed to rest in Him daily and to commit our every problem and difficulty to Him, as Peter wrote, "Casting all your care upon him; for he careth for you" (1 Pet. 5:7). Only in our great Redeemer is there rest for the restless heart of man from the threshingfloor of this world, with its chaff, stubble, and crowd.

> Reality, Reality,
> Lord Jesus Christ Thou art to me.
> From the spectral mist and the driving clouds,
> From the shifting shadows and phantom crowds
> From unreal words and unreal lives,
> Where truth with falsehood feebly strives:
> From the passings away, the chance and change,
> Flickerings, vanishings, swift and strange,
>   I turn to my glorious rest in Thee,
>   Who art the grand Reality.
>   —*Frances Havergal*

· 9 ·

In the Heart and Home of Boaz

She stood breast-high amid the corn,
Clasped by the golden light of morn,
Like the sweetheart of the sun,
Who many a glowing kiss had won,
On her cheeks an autumn flush
Deeply ripened—such a blush
In the midst of brown was born,
Like red poppies grown with corn,
Round dark eyes her tresses fell,
Which were blackest none could tell,
But long lashes veiled a light
That had else been all too bright.
And her hat, with shady brim,
Made her tressy forehead dim;
Thus she stood amid the stocks,
Praising God with sweetest looks.
"Sure," I said, "Heaven did not mean
Where I reap thou should'st but glean;
Lay thy sheaf adown and come,
Share my harvest and my home."[1]

[1]Joseph Parker, *The People's Bible* (New York; Funk and Wagnalls Co., n.d.), Vol. VI, p. 210.

From the very beginning there was a marvelous development in the status of Ruth. First, she was found
in the land of Moab, a stranger from the covenants of
promise without hope and without God in the world.
Next she was brought by providence into the field of
Boaz, under the wings of the God of Israel. Then she
was sent to the threshingfloor of Boaz, and there she
was seen asserting her claim for a kinsman-redeemer.
Finally, in this last chapter of the Book of Ruth, she is
seen as a bride for the heart of Boaz and as a mother
in his home. What splendid progress! What scriptural
evolution! From a very lowly beginning she was lifted
to the very pinnacle of blessing. All this was made
possible by a *goel* who loved her. She could indeed sing, "All the way my Savior leads me." In
this final chapter of the story of Ruth we have the
outcome of the action initiated by Boaz in the
preceding chapter. He set out upon the task of
redeeming Ruth. Herein is given the fruit of his
labors.

The first act of Boaz was to go early that morning to
the gate of the city, where he stationed himself in a
conspicuous place so that he might hail the unnamed
kinsman as he went out of the city into his fields to
harvest, or as he entered into the city from his
threshingfloor. Boaz eagerly awaited his passage so
that he might speak with him. Presently that one
came by, and Boaz greeted him as if he did not know
his name: "Ho, such a one! turn aside, sit down
here" (4:1). That Boaz knew his name is unquestionably
true, but why the record should withhold his name is
an enigma. "Such a one" is surely not a concrete
identification. The Septuagint threw some light upon

this by giving the word *Kρυοιt,* which means "hidden one." The Hebrew conveyed the same idea by the use of two words, the first meaning "to point out" and the second meaning "to conceal." It was the clear intention of the writer to conceal this name. The American idiom "so and so" corresponds more closely than any other expression. Why should the name of this kinsman be concealed? The next verse has resulted in a rather ingenious explanation, which is certainly the most satisfactory one considered: "And he took ten men of the elders of the city, and said, Sit ye down here. And they sat down" (4:2).

When this anonymous kinsman turned aside and sat down, Boaz already was prepared to have the matter settled at once. Ten elders of the city had been chosen to act as witnesses, perhaps as a sort of supreme court. The gate of the city of that day and place corresponded to the marketplace and forum of the cities of the West, and in some respects is equivalent to our present-day county courthouse. Certainly Boaz was proceeding in a way that was according to law, and the final decision in this case was sealed in the manner set forth in the Hebrew statute book. We will let another continue this explanation as to the omission of the name of the unknown kinsman:

> This powerless redeemer is the law. Ten witnesses are there confirming his inability to do it. These represent the Ten Commandments. The curse of the law rested upon the Moabitess for it is written, "An Ammonite or Moabite shall not enter into the congregation of the Lord, even to the tenth generation for ever." (Deut.

23:3). Therefore the law could not bring in Ruth, but only keep her out.[2]

This seems to be a satisfactory explanation for the concealment of the name of the nearer kinsman who bore the pseudonym "So and So." The name was surely known, and it was withheld purposely. This thought will be developed further in a succeeding chapter.

In the presence of these witnesses, Boaz presented the case to this kinsman. The expression used by Boaz concerning what Naomi intended to do with the property is translated in such a way that it is misleading: "Naomi ... selleth a parcel of land, which was our brother Elimelech's" (4:3).

Actually she could not sell it, according to the Mosaic precept: "The land shall not be sold for ever: for the land is mine; for ye are strangers and sojourners with me" (Lev. 25:23). She could only sell a jubilee estate in the property, which in most cases was less than a life estate today. But the tense of the verb precludes the possibility that it means even that. The tense is perfect, and the meaning is "has sold." Coverdale translated it, "offers for sale."[3] The American Standard Version retained the same translation here as the older versions. Dr. Driver said that a resolution or determination to do something in the future often required the perfect, and he cited this passage in Ruth as an instance of that.[4]

---

[2]A.C. Gaebelein, *The Annotated Bible* (New York: "Our Hope" Publication, 1915), Vol. II, p. 124.
[3]James Morison, *The Pulpit Commentary* (London: Kegan Paul, Trench, Trubner and Co., 1897), Vol. VIII, p. 60.
[4]*Ibid.*

It seems to us that the best interpretation is offered by the *Preacher's Homiletic Commentary*, namely that the stress and strain of the years of famine had forced Naomi to sell her property some time subsequent to her return to Bethlehem.[5] Dr. Elliott suggested that Elimelech had done this before he died.[6] In any case, the land needed to be redeemed, as adverse circumstances had forced it out of the hands of the family.

When Naomi first returned from Moab, she was in no position to have the property turned over to her, but as the clouds began to leave her sky, she felt inclined to get the family estate back into its proper channel. Since it was part of the estate of Elimelech and he was a brother to the unnamed kinsman and to Boaz, it was their prerogative to redeem—the first, the "so and so" kinsman, and then Boaz, if the other refused. The term "brother" that was applied to Elimelech by Boaz implied no such strict interpretation as is given the word today. It was a loose term which could refer even to a nephew or cousin. We shall show in a succeeding chapter that the kinsman with a pseudonym was a brother of Elimelech and that Boaz was a nephew of Elimelech. The point to note here is that both men were related by blood to Elimelech and were therefore *goels*.

Most commentators omit this passage, which must be explored if we are to discover the subtle method of Boaz. He did not approach the anonymous kinsman in the same way that Ruth had approached him. She

---

[5]Walter Baxendale, *The Preacher's Homiletic Commentary* (New York: Funk and Wagnalls Co., 1892), Vol. VIII, p. 166.
[6]*Ibid*.

claimed her rights as a widow under the statute regarding the *goel*. She did not mention the property. Evidently Boaz had discussed that angle of the case with her. When Boaz presented the case to this unnamed kinsman, he made the property the important issue. There was a clear change of tactics on the part of Boaz. He mentioned first a *goel* for the property and then presented the case of a *goel* for Ruth as a last alternative to deter this kinsman.

This change of emphasis is essential in revealing the eagerness of this man to have Ruth for his wife. The kinsman expressed a willingness to redeem when he thought it only involved the property, but Boaz was prepared to present the supreme difficulty in order to discourage him. Certainly Boaz was tending to this matter speedily, expeditiously, and righteously, but he was also using some of the wisdom of the serpent. He raised this final objection as a natural barrier, which was destined to cause this kinsman to relinquish all claims.

"Then said Boaz, What day thou buyest the field of the hand of Naomi, thou must buy it also of Ruth the Moabitess, the wife of the dead, to raise up the name of the dead upon his inheritance" (4:5). That which Ruth presented as the foremost claim for a kinsman-redeemer, Boaz reserved last, as a climax. Ruth had a claim upon the estate of Elimelech. The two sons of Elimelech were the natural heirs to the estate. If either one had left a son, he would have been the natural heir to the estate. They did not leave children, so their wives could pass the estate on to any child born to them by a kinsman-redeemer of the family of Elimelech.

Delitzsch and Keil explained the legal side of this affair, which took place at the city gate, in this way:

> So far as the fact itself was concerned, the field, which Naomi had sold from want, was the hereditary property of her deceased husband, and ought there- fore to descend to her sons according to the standing rule of right; and in this respect, therefore, it was Ruth's property quite as much as Naomi's. From the negotiations between Boaz and the nearer redeemer, it is very evident that Naomi had sold the field which was the hereditary property of her husband, and was lawfully entitled to sell it. But as landed property did not descend to wives according to the Israelitish law, but only to children, and when there were no children, to the nearest relatives of the husband (Num. 27:8-11), when Elimelech died his field properly descended to his sons; and when they died without children, it ought to have passed to his nearest relations. Hence the question arises, what right had Naomi to sell her husband's field as her own property?[7]

There is a technical problem here that is made more difficult because of the lack of sufficient data on other cases in Israel. Although it seems clear that neither Naomi nor Ruth could dispose of the property of the estate of Elimelech, yet both possessed certain rights to it. They were able by birth to convey the title of the property to their sons. Ruth's son by Boaz is called by the women of the city the "kinsman-redeemer of Naomi." Such he was, for he inherited the estate of Elimelech, the husband of Naomi. He did not inherit it from Ruth, Naomi, or Boaz, but from them he

---

[7]Keil and Delitzsch, *Biblical Commentary on the Old Testament* (Edinburgh: T. and T. Clark, 1865), Vol. IV, pp. 488, 489.

received the title to it. Ruth was the only one who could raise up a son to inherit the estate of Elimelech. Therefore, she was not only an important link in the chain of geneaology, but she sustained certain rights over the property which Boaz was discussing with the other kinsman. To redeem the property therefore would involve the *goel* in the affairs of the foreigner from Moab. The one who redeemed the estate would have to redeem Ruth also, as she and her affairs were legally bound up in the field of Elimelech. This was the legal technicality upon which Boaz was depending for his victory.

When the attention of Mr. "So and So" was called to this serious difficulty possessing legal implications, he declared that he could not redeem the stranger of Moab without involving his own estate: "And the kinsman said, I cannot redeem it for myself, lest I mar mine own inheritance: redeem thou my right to thyself; for I cannot redeem it" (4:6). The Targum stated that he had a wife and child, which fact would cause a marriage with the gentile girl to jeopardize their interests.[8] Lange inferred that it was merely superstition on his part, as Ruth was associated with the extinguishment of one estate.[9]

The more normal interpretation to place upon his words appears to be that the presence of the Moabitess as an inescapable appurtenance to the property aroused in his mind fears concerning a clear title to any estate in which anyone who was condemned in such unmistakable terms by the Mosaic system (Deut. 23:3) had

[8]Baxendale, p. 166.
[9]*Ibid.*

an interest. This law prevented a Moabite from entering the congregation, even to the tenth generation. It was this law, so it seems, that prevented him from prosecuting his preferred claim. He was evidently frightened by the presence of Ruth, and he immediately surrendered his rights as a redeemer to Boaz.

As further evidence that this agreement between Boaz and the other kinsman was accomplished in a legal manner, the method by which they sealed the bargain presents irrefutable proof. In order to make a contract or agreement binding, it was necessary to follow an unusual procedure. The law was given in Deuteronomy 25:7-9 in connection with a case which was similar to Ruth's. The law is repeated in the last chapter of Ruth, with a few minor omissions: "Now this was the manner in former time in Israel concerning redeeming and concerning changing, for to confirm all things; a man plucked off his shoe, and gave it to his neighbour: and this was a testimony in Israel" (4:7).

The removal of the shoe and the placing of it in the hands of the first party was a legal document of great significance in that day. In Deuteronomy there is mention made that when the kinsman-redeemer refused to marry the widow of the deceased, she was to take the shoe off his foot and to spit in his face. The man who refused to perform the part of a kinsman-redeemer was thereafter called "the house of him that hath his shoe loosed." It is easy to see why the other part of the law did not survive. Boaz did not spit in the man's face, but he did draw off his shoe. Another detail that is worth noting is that this action was to be performed by the widow, which in this instance, would have been Ruth. Instead, Boaz was acting for Ruth. In view of the fact that she was a Gentile, and that she was too modest to push the matter publicly, Boaz acted in her place and on her behalf. This fact is usually overlooked.

Boaz now possessed the shoe of the anonymous kinsman, which was in one sense his marriage license, for it was a legal document bearing all the seals of a court order. This kinsman who has not borne a name up to the present must now be dubbed with the euphemistic nickname "Barefoot." It is a name of reproach. Henceforth he is a "barefoot" redeemer.

This barefoot redeemer represents the law which is unable to redeem the sinner, for Scripture says, "For what the law could not do, in that it was weak through the flesh" (Rom. 8:3). The law is barefoot as far as the sinner is concerned, for it cannot clothe him or put shoes on his feet. It is the gospel of grace that clothes a sinner in the righteousness of Christ and puts shoes on his feet: "And your feet shod with the preparation of the gospel of peace" (Eph. 6:15). The law cannot redeem and must retreat in shame and disgrace, but Christ, our Boaz, can redeem in grace.

With the legal document in his possession (the shoe of "Barefoot"), Boaz concluded the transaction by calling the ten elders to witness that he now was the one who had that day redeemed the estate of Elimelech, Mahlon, and Chilion. Not only was he the redeemer of the estate, but he was the kinsman-redeemer of Ruth. "Moreover Ruth the Moabitess, the wife of Mahlon, have I purchased to be my wife, to raise up the name of the dead upon his inheritance, that the name of the dead be not cut off from among his brethren, and from the gate of his place: ye are witnesses this day" (4:10).

What far-reaching consequences that transaction was to have! The immediate accomplishments seem unspeakable. It changed the status of two very sad and poor widows. It made one of them a bride and a mother, and it lifted the veil of bitterness from the other and made her truly Naomi—"pleasant." It lifted Boaz out of the commonplace existence of a monotonous farmer's life, which he was living alone, into the realm of great blessing and joy. It paved the way for David and, ultimately, for Christ.

Before the close of the day that had begun so auspiciously, Boaz had concluded all his work of a kinsman-redeemer. He became the bridegroom-redeemer. Walter Baxendale called attention to a very interesting fact about this transaction.[10] It was concluded with prayer by the elders of the city. "And all the people that were in the gate, and the elders, said, We are witnesses. The LORD make the woman that is come into thine house like Rachel and like Leah, which two did build the house of Israel: and do thou worthily in Ephratah, and be famous in Bethlehem: and let thy house be like the house of Pharez, whom Tamar bare unto Judah, of the seed which the LORD shall give thee of this young woman" (4:11,12).

The business transaction and the marriage were concluded with prayer. Just as business is not solely a secular affair divorced from God, neither is marriage separated from the life of God. Marriages are made in heaven, and if not, they become an earthly hell. This

---

[10]*Ibid.*

entire story illustrates the great truth that God is interested profoundly in the love of men and women for each other when it blossoms forth into a happy marriage that has His blessing.

Ruth was the sole object that prompted Boaz to conclude this business with such alacrity and expediency. His love for the young maid of Moab afforded him sufficient reason to become the kinsman-redeemer. The story concludes quite properly with the succinct statement, "So Boaz took Ruth, and she was his wife" (4:13). This is the happy ending of every good story. God places in the heart of a man love and affection for a woman, and He makes the feeling between them mutual. His divine intention is that they be united in marriage in His presence with His blessing invoked upon the union. The divorce of marriage from the plan of God, as if it were something with which He took no interest or of which He heartily disapproved, is detrimental to marriage and unfair to God. When marriage is alienated from the plan of God, it ends always in divorce.

The happy marriage of Boaz and Ruth illustrates the glorious ending of the earthly career of the church, when she will be removed from this world and brought into His presence, where she will be united to Christ in marriage.

> Let us be glad and rejoice, and give honour to him: for the marriage of the Lamb is come, and his wife hath made herself ready (Rev. 19:7).

The church will someday be united to Christ as the redeemed gentile bride of the Lamb. Although he was not a Christian, the poet Shelley glimpsed that perfect love:

Love he sent to bind
The disunited tendrils of that vine
Which bears the wine of
life, the human heart.

However, there is another chapter to our story which, although it is not meant to contribute to its beauty, does contribute to one of the supreme objectives. The remainder of chapter 4 tells of the birth of Obed to Ruth and Boaz. This gives occasion for the inclusion of the great genealogy at the end. This genealogy is transferred in its entirety to the opening of the New Testament in the Gospel of Matthew. It sets forth the incidents of this humble story as a link in the great plan and purpose of God. The birth of Obed to Ruth and Boaz at Bethlehem foreshadows the birth of Another, whose coming was to reverberate to the ends of the earth and was to have ecumenical and eternal effect upon this world.

The name *Obed* means "servant" or "worshiper." The women of Bethlehem named him according to his relationship to Naomi. Although he was of no blood kin to Naomi, he was legally her grandson. He was a little servant to Naomi in her old age and took the place left vacant by the death of a husband and two sons. Now her estate would go to the little servant. This one who was the offspring of a Moabitess was a worshiper of the true God, even as his mother was.

The Book of Ruth, coming from the times of the judges, is like a lovely flower in a weed patch. The fragrance of this story has been wafted by the winds to the farthest corner of the earth.

· 10 ·

The Kinsman-Redeemer

In most works on redemption, very little attention, if any, is given to the *person* of the redeemer. Consequently the Book of Ruth is ignored, for the person of the redeemer is of primary importance in this narrative. Jonathan Edwards, in tracing the history of redemption from Moses to David, absolutely ignored Boaz as a type of Christ, the great Redeemer.[1] He mentioned many of the judges in this commendatory language:

> The deliverers that God raised up from time to time were all types of Christ, the great Redeemer of His Church; and some of them very remarkably so; as particularly, Barak, Jephthah, Gideon, Samson, in many particulars.[2]

Having included Samson, he passed over the Book of Ruth entirely, paid no attention to Boaz, and

---

[1]Jonathan Edwards, *History of Redemption* (London: Jones and Co., 1835), p. 84.
[2]*Ibid.*

discussed Samuel as the next in order as a type of the Redeemer. A. H. Strong, in his *Systematic Theology*, defined the section of theology under "Christology" as "the redemption wrought by Christ," and he did not even allude to Boaz as a type of Christ. There is no reference to the Book of Ruth in his entire work on theology. Calvin, in the *Institutes*, made no reference to the Book of Ruth when contemplating redemption. In any biblical history of redemption that seeks to trace the types through the Scripture, there ought to be a reference to Boaz in the Book of Ruth.

The entire scheme of scriptural redemption is posited upon the person of a redeemer. The redeemer is essential to any satisfactory system of redemption. In the Book of Ruth, the person of the redeemer is fully illustrated in the person of Boaz. He is the only example of a Hebrew *goel* in the Old Testament. Boaz was the kinsman-redeemer and is "the plain figure of Christ."[3] Naomi identified Boaz as the *goel* of their family (see 2:20).

The Hebrew *goel* is translated by the English word "kinsman" (3:9) and by the word "redeemer" (Job 19:25). Probably the best translation which combines both thoughts is "kinsman-redeemer." Simply stated, the word means "to set free."[4] Gesenius gave three meanings for the root word which define the different aspects of the word:

---

[3]F.W. Grant, *The Numerical Bible* (New York: Loizeaux Brothers, 1894), Vol. II, p. 274.

[4]C.I. Scofield, *Synthesis of Bible Truth* (Chicago: Moody Bible Institute, n.d.), p. 488.

1. To redeem, buy back. The simple thought is to purchase by paying a price for that which was lost by some reason.
2. To require blood, i.e., to avenge bloodshed. This had reference to someone who was near of kin, as only such a one would seek vengeance.
3. "Since both the right of redemption (1) and the office of avenging bloodshed (2) belonged to the nearest kinsman, this Hebrew word denotes near of kin, near relative."[5]

There are two thoughts in this word which the various meanings suggest. The first refers to the *person* of the redeemer. The redeemer must be a kinsman. This requires the redeemer to be a blood relation, and if he is unable to meet this stipulation, he forfeits all legitimate claims to the title. This is of tremendous importance in consideration of the blood redemption for the sinner provided by Christ. Not only did He shed His blood, but He was blood kin to us. Even on the human plane, not every person could qualify as a redeemer for another. The person of the redeemer is uppermost in any consideration of redemption.

The second thought in the Hebrew word *goel* refers to the *process* of redeeming. Redemption may refer either to the person or to the property or to both. A person who has sold himself or who has been sold into slavery can be redeemed by a kinsman. The property of a person can be redeemed by a kinsman. He can recover from penalty both the person and

[5]William Gesenius, *Hebrew and Chaldee Lexicon*, *Tregelles Translation* (Grand Rapids, Mich.: William B. Eerdmans, 1949).

property, recovering the property to the rightful owner and restoring the person to a place of freedom. According to the Law, if a man through misfortune or untoward circumstances was forced to mortgage his property, and then was unable to recover it at the date of maturity of the mortgage, the property passed into the hands of the mortgager until the Year of Jubilee. In any period during that interval, a kinsman of the mortgagee could pay the mortgage and restore the property to the rightful owner. This same thing applied to the person himself. If he did not have any property, he could sell himself into slavery. The kinsman could at any time restore him to freedom by paying the sum required to meet the debt. The *goel* could move into civil court and recover the property, and he could go into criminal court and deliver the person from the penalty of the law. We see that only a kinsman could perform this peculiar but vital work for a poor relation.

The second meaning of the term *goel* does not figure in this consideration of redemption as it is in no way connected with the Book of Ruth. There is, however, a thought in it that we wish to indicate at this time in connection with the kinsman-redeemer. This is mentioned in connection with the cities of refuge, where a man could flee if he killed another person accidentally. In the city of refuge he was to be protected from the *goel* of the man he had inadvertently slain. The close blood kin of the murdered man would want revenge, and the slayer would be protected in that event. If the slaying was premeditated and the murderer had intentionally killed another, it was allowed under the law for a *goel* to take revenge by slaying him in turn. This was the expressed language of the code of Israel:

> The revenger [*goel*] of blood himself shall slay the murderer: when he meeteth him, he shall slay him (Num. 35:19).

This aspect of the meaning of the *goel* was wonderfully fulfilled in Christ. Sin and Satan have killed man and are therefore murderers. Satan is called a murderer in Scripture, and man is his victim. In the Garden of Eden he led man to eat of that which brought death to the human family. Sin today is a partner in the crime, for "the wages of sin is death." And Paul speaks of sin as an actual murderer: "For sin, taking occasion by the commandment, deceived me, and by it slew me" (Rom. 7:11).

The law is the third party to this unholy trinity. The law is not evil in itself, but it is a horrible taskmaster: "For I was alive without the law once: but when the commandment came, sin revived, and I died" (Rom. 7:9). Man must be redeemed from the law also, for it has become innocently a partner in the crime of murdering the human race. Man had no kinsman to avenge him of this dastardly deed, but One was promised who would be an enemy of Satan and his destroyer:

> And I will put enmity between thee and the woman, and between thy seed and her seed; it shall bruise thy head, and thou shalt bruise his heel (Gen. 3:15).

In the fullness of time, the avenger of blood came "...that through death he might destroy him that had the power of death, that is, the devil" (Heb. 2:14). He came to redeem us from sin and the law. He

hates sin and Satan because they have been the cause
of man's undoing. As we shall presently see, Christ
did not pay a ransom to the Devil, but He did ransom
us from the power of the Devil. Christ, in dealing
with Satan and sin, is the avenger of the blood
kinsman. Our Redeemer loved us when we were
dead in sin, but He hated sin and Satan.

God is seen in Scripture as the Redeemer of both
persons and property. God told Moses that He would
be the Kinsman-Redeemer of Israel. He identified
Himself as the *Goel* of these people: "I will redeem
you with a stretched out arm" (Ex. 6:6). He redeemed
their persons from the slavery of Egypt, but He likewise was the Redeemer of their property. The gifts
that they made to the construction of the Tabernacle
in the wilderness reveal that they left Egypt a rich
nation. That did not conclude God's redemption of
these people. He was not only redeeming them from
Egypt; He also promised to deliver them into the land
pledged to Abraham: "And I will bring you in unto
the land, concerning the which I did swear to give it
to Abraham" (Ex. 6:8). The redemption included the
land. God was the *Goel* of both their persons and
their property.

In the Book of Ruth there is an instance of each of
these aspects of redemption. There is, primarily, a
redemption of the property of Elimelech, but the *goel*
in this particular case had to redeem the maid from
Moab, according to the penal code in Deuteronomy
25:5–10. The *goel*, as a near kinsman, had to marry the
widow of the deceased to raise up the name of the
brother. There could have been no redemption of the
property of Elimelech without a redemption of Ruth,

as Boaz clearly indicated in his answer to the barefoot kinsman: "Then said Boaz, What day thou buyest the field of the hand of Naomi, thou must buy it also of Ruth the Moabitess, the wife of the dead, to raise up the name of the dead upon his inheritance" (4:5).

The refusal of the barefoot kinsman to redeem the property if it involved the redemption of the person of the gentile girl abundantly confirms that both must be done. There could be no separation of the person and the property.

Boaz qualified as a bona fide kinsman-redeemer. He was a blood relation of Elimelech. He was willing to redeem, and he was able to redeem. He was free from any involvement or entanglement that would compromise his person, position, or property. Boaz was a capable redeemer who was endowed with all the qualifications that could be asked of him in this function. As such, he is a worthy figure of Christ, who is greater than Boaz. The credentials of Boaz will be examined in the next few chapters. We are stressing here the first thought concerning the word *goel*; that is, the person who acts as a redeemer must meet every specification, for the entire structure of redemption rests upon him.

In order to make clear in our minds God's method of redeeming, it will be necessary to examine the method by which property and persons were redeemed under the Mosaic system. In a preceding chapter we made reference to the marriage of a widow, which was a redemption for her, according to Deuteronomy 25:5–10. The law concerning the redemption of property is stated in the following way:

And in all the land of your possession ye shall grant a redemption for the land. If thy brother be waxen poor, and hath sold away some of his possession, and if any of his kin come to redeem it, then shall he redeem that which his brother sold (Lev. 25:24–25).

There were two things that were true regarding all real estate in Israel. First of all, God was the owner, and the inhabitants had no such relation to the land. God carefully instructed them in this great fact: "The land shall not be sold for ever: for the land is mine; for ye are strangers and sojourners with me" (Lev. 25:23).

The individuals were tenants upon the land. They merely rented from God; therefore they could not finally dispose of the property. No man could grant a clear title to land, and there were no fee-simple deeds. The nation Israel held an eternal title in the land of Canaan, but the individuals possessed only temporary rights, which were forfeited when they sinned. When God sent the entire nation into captivity, He did not abrogate the title deeds to that land, and the nation did not default in such a way as to lose their right to it. But the individuals who composed the nation at that time were removed off the land, for after all, they had only squatters' rights, which they forfeited for sin.

The second and final fact that was true regarding real estate in Israel grows out of the first. As they were not owners of the land, they could not make a final disposition of it. It was impossible for a person to let the real estate of his family pass out of the hands of himself and his children. He might mortgage it, but the one who held the mortgage understood that in the Year of Jubilee the land returned to the rightful heir of the family who originally had possessed it. Between the time of the mortgage and the Year of Jubilee it was possible for a kinsman to redeem it by paying the mortgage and restoring the property to the family estate. It was not incumbent upon the kinsman to redeem, but the Mosaic system granted him the prerogative if he cared to exercise it.

The other class to which redemption applied is that of persons. This phase of the law is stated in these terms:

> And if a sojourner or stranger wax rich by thee, and thy brother that dwelleth by him wax poor, and sell himself unto the stranger or sojourner by thee, or to the stock of the stranger's family: after that he is sold he may be redeemed again; one of his brethren may redeem him; either his uncle, or his uncle's son, may redeem him, or any that is nigh of kin unto him of his family may redeem him; or if he be able, he may redeem himself. And he shall reckon with him that bought him from the year that he was sold to him unto the year of jubile: and the price of his sale shall be according unto the number of years, according to the time of an hired servant shall it be with him. If there be yet many years behind, according unto them he shall give again the price of his redemption out of the money that he was bought for (Lev. 25:47–51).

If a man through unfortunate or untoward circumstances found himself in poverty, and a stranger next to him during the same interval had become wealthy, it was likely that the Israelite would find himself at the mercy of his rich neighbor. He would probably find himself on the short end of a hard bargain, which would terminate in his selling himself into slavery to the rich man. This was a terrible plight for an Israelite, but it became the unhappy lot of many. In this hopeless position he would have forever remained if it had not been for a clause in the Mosaic law.

In the Year of Jubilee, every slave was freed in the land of Israel. This year occurred only twice a century; because death might come before the Year of Jubilee, another clause brought hope to the heart of the Israelite and redemption to his person. A *goel* could redeem him from the horrible condition of slavery. In such a time and under such circumstances, a rich kinsman must have been a wonderful deliverer to an Israelite, for the *goel* could break the shackles of slavery. The *goel* was a savior for every Israelite in slavery.

Another important feature of redemption is found in the legal tender. The legal tender of redemption was the coin used in any business transaction. The *goel* paid for the release of the property and person with the money that would have been required in any transaction. In other words, the *goel* had to have the *price* of redemption.

In this same connection, the nation Israel was a redeemed people. In what sense were they a redeemed people? The answer that is commonly given to this question is rather stereotyped. They were redeemed by blood and power. The blood of the Passover lamb marked the first stage of their redemption. The Death Angel passed over the land of Egypt, and in every home where there was not the blood upon the doorposts and lintel, he smote the firstborn of man and beast. The blood on the entrance of the home kept the Angel of Death on the outside, and he passed over. The occupants therein partook of the feast that night in joy and afterwards passed out of the land of Egypt. In the midst of the sorrow of Egypt, they went out rejoicing. They were delivered from death. They were redeemed by blood. That was the first coin of redemption.

Then the Red Sea blocked the Israelites' exodus from Egypt. The Egyptians were pursuing them in order to slay them. Again, God became their Redeemer, but the type of exchange used was different. With mighty power He opened the Red Sea so that they might cross dry-shod. The power of God was the toll that Israel used in crossing. As the Egyptians could not pay this toll, they were drowned. This marked the second stage of redemption, but it does not exhaust the truth concerning Israel's redemption. Up to this point, the people of Israel were only freed slaves, and a motley mob they were. They were not prepared to worship God. Redemption is not complete until it brings a lost sinner from the slavery of Egypt into the presence of the Holy God. The lost sinner must be given a heart with which to worship, and he must be redeemed individually. It was necessary, therefore, for each Israelite to pay the price of his redemption, even from the poorest to the richest, about twenty years old and upward. This was the law:

> And the LORD spake unto Moses, saying, When thou takest the sum of the children of Israel after their number, then shall they give every man a ransom for his soul unto the LORD, when thou numberest them;

that there be no plague among them, when thou
numberest them. This they shall give, every one that
passeth among them that are numbered, half a shekel
after the shekel of the sanctuary: (a shekel is twenty
gerahs:) an half shekel shall be the offering of the
LORD. . . . The rich shall not give more, and the poor
shall not give less than half a shekel, when they give
an offering unto the LORD, to make an atonement for
your souls (Ex. 30:11–13,15).

Exodus 30 is the great worship chapter of the
Hebrew economy. A peculiar kind of redemption was
required by those who worshiped God, and it was
paid by the Israelite himself. This constituted a sort of
poll tax which reminded him that he had been
redeemed with a price. Israel was redeemed by blood,
power, and a price. The price was the payment of the
silver half shekel. Redemption always involved the
payment of a price. There could be no redemption in
Israel without the payment of the stipulated price.
Therefore, redemption required that the redeemer be
able to pay the price.

This is further emphasized in the redemption of
persons and property. In the case of property, the
price of redemption was measured in money or in something of value that was in turn measured in money. In the case of persons, the price was measured
always in terms of money. Redemption always involved the payment of a price. There were three
essential characteristics of redemption which were
vital to its accomplishment. Redemption required that
there be a redeemer, a *goel*—one who was a kinsman.
The next requirement was the method of redeeming.
Property or a person could be redeemed only under

certain conditions. Finally, the redeemer had to have
the price of redemption. Each of these requirements
of the Hebrew *goel* was included in the very word
itself. If any one of these was absent, then there was
no *goel*; (e.g., a man might have been a brother to
some poor slave, but if he did not have the price of
redemption he was not a *goel*).

These three characteristics of the *goel* demonstrate
conclusively that the whole doctrine of redemption
rests upon one foundation: the Redeemer Himself.
"For other foundation can no man lay than that is
laid, which is Jesus Christ" (1 Cor. 3:11). The Kinsman-
Redeemer is the hope of the sinner. There is no
redemption for him without Christ. A.H. Strong is
correct in declaring that Christology is Redemption
and Redemption is Christology.[6] We shall consider
the subject of redemption in connection with the
person of the redeemer.

There are five facts concerning the person of the
redeemer which must be true or else he cannot qualify as a legitimate redeemer under God's program:

1. The redeemer must be a near kinsman.
2. The redeemer must perform in willingness his
   work of redemption.
3. The redeemer must possess the ability to redeem.
4. The redeemer must be free himself.
5. The redeemer must have the price of redemption.

Boaz met all of these qualifications in the case
concerning Ruth. He is but a type, and Christ is the

---

[6]A.H. Strong, *Systematic Theology* (Philadelphia: The Judson Press, 1907),
p. 665.

true figure. All of these find their final and complete fulfillment in Christ. In His humanity, He met the first two qualifications. In His deity, He fulfilled the next two requirements. As the God-Man, He met the final qualification. We shall examine each one of these requirements in a separate chapter. First, we shall consider each in its relationship and fulfillment in the Book of Ruth, and then we shall see how this fore-shadows Christ. Boaz met all of these requirements for Ruth and became her kinsman-redeemer; Christ, on a higher plane and in a more complete way, meets all of these for the sinner. We have a Kinsman-Redeemer who satisfies the heart of every redeemed sinner, and who meets all his needs.

> I will sing of my Redeemer
> And His wondrous love to me;
> On the cruel cross He suffered,
> From the curse to set me free.
>
> I will tell the wondrous story,
> How my lost estate to save,
> In His boundless love and mercy
> He the ransom freely gave.
>
> —P. P. Bliss

· 11 ·

The Near Kinsman

O God, O kinsman loved but not enough!
    O man, with eyes majestic after death,
Whose feet have toiled along our pathways rough,
    whose lips drawn human breath!
By that one likeness which is ours and Thine,
    By that one nature which doth hold us kin;
By that high heavens where sinless Thou dost shine,
    To draw us sinners in.

—Jean Inglelow

Anselm, in *Cur Deus Homo*, reduces to one well-defined point the problem of why God became a man. That point is defined by one word: redemption. The Word was made flesh in order to pay the ransom for man's sin. John the Baptist called the Word "the Lamb of God, which taketh away the sin of the world" (John 1:29). His problem resolves itself into the declaration that the Redeemer must be a near kinsman.

In Ruth 2:1, Boaz is first mentioned as a kinsman of Naomi. This word does not designate the *goel* but is a

129

term that probably does not even suggest blood relationship. It can mean no more than "acquaintance."[1]
But when Naomi spoke of Boaz as a kinsman in verse
20 of the same chapter, the word *goel* was employed.
In order that it might not become an ambiguous
word, she prefaced this name with the following:
"The man is near of kin unto us, one of our next
kinsmen [*goel*]."

The difference in the usage of the two terms to
describe the relationship between Boaz and the family
of Elimelech is explained in the meaning of the word
goel. In the first verse of Ruth 2 the writer is making a
general statement regarding Boaz. He actually was no
blood relation of Naomi, and the first word helps to
keep that clear. *Goel* is a technical term and is employed
by Naomi to designate the position of Boaz in relationship to them. Although he was no blood relation
of either Naomi or Ruth, he stood in the place of a
goel because of his kinship to Elimelech. In the first
verse the statement is made that he was "of the
family of Elimelech." This is an indefinite generaliza-
tion. In Ruth 2:20, Naomi says that he is "near of kin
unto us." Technically, he was in the position of a
kinsman-redeemer because of his blood relationship
to Elimelech. It was the family estate of Elimelech that
was in need of a redeemer. It was the widow of a son
of Elimelech who was in need of a redeemer. Boaz
was this *goel* because of blood connection; he was in
this technical position of a *goel* because of his blood
tie with the family of Elimelech.

---

[1]James Morison, *The Pulpit Commentary* (London: Kegan Paul, Trench,
Trubner and Co., 1897), Vol. VIII, p. 29.

Boaz recognized that he was a kinsman-redeemer for these two widows, for he gladly made the acknowledgment, "And now it is true that I am thy near kinsman..." (3:12). Boaz never denied this technical position, which he occupied by blood. Just what the relationship of Boaz to the family of Elimelech was is problematical, but Scripture affords us some suggestions. When the definite relationship of the *goel* was given that there might be some order followed, the uncle of the man who needed to be redeemed exercised seniority, and then next, the son of the uncle or the cousin of the man who needed to be redeemed. After these two, any kinsman could step forward and assert his claim (Lev. 25:49). Boaz mentioned another kinsman who was nearer than he. The implication is that the barefoot kinsman was a brother of Elimelech. Boaz evidently was the son of a third brother, and therefore a nephew of the other kinsman and of Elimelech. This would mean that he was a cousin of Mahlon, the first husband of Ruth. Keil and Delitzsch confirmed this position by stating: "According to the rabbinical tradition, which is not well established however, Boaz was a nephew of Elimelech."[2]

In speaking to the barefoot kinsman who was nearer than he, Boaz recognized that he did not have the first claim but that the other kinsman had prior rights. Boaz acknowledged that "I am after thee" (4:4). In speaking to the anonymous kinsman concerning Elimelech, Boaz called him "our brother Elimelech's" (4:3). Both of these men were *goels* for the estate of

---

[2]Keil and Delitzsch, *Biblical Commentary on the Old Testament* (Edinburgh: T. and T. Clark, 1865), Vol. IV, p. 477.

Elimelech, with Boaz in second position. The other had legal precedence.

The presence of this other kinsman, and his primary rights as a kinsman, demands attention. The only fact that is stated concerning him is that he was a nearer kinsman than Boaz. Although he retained a superior claim and was willing to redeem, apparently with Ruth in the case he did not have the ability to consummate the act of redeeming without endangering his private estate. His willingness was not the eagerness which characterized Boaz, for Boaz apparently endangered his inheritance when he married Ruth (Deut. 23:3). If he did, he was able to overcome any existing barriers. The barefoot kinsman lacked any intention of playing the part of the kinsman-redeemer until reminded by Boaz; then when the danger involved was pointed out to him, he withdrew his generous offer in a state of alarm. He was frightened away by the presence of the gentile girl. On the other hand, she was the magnetic power that attracted Boaz, and the withdrawal of the claims of the other kinsman paved the way for Boaz to become the *goel*. Boaz was the *goel* per se, but it was necessary for the other kinsman to retire in his behalf.

When Boaz went down to the gate of the city of Bethlehem, he sat down to wait for the coming of the anonymous kinsman through the gate. This was more than a convenient place to locate the kinsman; otherwise Boaz would have gone to his home to wait. The gate was the place where contracts were made legal. The procedure of Boaz was equivalent to that which occurs today when a notary public attaches his seal to a document to make it binding in a court of law. The city gate of an Eastern city was similar in many respects to the present-day courthouse. Stone benches were placed there for the accommodation of the crowd, and the gateway became a marketplace and a forum.[3] Ten elders of the city were summoned. These men evidently sat upon these stone benches when they gave legal advice in reference to problems of law which arose from time to time. The elders were apparently already present at the gate, for that represented their place of business. These men acted in this case as witnesses, judges, and attorneys. If it had been necessary to have an opinion rendered in this case, these judges would have done it. In the event of any disagreement, they would have handed down a decision.

Boaz notified the other kinsman that Naomi was going to sell part of the estate of Elimelech. It is apparent that there had been a consultation beforehand between either Boaz and Ruth or between Boaz and Naomi. Perhaps Naomi had instructed Ruth to inform Boaz privately of the financial affairs of the family. Boaz gleaned this information in confidence and wanted to pass it on in the same way, as his speech with the other kinsman indicates: "I thought to advertise thee" (4:4). This reflects very unfavorably upon Boaz; but a more literal rendering has it, "I will uncover thine ear."[4] Our idiom corresponding to this is: "I will whisper it in your ear." It was the financial condition of Naomi that he had learned in private. It was not ready for publication until a kinsman was

---

[3]Morison, p. 60
[4]*Ibid.*, p. 61.

ready to act upon it, and then necessity forced it to be made public: "Buy it before the inhabitants, and before the elders of my people" (4:4).

Then Boaz acknowledged the right of this unknown kinsman to redeem and graciously admitted him to his legal right: "If thou wilt redeem it, redeem it" (4:4). The remainder of this legal transaction brought. out the inability of this kinsman to redeem, under the extraordinary conditions which existed in this case. This kinsman was not willing to expose himself to any legal difficulty. Boaz alone was willing to pay the price, which made him the only competent kinsman-redeemer of the estate and of Ruth.

The redemption of the estate involved the redemption of Ruth the Moabitess. The presence of Ruth cast a dark shadow over the entire transaction, for she was the widow of Mahlon and the only one at this time who could raise up an heir for the estate. Nevertheless, the Mosaic law rejected Ruth and not only treated her as an outsider but kept her from enjoying the covenant relation that the nation Israel possessed (Deut. 23:3). The *goel* who redeemed the property had to redeem her. There was no other alternative. She was rejected until there could be found one who was willing to pay the price.

Boaz was the only one who would pay the price. Boaz was the kinsman-redeemer in a twofold manner: he was a near kinsman by blood relation, and he was a redeemer by exclusion. The presence of Ruth excluded the other kinsman. Boaz occupied a unique position.

This story on the human plane finds full fruition in One who is greater than Boaz. The Lord Jesus Christ is the great Kinsman-Redeemer. Job's heart cry finds perfect fulfillment in Him: "I know that my redeemer liveth, and that he shall stand at the latter day upon the earth" (Job 19:25). Boaz is the only kinsman-redeemer who is a type of Christ as our Kinsman-Redeemer. Boaz occupied a peculiar place in reference to Ruth and Naomi. Christ occupies a unique place in reference to man.

When the covenant of redemption was under consideration, the Son, the Second Person of the Godhead, agreed to come to this earth and provide a redemption for lost sinners in the very place where God had permitted sin to enter. When the covenant of redemption was in the process of fulfillment, Christ did not resort to any of the theophanies or Christophanies of the Old Testament. He did not come as the Angel of the Lord or the Angel of the Covenant, but "we see Jesus, who was made a little lower than the angels for the suffering of death" (Heb. 2:9). When the redemption of man engaged the attention of the Godhead, "God sent forth His Son, made of a woman, made under the law, to redeem them that were under the law" (Gal. 4:4,5).

Christ became a man. God appeared in the tent of human flesh. The Son took upon Himself the form of a servant. The One who was in the *morphe* of God was made in the similitude of man. Christ, who is the image of the invisible God, became a visible man that all might behold His glory. God created man in the image of God, and that was the consummation of the work of creation. God took upon Himself the likeness of man, and that was the initiation of the work of redemption. When man, the creature, sinned, God

did not withdraw from man, but He came down first
to seek the sinner, and finally He came down in the
likeness of sinful flesh to redeem the sinner.

In the Garden of Eden, man sought to be like God
and failed. In the sinful world, Christ sought to
become like man and succeeded. He came down
where we were and got close to us. God became kin
to us that He might redeem us. One of the identifying
marks of the sons of Adam is death: "As in Adam all
die." They are all made of the same flesh and cast in
the same mold. "Christ died" is another way of
saying that He was a son of Adam, and as such, He is
kin to the race of man and is a part of the human
family.

> Forasmuch then as the children are partakers of flesh
> and blood, he also himself likewise took part of the
> same; that through death he might destroy him that
> had the power of death, that is, the devil; and deliver
> them who through fear of death were all their lifetime
> subject to bondage. For verily he took not on him the
> nature of angels; but he took on him the seed of
> Abraham (Heb. 2:14–16).

In the genealogy in Luke's Gospel, Christ's lineage
is traced to Adam, the father of the race (3:38). After
the flesh, Christ was a son of Adam. In addition, the
writer to the Hebrews mentions that "he took on him
the seed of Abraham." The genealogy that opens the
New Testament in the Gospel of Matthew declares in
the first verse that Christ was the son of David and
the son of Abraham. As a son of David, He is related
to the nation of Israel. As a son of Adam, He is
related to the Gentiles. As a son of Abraham, He is
related to the believers in the church. Abraham was

not racially a Jew, although he was the father of that race. He was not any more a Jew than he was an Arab or an Ishmaelite, for he was the father of all three nations. He was a Syrian, racially, according to the Bible (Deut. 26:5).

However, God made a covenant with Abraham that was postulated on grace. Abraham was saved by faith, as is every other lost sinner who receives salvation. Believers are, in this sense, called "children of Abraham." Christ is related, on the human side, to every great family division of the family of men. God came very close to us in the Person of Christ. He could not have come any closer if He had chosen to become our personal brother in our immediate family.

The writer of Hebrews presents two qualifications for a priest (see ch. 5). He shows that Christ met both of these requirements in order to become the Great High Priest. First, the priest must be taken from among men. He must be related to man so that he might have a kindred feeling. He must be a man, for the priest represented man before God, and he must "have compassion on the ignorant, and on them that are out of the way; for that he himself also is compassed with infirmity" (Heb. 5:2). Secondly, the priest must be divinely appointed. Christ likewise meets this requirement, as the writer demonstrates with an abundance of quotations from other Scripture. We need not dwell on the second, as it has no direct bearing upon our subject, but the first bears on the kinship of Christ to the race of man. The writer to the Hebrews offers the kinship of Christ to the race as a proof of His priesthood. "The Word was made flesh" is the simple yet sublime statement of John. It tells of the mighty passage of Deity to humanity, from heaven's glory to earth's gloom. Paul expresses the idea of the redeemer being near of kin when he gives this comprehensive account of the Kinsman-Redeemer:

> But when the fulness of the time was come, God sent forth his Son, made of a woman, made under the law, to redeem them that were under the law, that we might receive the adoption of sons (Gal. 4:4,5).

There could be no real redemption if Christ had not become our kinsman after the flesh. Redemption would only be a theological theory, tending to support a deistic and materialistic philosophy of life. The fact of the kinship of the redeemer puts a heart into this doctrine of redemption and delivers it from the coldness of rationalism. The universe in which we live is theocentric. God is the great central Person of the universe, and all things are for His glory. What man thinks and does is unimportant. God is the only One who matters. His pleasure, His glory, His plan, and His thoughts make the difference. Everything else is secondary. Modernism, in revolting from this seemingly cold position, made the universe Christocentric. This offered no final solution to the problem, for these split into two schools of thought. The deists at first held sway and robbed Christ of His deity, making Him a philanthropic person. The pantheists then assumed control, and they spoke of the divinity of Christ. The divinity that they contemplated was common to all men. At present the deists are becoming the more vigorous group.

There is a deliverance from the horns of this dilemma. The universe is theocentric, but it is not a formal affair. God became a man and came close to us for purposes of redemption. The universe is also, as Henry Mabie put it, "redemptocentric."[5] This enables man to retain his mental equilibrium in a universe suffering from the sting of sin. God did not leave man alone to beat his music out, but He came forth from heaven and became a man in order to redeem. He made Himself kin to the man who had turned his back upon God. Man was marred by sin, but Christ became the perfect man. The man created in the Garden of Eden was made in the likeness of God. There was kinship in creation, for Adam is called "the son of God." Man alienated himself from the life of God, repudiated his right of kinship, and erased through spiritual death any likeness to God. God moved to restore the relationship in a more permanent way by coming down into flesh to redeem man from sin. He re-created a more binding kinship where man might become the son of God through regeneration. The act was "God . . . in Christ, reconciling the world unto himself . . ." (2 Cor. 5:19). Those who have been redeemed by Christ are in a position where now He "is not ashamed to call them brethren" (Heb. 2:11).

A mother is willing to sacrifice herself for the child of her bosom because the little one is flesh of her flesh. A brother will fight for brother, even avenging any wrong done to him. Blood relationship begets in the heart an affection and love that is sometimes beyond human comprehension. There is an old bro-

---

[5]Henry C. Mabie, *The Divine Reason of the Cross* (New York: Fleming H. Revell Co., 1911), p. 34.

mide that recognizes this: "Blood is thicker than water." Human relationship is nothing in comparison
with the love of God for lost sinners. He deliberately
chose the place of kinship to us. His love not only
compares with love of brother for brother but transcends it. Christ is the Kinsman-Redeemer of the
world: "For God so loved the world that he gave his
only begotten Son..." (John 3:16).

We sinners have lost the right to claim any kinship
to God, but God has restored a stronger tie through
redemption. On the authority of God, we can claim to
be sons of God if we are born again. There is one
relationship that is not specifically granted to us to
acknowledge, and that is to call Christ "our elder
brother." Even James and Jude, who could have boasted
of such a relationship, were satisfied to call themselves "servants of Jesus Christ." Certainly we are
forbidden such liberty. But He is not ashamed to call
us *brethren.*

· 12 ·

The Willing Redeemer

Looking unto Jesus the author and finisher of our
faith; who for the joy that was set before him endured
the cross, despising the shame, and is set down at the
right hand of the throne of God (Heb. 12:2).

The impressive feature about the story of Ruth and
Boaz, which was emphasized in previous chapters, is
the eagerness with which Boaz responded to the
responsibility of a redeemer and his glad assumption
of that role. Most evidently he was intent upon paying
whatever price was necessary, and in this he was in
direct contrast to the barefoot kinsman. The other
kinsman never exerted any initiative in the matter of
redemption. Not until Boaz had called it to his attention did he express any willingness at all to redeem,
and then he relinquished all his rights when he
discovered that his inheritance would be endangered
by his act of redemption. "And the kinsman said, I
cannot redeem it for myself, lest I mar mine own
inheritance: redeem thou my right to thyself; for I
cannot redeem it" (4:6).

There was no compulsion placed on the redeemer by the Mosaic statute. He could of his own volition act as a *goel*, or he could desist from exercising any rights that accrued to him under this law. The language of the law was specific: "After that he is sold he *may* be redeemed again; one of his brethren *may* redeem him" (Lev. 25:48).

The only constraint was the blood tie. If love for his more unfortunate brother did not prompt him to act, then there was no law which could force him to do so. The barefoot kinsman's interest in Ruth and Naomi was nil and he was not legally bound to act, although a moral obligation might rest upon him. Seemingly, nothing moved him, and there was no power to make him move.

This is the first point of difference between Boaz and the other kinsman. There was a willingness on the part of Boaz. The urgency of the man in the whole matter is patently evident. The source of his inspiration does not have to be sought afar. When Naomi and Ruth returned from the land of Moab, Boaz was apparently not one of the townsfolk to greet them. He did not know who Ruth was when she ·came into his field, although he had heard of her. Jamieson, Fausset, and Brown offered the explanation that Boaz was away upon some military expedition at the time of their homecoming.[1]

The first information that Boaz had concerning the return of Naomi was a report that contained a favorable and complimentary estimate of the stranger who

---

[1]Jamieson, Fausset, and Brown, *Commentary on the Old and New Testaments* (Chicago: National Publishing Co., 1871), p. 174.

had come with her: "And Boaz answered and said unto her, It hath fully been shewed me, all that thou has done unto thy mother in law since the death of thine husband: and how thou hast left thy father and thy mother, and the land of thy nativity, and art come unto a people which thou knewest not heretofore" (2:11).

The return of Naomi and the presence of a delightful stranger did not prompt Boaz to go immediately to the aid of his distressed kinsfolk. An apology may be found for Boaz in the probability that not enough time had elapsed between their return and his meeting with Ruth to enable him to do anything tangible.

It was the meeting of Boaz with Ruth in the field that led the *goel* to set the wheels of redemption in motion. As stated earlier, the inquiry that he made of his servant in charge of the reapers is significant: "Whose damsel is this?" (2:5). His evident interest in Ruth from the moment of meeting must have been apparent to all, and certainly it did not escape the attention of Ruth. Her question to him was surely guileless and artless, but it revealed an undue attention on his part. "Then she fell on her face, and bowed herself to the ground, and said unto him, Why have I found grace in thine eyes, that thou shouldest take knowledge of me, seeing I am a stranger?" (2:10).

Boaz insisted that Ruth continue to glean in his fields so that he might make adequate provision for her. The first day's gleaning was so much that Naomi did not let it go unnoticed but was provoked to inquire, "Where hast thou gleaned today?" (2:19). Naomi could see, with her mother's heart of experience, all the evidence of a man who had fallen desperately in love with a woman. Nothing but love could have led to the manifestation of such grace. The name Ruth may not sustain the meaning of "beauty" that is sometimes given to it, but most assuredly the story of this book would lead us to ascribe that characteristic to the one who bore it. The Moabitess stirred the heart of Boaz. John Lord makes Heloise, loved by Abelard, the symbol of love among women.[2] In our feeble judgment, Ruth surpasses Heloise as a fitting symbol of the noblest passion among mankind. Ruth of the Bible transcends Heloise of secular history as a living example of what is finest in human affection.

Naomi, recognizing the implications, was bold enough to suggest that Boaz was in love with her pretty daughter-in-law. "Then Naomi her mother in law said unto her, My daughter, shall I not seek rest for thee, that it may be well with thee?" (3:1). The "rest" to which Naomi referred was that of a home for her widowed daughter-in-law. "It was a home to which Naomi pointed, a home for her daughter's heart."[3] That it was the intention of Boaz to marry Ruth was the accurate assumption of Naomi, and the story of chapter 3 is predicated upon that supposition. The Authorized Version does not bring out that idea sharply, but Gesenius' translation of Ruth 3:13 made it clear. "If he will marry thee by right of

---

[2]John Lord, *Beacon Lights of History* (New York: Fords, Howard, and Hulbert, 1886), Vol. IV, pp. 23–65.
[3]James Morison, *The Pulpit Commentary* (London: Kegan Paul, Trench, Trubner and Co., 1897), Vol. VIII, p. 46.

relationship, let him marry thee, but if he will not, I will marry thee."[4]

Gesenius gave a fourth meaning for the Hebrew word *goel* which was known by those in the Book of Ruth and which was acted upon by them. According to the law of Moses, when a man died, it was the office of the next of kin to marry his widow (Deut. 25:5–10). When Ruth went to the threshingfloor of Boaz, she was not breaking through the bounds of modesty and propriety. She was entirely within the moral code of Israel. She was following it to the very letter and according to the instructions of Naomi. It is evident from Gesenius' translation in the preceding passage that Boaz recognized this obligation under the Mosaic code, and it may be said to his credit that he had no intention of transgressing the Mosaic law at this point. The language of Boaz corresponds to our present-day proposal of marriage, although it is couched in a form to comply with the law and custom of that day. Naomi so interpreted his language and action, as she intimated in her admonition to Ruth: "Then said she, Sit still, my daughter, until thou know how the matter will fall: for the man will not be in rest, until he have finished the thing this day" (3:18).

The fourth chapter of Ruth outlines the action of Boaz on behalf of the stranger. He immediately started the legal wheels moving. He hauled the other kinsman into court and laid upon him the necessity of action in regard to the parcel of ground of Elimelech. The other

---

[4]William Gesenius, *Hebrew and Chaldee Lexicon, Tregelles Translation* (Grand Rapids, Mich.: Wm. B. Eerdmans, 1949), p. CLI.

kinsman was perfectly willing to redeem the land
until Boaz revealed to him that there was more involved than the property. Besides the ground, there
was the woman. She was the one who moved Boaz to
action, and she was the one who prompted the anonymous kinsman to desist. The unknown kinsman
relinquished all his claims, and immediately Boaz
seized them. A contract was made then and there to
convey to Boaz, the party of the second part, all
rights as redeemer appertaining to the estate of
Elimelech.

Boaz was more than willing to become the redeemer; he was eager to function in that capacity. He acted
with enthusiasm in that relationship. The motive which
prompted him to act was love for the Moabitess.
Although a stranger, she possessed a beauty, a charm,
and character that had rightly earned for her a worthy
name in her adopted land. Her excellent treatment of
her mother-in-law and her sincere passion for her
must have moved the citizens of Bethlehem in that
day, and even today she stands out as one of the
loveliest characters in the Bible. Willingness is a feeble
word to describe the attitude of Boaz in the role of a
kinsman-redeemer. *Eagerness* is a more appropriate
term.

The One who is greater than Boaz committed His
will fully to the task of the great Kinsman-Redeemer
of the human family. Christ was in no way an unwilling Redeemer, nor was He forced into that position
by circumstances over which He had no control. He
defined His own attitude toward the Cross: "No man
taketh it [life] from me, but I lay it down of myself. I
have power to lay it down, and I have power to take

it again" (John 10:18). The Cross was not something
He sought to avoid, but He "for the joy that was set
before him endured the cross" (Heb. 12:2). Again He
said in reference to His death: "Even as the Son of
man came not to be ministered unto, but to minister,
and to give his life a ransom for many" (Matt. 20:28).

There are two extreme positions regarding the death
of Christ that need to be avoided. While we attempt
to avoid one extreme, the danger of falling into the
other is always present. The first extreme is the assumption that Christ was forced to die on the Cross.
This is a grievous error. Christ was not compelled to
die on the Cross by outside forces which He could not
control; otherwise, God would have been guilty of
murder, for "it pleased the LORD to bruise him;
he hath put him to grief..." (Is. 53:10). Christ was a
willing sacrifice. He was obedient unto death, it is
true, but that obedience had gained the permission of
His volition.

The other extreme is the supposition that the death
of Christ was a suicide. This, too, is a glaring false-
hood. His willingness to die was not born of a desire
to leave off living. He did not love death but dreaded
it as such, a fact the experience in the Garden of
Gethsemane indicates. A mother who plunges into
the flames of a burning house to rescue her baby,
knowing full well that the holocaust will be her deathbed, is not a suicide. She goes willingly and gladly
because her child must be rescued from the flames,
and this woman with such a motive is praised as a
martyr. If she deliberately chooses death merely for
the sake of dying, then she is a poor, miserable
wretch of a suicide. Again, if she is pushed into the

fire against her will, the hand that pushed her belongs to a murderer. But when she willingly enters
the fiery furnace the moral problem is removed, and
she is acclaimed as a heroine.

Isaiah, the prophet who more clearly than any
other depicted the death of Christ, declared, "He was
oppressed, and he was afflicted, yet he opened not
his mouth" (Is. 53:7). The gospel affirms this statement in a striking manner. Christ did not protest at
His own trial. It was evident that He was not trying
to escape the penalty which His enemies sought to
inflict upon Him. Calmly He faced the issue, accepted
the verdict, made no appeal for help, bore in silence
the unjust penalty imposed upon Him, and died as
"the Lamb of God, which taketh away the sin of the
world" (John 1:29). All this was in fulfillment of the
Old Testament declaration: "As a sheep before her
shearers is dumb, so he openeth not his mouth" (Is.
53:7). Paul appealed to Caesar for justice, but Christ
made no appeal from an unjust sentence to a higher
authority, for the sinner deserved to die, and Christ
was bearing the penalty of sin willingly.

His life was the ransom for many. That is the
scriptural explanation for the death of Christ, coming
from His own lips before the excitement of the last
few days of His earthly life. His passivity in the hands
of His captors would be tantamount to suicide if it
were not for the fact that He was dying for another.
He was a Kinsman-Redeemer, paying the price of
redemption. The only position that can be maintained
regarding the death of Christ is to see Him as the
Kinsman-Redeemer, performing the work of redemption willingly. He deliberately drank the cup. With

eagerness He endured the Cross, and with joyful anticipation He accepted His Passion. Tears of joy were mingled with His tears of suffering. He willingly bore my sin and paid the price for my redemption. He not only endangered His inheritance but He sacrificed His life. Love made Him willing to die, for He "first loved us." He did not find the motive for redemption in us, but He found it in His own Person. We were not lovely, but He was wonderful. He redeemed us because of His yearning love. Now we can say exultantly with Paul, "I live by the faith of the Son of God, who loved me, and gave himself for me" (Gal. 2:20).

·13·

The Able Redeemer

Regardless of the translation placed upon the first verse of chapter 2 where Boaz is called "a mighty man of wealth," the evident implication is that he was thoroughly capable of performing the part of kinsman-redeemer per se. There is not a scintilla of suggestion that Boaz was unable to render the service of a kinsman-redeemer. Rather, the tenor of the story suggests that he was more than able to redeem. As a man of wealth, he could pay the price; as a man of valor, he possessed the strength necessary to enforce his claim; and as a man of the law, he was fully prepared to fulfill all legal requirements.

The presence of another redeemer with prior claims *de jure* was the only obstacle that seemed to preclude the possibility of Boaz' acting the kinsman's part. The anonymous kinsman presents to us the major problem in the story of Ruth. The story recognizes that he was the kinsman nearer than Boaz. Not only did he lack a willingness to redeem, but he lacked the ability to redeem. The problem resolves itself upon the abili-

150

ty of the two redeemers. Both of them were in the unique position of kinsmen-redeemers, with the unnamed kinsman possessing the advantage in that he was nearer of kin than Boaz. Yet in the final analysis, this kinsman confessed that he could not redeem Ruth without affecting his own inheritance. At the same time he stated that Boaz occupied no such anomalous position. He urged Boaz to redeem her.

Now, what made the difference between these two redeemers so that one had difficulties which prevented him from acting, while the other had these difficulties obviated? There is nothing in the story that offers any explanation, nor in the Mosaic system is there anything that throws any light upon this problem. This is a difficulty largely ignored by commentators, for the sufficient reason that there is no explanation. We raise the question not to answer it but to recognize it. The recognition of this problem furnishes an understanding of the kinsman-redeemer. The redeemer had to be a kinsman and had to be willing, but he might meet these two requirements and still be wholly inadequate because of inability.

The barefoot kinsman possessed the first two essentials. Boaz possessed an ability that the unnamed kinsman lacked. It was something besides a willingness, for this kinsman did not refuse to redeem but expressed his willingness when the matter was called to his attention: "I will redeem it" (4:4). The kinsman went on to declare that there was a difference between himself and Boaz. Although he was closer of kin and possessed all claims of priority, Boaz could redeem without incurring the liability that was placed upon him. The presence of the Moabitess and her rights to the property indicated that it would be difficult for an Israelite to get a clear title to the property. Quite probably this other kinsman had a wife and children, and if he had redeemed the property in which Ruth had an inheritance, it would have affected the inheritance of his own children.

Boaz was unmarried; therefore there was no such difficulty for him. When he married the Moabitess, he brought her into the congregation of the Lord by giving her his name and all the rights appertaining thereto. This reasoning is merely conjecture and is offered not as the interpretation of the story but to demonstrate a probable explanation.

Although it is difficult to offer a solution to this problem, it is not impossible. The Mosaic law did not treat this matter. The Mosaic system dealt with great legal principles and with the most important issues touching life, but it did not offer detailed laws touching every relationship of life.

For example, the sixth commandment said, "Thou shalt not kill" (Ex. 20:13). The penalty for committing murder was also given, but none of the details were given as to how to determine what constituted murder, and no distinction between manslaughter and murder was given. It was evident, however, that some such distinction was made, as is seen in the law concerning the cities of refuge (see Num. 35:1–34; Deut. 19:1–6). Custom must have established some sort of precedent which had the sanction of God.

Boaz possessed the power to redeem, and he exercised his power on behalf of Ruth. The law kept her out (Deut. 23:3), but Boaz used his ability to redeem her from the power of the law. She was a stranger, far

removed from the privileges granted to God's people
and unable to extricate herself from the meshes of the
law, but a mighty man of wealth paid the price and
brought her into the nation, into his home, and into
his heart. This absorbing and captivating story of
redeeming love was but a faint foreshadowing of the
One who was mightier than Boaz and who paid a far
greater price.

The highest title borne by Jesus Christ is that of
Redeemer. It is far greater than that of Rabbi, Lord,
Master, or King of kings and Lord of lords. He was
the greatest teacher that the world has ever seen.
Even the enemies of the Cross have been unanimous
down through the ages in asserting that He was *the*
great Teacher. He set an example that has been un-
paralleled in the annals of history. His life has been
the subject of admiration by even the skeptic. Renan,
the great French agnostic, admired the life of Christ,
for he made that the subject of his greatest work. Yet,
as Example and Teacher, Christ does not possess His
highest title. These titles are not to be ignored or
taken from Him, but it is in the title of *Redeemer* that
all the others receive life and meaning. Frederick A.
Noble expressed it in this language:

> It is not to be denied that Christ is much other to us
> than a Redeemer. . . . In the first place, both His in-
> struction and His example miss their highest value
> without the large and crowning benefit which comes
> from His death. For grant, what has just been claimed,
> that in His words He plucks and brings to us the
> flower of knowledge, that in His perfect demeanor, in
> the midst of friends and foes alike, under favoring
> circumstances and also under perplexities and tempta-

tions and trials, He illustrates for us the ideal of daily conduct; yet of what service would it all be to us without atoning blood to wash away the defilements that are in us, and to emancipate our souls from the dominance of sin? If knowledge is to be of advantage to one, he must be in condition to use knowledge. If a perfect example is to be of worth, one must somehow be possessed of ability to imitate the example.[1]

The title of Redeemer enhances the meaning of the others. It is one of the prophetic titles given to Christ in the Old Testament. It was first given to Him by Job through prophetic inspiration: "For I know that my redeemer liveth, and that he shall stand at the latter day upon the earth" (Job 19:25). This comes from what is probably the oldest book in the Bible and expresses the heart cry of man from ancient days. The prophet looked down the vista of time to the end of man's sorry attempt to rule this earth and saw Him in the last days bearing this high title: "And the Redeemer shall come to Zion" (Is. 59:20). Israel, in view of this and similar prophecies, anticipated the coming of a Redeemer. Jehovah came to be in every sense their Redeemer. The coming Redeemer could be none other than Jehovah. Although these two ideas were never merged into one definite statement, it was, nevertheless, the heart-hope of Israel.

Nowhere in the New Testament is Christ given the title of Redeemer, but He was given a name that bears all the significance of the appellation. The announcement of the angel Gabriel to Mary revealed

---

[1]F.A. Noble, *Our Redemption, Its Need, Method and Result* (New York: Fleming H. Revell Co., 1897), p. 142.

that name. It was the name *Joshua* which in the Greek is *Jesus*. Simply stated, it meant "the salvation of Jehovah," or "Jehovah is a Savior." The name was not spoken the first time by Gabriel. Joshua, the man who succeeded Moses, was the first to bear this name with distinction, and after him there must have been many boys who bore that name. At the time of our Lord's birth there must have been a great company of boys bearing that name. Every Hebrew mother anticipated that the son born to her would be the Deliverer. It was only in Jesus Christ, however, that the name found adequate fulfillment. The angel announced to Joseph that the name signified that Jesus would "save his people from their sins" (Matt. 1:21). Redemption became the subject of the spiritual songs of prophecy uttered at His birth; first by Zacharias (Luke 1:68) and then by Anna (Luke 2:38).

Jesus bore that name in the unique way of Redeemer, and He alone so adorns it that it might find its final fruition. The name Jesus is reserved for only One today. That name belongs supremely to the One who hung on the Cross. It was the name *Jesus* that was written above the impaled figure. This is the name that He brought out of the tomb and glorified. Paul, in speaking of His transition from heaven to earth and the humiliation that such a movement entailed, also told of His passage back to heaven and the exaltation that such a movement involved. The round trip that He made between heaven and earth accomplished the work of redemption. He is today something that He could not have been before He came to this earth. He is a Redeemer today by virtue of the work accomplished on the Cross. He received a name that He would not otherwise bear if He had not come to this earth. It is the name *Jesus*. He came down to this place of humiliation to receive that name in order that He might bear it back and exalt it as the greatest name ever borne by man. Paul told of the conspicuous place that name occupied and will continue to occupy in God's program:

> Wherefore God also hath highly exalted him, and given him a name which is above every name: that at the name of Jesus every knee should bow, of things in heaven, and things in earth, and things under the earth; and that every tongue should confess that Jesus Christ is Lord, to the glory of God the Father (Phil. 2:9–11).

It is as the Redeemer that Christ received the name Jesus. That human name implied all that the term Kinsman-Redeemer could imply.

There was another implication in the name of Jesus which emphasized His deity as well as His humanity. The name meant that Jehovah was the Savior. *God* became a man, and that man bore the name Jesus. The Gospel of John, which sets forth His deity, uses the name Jesus almost exclusively. His human name occurs more than any other, which suggests that God became the man Jesus, or as Jesus expressed it in this Gospel, "I came forth from the Father, and am come into the world: again, I leave the world, and go to the Father" (John 16:28).

Jesus is mightier than Boaz because He is able to redeem lost sinners. He is able because He was God manifest in human flesh, and He can do all that God can do. He brought to bear on the work of redemption all the wisdom and power of God. Jesus was the omnipotent Redeemer. We will now consider two passages of Scripture which set forth Jesus as the Redeemer who is able.

The first passage of Scripture is an extended one and we shall forbear quoting it as there are only portions of it that we wish to examine. The entire passage is John 10:11–30, but the verses that bear on our subject are verses 11, 14–18, 27–30. In this section of Scripture, under the figure of a Shepherd, our Lord is set forth as the Redeemer who is able. He is the Good Shepherd who gives His life for the sheep. Three times over He emphasized the fact that the Shepherd will die for the sheep (vv. 11,15,17). He also emphasized the fact that His death for the sheep will not only be a willing death but a death over which He has the power. He had the power to lay His life down, and He had power to take it up again. His work of redemption is wrought in the power of deity.

These sheep, whom he redeems by His death, are the objects of eternal life vouchsafed to them by His death. Not only is the Redeemer omnipotent, not only is His redemption wrought in the power of deity, but the redemption itself is a mighty redemption. "They shall never perish" speaks of the new position into which the sheep are brought. The explanation for that is found in the power of the Redeemer, "neither shall any man pluck them out of my hand" (v. 28). Then, as if that were not enough, our Lord told of another hand, the hand of the Father, which is clasped over them for eternal security. He appears to be saying that He holds them in the left hand of deity and that the Father clasps the right hand of deity over them. The omnipotent Redeemer holds the redeemed. The final perseverance of the saints is possible on the basis of the holding power of God.

This passage reveals the limit to which God is going to redeem lost sinners. The extent appears to be infinitely extravagant and the price seems to be exorbitant, but the Good Shepherd is "a mighty man of wealth." The justification for this exceedingly lavish expenditure is found in the place to which the sinners are redeemed, even "eternal life."

The second passage that reveals the ability of our Redeemer is found in the Epistle to the Hebrews.

> Wherefore he is able also to save them to the uttermost that come unto God by him, seeing he ever liveth to make intercession for them (Heb. 7:25).

Some commentators have interpreted that the reference here is not to the depths of sin out of which the sinner is saved but rather to the other extreme of redemption, the consummation after it is once initiated. Jamieson, Fausset, and Brown gave "altogether" and "perfectly" as an interpretation of the expression "to the uttermost."[2] This is the interpretation that is concurred in here, but this does not preclude the other position that the reference is likewise to the depths to which the Redeemer went to save lost sinners. Kelly interpreted it as "the guarantee of a commensurate salvation." Delitzsch saw in this expression no reference to time, but of every want and need met in Christ.[3]

---

[2]Jamieson, Fausset, and Brown, *Commentary on the Old and New Testaments* (Chicago: National Publishing Co., 1871), p. 458.
[3]Ibid.

Regardless of which phase of redemption is con sidered—the place from which the Redeemer takes the sinner or the place to which the Redeemer brings the sinner—something of the great power expended in redemption is the evident intention of the writer here. "To the uttermost" implies *from* the uttermost. This is an a priori consideration, for redemption finds its cause in the lost estate of the sinner and its effect in eternal life. No matter how far down Jesus goes to get the sinner, He is able to bring him all the way to the consummation of redemption. Scofield suggested "completely" as a meaning for the expression "to the uttermost."[4] This again logically suggests that redemption is a process. The sinner is lost, "having no hope, and without God in the world." God lifts His mighty arm in redemption and begins to move on behalf of the sinner, and, lo! the lost sinners "who sometimes were far off are made nigh by the blood of Christ." For the sinner this may only consume a moment of time, as this is not a chronological process. The process begins with the sinner absolutely lost and leaves him absolutely saved. The sinner passes from death unto life, and it takes a long and mighty bridge to span the yawning chasm between these two extremes.

"Our Boaz" found us "aliens from the commonwealth of Israel," with sin preventing us from ever entering the congregation of the Lord. However, there was another kinsman who had an opportunity to redeem sinners. There is another way of salvation, theoretically. There is an hypothesis on which to erect

----

[4]*Scofield Reference Bible*, p. 1297.

a plan of salvation. Dr. Grant called attention to this assumed redeemer.[5] This hypothetical plan of salvation is stated in Scripture:

> Again, when the wicked man turneth away from his wickedness that he hath committed, and doeth that which is lawful and right, he shall save his soul alive (Ezek. 18:27).

This is a plan of salvation for a wicked man whereby he can become his own redeemer. God put Israel on the same sort of basis at Sinai:

> Now therefore, if ye will obey my voice indeed, and keep my covenant, then ye shall be a peculiar treasure unto me above all people: for all the earth is mine (Ex. 19:5).

This is the salvation by works. The law becomes the redeemer in this plan of salvation. In fifteen hundred years of Israel's history, it was proven obviously that this plan would not save a soul. It is evident that not one soul in Israel was saved by the law. This was a plan of self-recovery, given to Israel to see if man could redeem himself by law. The law became the despair of Israel and finally became their undoing. Law is the other kinsman who is even closer to man, just as the other kinsman was closer than Boaz. But in the final analysis, the law could not redeem man without endangering its own inheritance, which was its high standard.

Law today, as such, cannot redeem man without lowering its standards to conform to man's weak

---

[5]F.W. Grant, *The Numerical Bible* (New York: Loizeaux Brothers, 1894), Vol. II, p. 279.

ability. If it did come down to the low plane where
man could abide by its precepts, it would no longer
be law but a system of compromise with a very low
standard. God would have a law to pardon sinners
which would not change the sinner except to fill him
with blind pride in the idea that his sin was well
pleasing to God. Law demands a high standard to
conform to the character of God. This high plane is
above man and condemns man:

> For as many as are of the works of the law are under
> the curse: for it is written, Cursed is every one that
> continueth not in all things which are written in the
> book of the law to do them (Gal. 3:10).

Salvation by works is a plan of redemption, but it is
like the anonymous kinsman who had to retire on
behalf of Boaz. Salvation by works cannot save a lost
soul, for "by the deeds of the law there shall no flesh
be justified in his sight: for by the law is the knowledge of sin" (Rom. 3:20). Naomi and Ruth would
have been permanently undone if they had placed
any faith in the barefoot kinsman, for he was impo-
tent to redeem them. It was only in Boaz that they
found complete redemption. Salvation by works cannot save a lost soul, and to trust such a redeemer is
tragic. Salvation by faith in Christ Jesus is the only
plan that finally works.

> Knowing that a man is not justified by the works of
> the law, but by the faith of Jesus Christ, even we have
> believed in Jesus Christ, that we might be justified by
> the faith of Christ, and not by the works of the law: for
> by the works of the law shall no flesh be justified"
> (Gal. 2:16).

Faith in our Kinsman-Redeemer is the only plan of salvation which is effective, for we have a Kinsman-Redeemer who is able to save the last, the least, and the lost.

· 14 ·

The Free Redeemer

The redeemer must not only be a kinsman; he must belong to a higher branch of the family where he is not involved in the trouble of the family. The redeemer must not be under the curse that makes redemption essential for another. If an Israelite was himself in slavery because of untoward circumstances or misfortune, he could not act as a redeemer. Rather, he himself needed a redeemer.

Boaz, for example, could not have acted in the capacity of redeemer if he had sold himself into slavery or if he had been a Moabite. The demands of the law could not go unfulfilled in him, nor could the curse of exclusion by the law because of some defect in his life go unnoticed when he made application as a redeemer. A drowning man is in no position to rescue someone else who is drowning. A man who rescues people who are in a sinking ship cannot himself be in that sinking ship. The lifeline must be thrown by someone who is in a place of comparative safety. For someone to throw a lifeline from the upper deck of a sinking ship to someone on a lower deck will avail nothing.

The Chaldee translation of this phrase in verse 1 of chapter 2 is significant at this juncture. Boaz is called "a mighty man of law." Before the law, Boaz was a mighty man. This could mean the same thing that Paul intended when he wrote, "Touching the righteousness which is in the law, blameless" (Phil. 3:6). Boaz had met every demand of the law concerning offerings for sin. He had made all proper sacrifices. He had met every demand of the Mosaic law, and it had no claim upon him that would prevent his acting as redeemer.

Not only did he meet the law in his conduct; he met its just demands in his character. The genealogy in Ruth was David's genealogy and linked him with the tribe of Judah. This same genealogy was Christ's and gave Him the legal right to the throne of David. This genealogy belonged to Boaz also and conveyed to him all that was conveyed to David and to Christ. He was in the chosen line. He was an Israelite, and the prerogatives of the nation belonged to him.

> Who are Israelites; to whom pertaineth the adoption, and the glory, and the covenants, and the giving of the law, and the service of God, and the promises; whose are the fathers, and of whom as concerning the flesh Christ came, who is over all, God blessed for ever. Amen (Rom. 9:4,5).

There could be no objection to Boaz, racially, as a redeemer.

Boaz was a rich man. The implication is that he had never been forced to sell himself into slavery or to dispose of his property, even temporarily. As a slave he would have been under the curse, which would have incapacitated him to act as redeemer and would have put him in need of a deliverer. His hands were not shackled by slavery. He was free to act from the outside on behalf of the poor kinsman who needed redemption.

Christ fully met this requirement of a Redeemer. He was free from the curse of sin. He was not vulnerable at any point to its deadening effects, as he said explicitly, "Hereafter I will not talk much with you: for the prince of this world cometh, and hath nothing in me" (John 14:30). The law was not given to make Him silent, for He did not break it but kept it in all its points. "Think not that I am come to destroy the law, or the prophets: I am not come to destroy, but to fulfill" (Matt. 5:17). He was not a Gentile who never attempted to keep its precepts, but He was "made under the law" (Gal. 4:4). He kept it in all of its parts.

Christ was unique inasmuch as it could not be said of the other children of man, not even of Adam, that they were "holy, harmless, undefiled, separate from sinners" (Heb. 7:26). Before He was born the angel Gabriel said to His mother, "That holy thing which shall be born of thee shall be called the Son of God" (Luke 1:35). Mary had the most wonderful child in the world. There never was One like Him before, and there never has been One since. The first child born into the world inherited the fallen nature from his parents. His mother Eve thought he might be the one to bruise the serpent's head, and so she called him Cain, for she said, "I have gotten a [the] man from the Lord" (Gen. 4:1). However, this child was not a

redeemer but was the first murderer. All children
from that day on have manifested the propensities of
sin. That has been the indelible mark on the sons of
Adam.

The one exception to the rule is Jesus Christ. He
possessed no inherent sin. He had no sinful nature.
He was virgin born. In His lifetime He challenged
anyone to convict Him of sin, a challenge that was
never accepted. Nor was His claim to perfection
successfully refuted. He was the sinless Savior. He
was the impeccable Christ. As the only sinless Person, He was not subject to death as the race of man
is. He testified that He would "give his life a ransom
for many" (Matt. 20:28). He was outside the power of
death, but He moved under its power that He might
become the Redeemer, "And deliver them who through
fear of death were all their lifetime subject to bondage"
(Heb. 2:15). The Son of God was free to redeem
because He was not implicated in man's sin in any
way. When He went to the cross, our sin became
His, and He "was made sin for us, who knew no sin"
(2 Cor. 5:21).

Christ was not only the Kinsman-Redeemer; racially
He was an Israelite. He was the son of Abraham,
Isaac, and Jacob. He was descended from the line of
David. His mother was a daughter of Israel. He must
have resembled members of that race, for the woman
at the well in Samaria asked Him, "How is it that
thou, being a Jew, askest drink of me, which am a
woman of Samaria?" (John 4:9). Although He was
free from the sinful nature that belongs to the sons of
Adam, He was not a stranger but was identified with
the covenant people and the chosen nation. He was

not outside the human family because of His sinless nature.

Jesus Christ presented all the credentials of a Kinsman-Redeemer when He came to this earth. He was not like Moses, who attempted to deliver his brethren in Egypt without any instructions from God when he killed the Egyptian and buried him in the sand. Christ was not born under the slavery of sin. He was able to pay the penalty of sin because He was not Himself subject to it. When He throws the lifeline to some sinking soul, He is able to rescue, for He stands upon the vantage ground of a sinless life. When He went to the cross, He was not paying any penalty for Himself. He had absolutely no obligation to the curse and penalty of sin. He bore the slavery and the sin of *man* on the cross.

· 15 ·

The Wealthy Redeemer

Forasmuch as ye know that ye were not redeemed with corruptible things, as silver and gold, from your vain conversation received by tradition from your fathers; but with the precious blood of Christ, as of a lamb without blemish and without spot (1 Pet. 1:18, 19).

The kinsman-redeemer must have the legal tender of redemption. In other words, the redeemer must have the price that is the legal amount essential to make the deliverance. He must be able to discharge the obligation fully. In the case of Boaz this must have been a small matter. Redeeming the small estate of Elimelech was no difficulty for Boaz, the rich kinsman. In the text the question of the amount is never raised, nor is it discussed as a probable hindrance toward making redemption. Even the other kinsman was willing and therefore apparently was able to pay the amount that was required to free the property. In this matter he was unlike Christ, for the price paid by Christ for our redemption was tremendous. It bankrupted heaven temporarily. It drained all the resources of an omnipotent God. Christ could pay and He did pay, but at what a cost!

> For ye know the grace of our Lord Jesus Christ, that, though he was rich, yet for your sakes he became poor, that ye through his poverty might be rich (2 Cor. 8:9).

It is necessary to ascertain the legal tender Christ used in accomplishing redemption for man. Let us return, for the moment, to the redemption of Israel out of Egypt. The night of the Passover marked the time of the accomplishment of Israel's redemption. That night was the birthday of the nation. They were born at night in the brickyards of Egypt. God told them that it would be "the beginning of months" for them. They were instructed to take a lamb for each house and to slay it. The blood of the lamb was taken and sprinkled on the doorposts and lintels of the homes of the Hebrews that evening. The Death Angel visited every home in Egypt that night, and at each home where he found the blood sprinkled, he passed over. But where the blood was not sprinkled, death seized the firstborn of that family, both man and beast. The sign of the Passover was blood. The nation of Israel began on a bloody basis. They were redeemed that first Passover night by blood.

Why was blood brought into such prominence? It could never be a beautiful thing to see. The sight of blood produces nausea in most people. It is repulsive to the thought of man. Blood could not have been chosen because of its appeal to the aesthetic nature of man. Blood repels because it is abhorred by the normal person. Redemption by blood has been ab-horred by the natural man from the time that Cain brought the lovely fruit of the cursed ground as a sacrifice for his sin up to the bold modernism of the present hour. The hideous specter of a bloody lamb offended Cain's nobler feelings, but in reality it was his fallen nature rebelling against God's way. Dr. Coffin quoted from the work of an unnamed poetess to give expression to the modern reaction to the blood of Christ:

> Go, bitter Christ, grim Christ! haul if Thou wilt
> Thy bloody cross to Thine own bleak Calvary!
> When did I bid Thee suffer for my guilt
> To bind intolerable claims on me?
> I loathe Thy sacrifice; I am sick of Thee.[1]

Certainly God was not seeking to emphasize beauty in religion, nor was He attempting to please the natural man when He instituted the bloody sacrifice. The explanation was contained in the Levitical ritual:

> For the life of the flesh is in the blood: and I have given it to you upon the altar to make an atonement for your souls: for it is the blood that maketh an atonement for the soul (Lev. 17:11).

The blood is the life principle of man. The blood represents the life. The shedding of the blood of animals sets forth the sacrificing of life in substitution for the one making the sacrifice. But why should it be necessary for man to have a substitute to shed blood for him? Why was man's life demanded? The human race stood in disobedience to the will of God, in

---

[1] H.S. Coffin, *Evangelistic Preaching* (New York: Geo. H. Doran Co., n.d.), p. 22.

rebellion to the authority of God, in treason to the government of God, and in ingratitude to the love of God. The simple but satisfactory statement of Scripture is: "All have sinned, and come short of the glory of God" (Rom. 3:23). Man is a sinner in any way you care to look at him. Before God, man is guilty. There must be some penalty for a sinner, or else God is not the moral ruler of this universe. There is such a penalty, for there comes thundering down from the throne of justice, out of the presence of a Holy God, the eternal and irrevocable law: "The soul that sinneth, it shall die" (Ezek. 18:20). This places every man under the sentence of death, for "the wages of sin is death." The sons of Adam have drawn wages faithfully for the penalty of sin, as every cemetery silently testifies. Physical death is the outward evidence of the accuracy of this law. Physical death is not all, for spiritual death is included, which means eternal separation from God.

The only hope for man is to get someone to pay a penalty for him that is satisfactory to God. It is reasonable that the death of animals could not atone for sins, "For it is not possible that the blood of bulls and of goats should take away sins" (Heb. 10:4). There must be found some man who is satisfactory to God and who is willing to pay with his blood the price of redemption for the penalty of sin. The big problem is to find someone satisfactory to God. We have noted that he must be related to the human family by blood, but if he has the blood of Adam flowing through his veins, he, too, would need a substitute. It is impossible for man to produce a redeemer who can pay the price of redemption. No man could be free from the guilt of sin, and no man could escape its penalty for himself. As far as man is concerned, redemption is an impossible achievement. No man could present anything that would be legal tender in heaven; no man could even redeem himself. In his own strength, man is hopelessly lost for eternity.

At this juncture, God steps into the picture with a price that was legal tender in heaven. God issued the currency that redeemed man. That story is told in this sublime language:

> Wherefore when he cometh into the world, he saith, Sacrifice and offering thou wouldest not, but a body hast thou prepared me (Heb. 10:5).

The blood of bulls and goats could not redeem man. The blood of man could not redeem man. So God took upon Himself a human body. This body was not contaminated with the sin nature. No tainted blood flowed through His body. This blood, which was free from sin, was the source of His earthly life. He shed this blood and thereby sacrificed the life of this earthly body for the payment in full of man's redemption. Twenty-one times Scripture identified the blood of the Lord Jesus Christ as the legal tender of redemption.[2]

The value of any currency is measured in what it can accomplish. Currency is worthless when it is not acceptable for articles of value. Currency is valuable when it is accepted for things of value. The only worthwhile question regarding money is, what is its

---

[2]C.E. Putman, *The Power of Jesus' Blood and Its Relation to Sin* (Chicago: Bible Institute Colportage Association, 1920), p.55.

purchasing power? Some express their philosophy in this way: "I am not interested in money as such but in what money can buy." This test may be applied to the blood of Christ. Putnam mentioned ten wonderful priceless objectives made possible by the blood of Christ.[3] Wilkes enumerated fourteen marvelous accomplishments made available to man by the blood of Christ.[4] Each one of these is a spiritual blessing that can not be measured in terms of dollars and cents. Nothing in this world can buy any one of them. We do not wish to deal with these items; but we do wish to mention one blessing that has been bought by the blood of Christ, which has been omitted by all works on redemption consulted for this book.

> And they sung a new song, saying, Thou art worthy to take the book, and to open the seals thereof: for thou wast slain, and hast redeemed us to God by thy blood out of every kindred, and tongue, and people, and nation (Rev. 5:9).

In my thinking, every normal individual entertains a desire to go to heaven. Man often has a very limited and faulty conception of heaven and perhaps is devoid of any spiritual appreciation of it, but he secretly cherishes a wish to go there someday. Even the worst sinner would like to go to heaven, if it only means escape from punishment. Heaven is a place in the thinking of all peoples, whether they expect to go there or not, and to them it is a place of unspeakable pleasures and joys forevermore. The human race is characterized by a deep urge to gain heaven. As man

[3]*Ibid.*
[4]A. Paget Wilkes, *The Dynamic of Redemption* (London: Japan Evangelistic Bank, 1924), p. 7.

approaches death, the desire for heaven increases. Man on his deathbed will give all he possesses to be assured that he will go there. Anyone who could assure the members of the human race that they would go to heaven on the payment of a stipulated sum to him would find himself the richest man on earth, able to gratify the avarice of any Midas.

In the final analysis, man will pay more for the chance of going to this cherished place than for any other thing. The millions of dollars paid annually into the coffers of the Roman Catholic Church to get some loved one out of purgatory is a witness to this innate yearning of the heart of man. What a ghastly and awful thing it is to traffic in human souls as if some human agency had divine authority over their place of abode after death! This fiction of purgatory has created the wealthiest organization on earth. Billions are spent annually for pleasure and security. These two objectives are present in every conception of heaven, and this money would be gladly diverted into a channel that could guarantee heaven to the natural man, apart from God's plan of salvation. Every man will invest money in a feasible human plan which will make heaven available to him.

In Revelation 5:9, there is presented a company of people from every nook and corner of the earth. Every race, class, and condition of man is present. This company is present in heaven. They are singing because of the fact that they have been brought into the blessings of this place heaven. They do not attribute their presence there to anything that they have done or to any payment that they have been able to make to gain this exceedingly great privilege. Yet they acknowledge that Someone did pay a price to make it possible for them to be there. The purchase price that made heaven available to them is not in the coin of earth, such as silver and gold. They are there on their own confession that they have been redeemed by the blood of the Lamb. The blood of Christ is the most valuable thing in this universe because it has purchased what silver and gold cannot; yet man would be willing to sell all his possessions to buy heaven. Another sold all that He had and paid the price of redemption.

There is another fact that gives value to any currency. This is the scarcity of it. Inflation destroys the value of any money. There has been only one Person who ever lived who could "give his life a ransom for many" (Mark 10:45). Only one Person out of the millions of the earth ever shed blood that availed before God. There have been literally millions of martyrs, but only the death of One was able to redeem sinners from the penalty of sin. The blood of Christ is today, and has always been, the only avenue by which a sinner can obtain salvation: "no man cometh unto the Father, but by me" (John 14:6).

It is reported that when the *Titanic* was sinking, a millionaire came to a man sitting in one of the lifeboats, which was about to be lowered, and offered him one hundred thousand dollars for his place in the boat. The man in the boat refused. The scarcity of places made the value of one priceless. The only avenue of escape was the lifeboat. Christ is the only lifeboat that can be launched from a doomed and sinking world, and His blood buys the only seat in the lifeboat. He paid the price and offers salvation to any lost sinner who will take it. It costs the sinner nothing, but it cost Him everything. The blood of Christ alone suffices to purchase redemption for the sinner. It alone has merit before God. The blood of Christ opens the gate of heaven and lets the sinner in, and it will be the subject of every song in heaven.

> What can wash away my sin?
> Nothing but the blood of Jesus.
> —*Robert Lowry*

· 16 ·

Sin and Redemption

In whom we have redemption through his blood, the forgiveness of sins, according to the riches of his grace (Eph. 1:7).

Redemption is one of the high terms of salvation. It is sometimes used to connote the entire field of Christology, as in Strong's *Theology*.[1] In its broader sense, it speaks of the Person and work of Christ. However, it is a more specific term than that, and there is a danger of losing the technical meaning if such a broad application is made. It requires restriction to keep it in proper bounds. This can be attained when redemption is kept related to the Hebrew *goel*, as we have previously indicated. When so restricted, it is as Wilkes declared: "There is no theme so solemn and yet so blessed as that of redemption."[2] Redemption means "to purchase by paying a price." In the case of the

---

[1]A.H. Strong, *Systematic Theology* (Philadelphia: The Judson Press, 1907), pp. 665-776.
[2]A. Paget Wilkes, *The Dynamic of Redemption* (London: Japan Evangelistic Bank, 1924), p. 127.

sinner, the price is the blood of Christ. Redemption
has been defined as:

> The act of Deity in which Jesus Christ pays the whole
> demand of the law against the sinner, redeeming him
> from the curse and bondage of the law: the Father
> receives him as son and heir, and the Holy Spirit
> delivers him from the bondage to indwelling sin.[3]

Redemption is postulated on the fact of sin. If sin
does not exist, then redemption is a useless work and
a meaningless word. The entire plan of redemption
rests upon the reality of sin. Therefore, the reality of
sin must be established as actually existing in the life
of the race. It must be demonstrated that sin is
something over which man has no power. The Redeemer is made necessary because man is helpless in
the presence of sin.

First, we wish to discuss the fact of sin. When man
sinned in the Garden of Eden, God put this question
to Eve: "What is this that thou hast done?" (Gen.
3:13). It was a question that neither the man nor the
woman could answer adequately. This question is
handled satisfactorily only in the New Testament.
There it is possible for us to gain an adequate conception
of sin. Tholuck, in his address celebrating the fiftieth
anniversary of his professorship at Halle, made this
poignant statement: "In review of God's manifold
blessings, the thing I seem most to thank Him for is
the conviction of sin."[4] God's revelation concerning sin

---

[3]C.I. Scofield, *Bible Correspondence Course* (Chicago: Moody Bible Institute,
n.d.), Vol. III, p. 491.
[4]Strong, p. 576.

and six thousand years of human history give some conception of the "exceeding sinfulness of sin."

There is no excuse for feeble ideas about the sin problem. Liberal theology in America has entertained light notions about sin during the entire history of our republic. This psychological religion has called man "a momentary figure in the dance of the atoms." Sin is described as a "relic of the theological jungle." Sin has been outmoded, according to some. Dr. Shaler Matthews defined sin as "the backward pull of an outworn good." In other words, there was a time when sin was good. It at least has a good background, according to this definition. The light of revelation and history will not yield to these feeble notions.

A full-orbed conception of sin is presented to us in the Bible, and sin can be seen in its effect upon man and upon God. First, let us see the effect of sin upon man. This is revealed in a threefold manner.

1. *The extent of sin.* "For there is no man that sinneth not" (1 Kin. 8:46). Sin extends to each member of the human family. No individual has escaped the corruption of sin. This is another way of saying that sin is universal. No member of the race is immune to it, nor is it possible to be inoculated against it. Cancer is a dreadful and dreaded disease, yet very few of the race, comparatively speaking, suffer from it. Poverty is a terrible existence, yet some have escaped its meshes. But sin is far-reaching in its consequences, for it has touched each member of the race. Every baby born into the race inherits a sinful nature. Men are sinners by birth, and not by act. Where the

revelation of God's Word has gone, men have been made aware of this. Goethe said, "I see no fault committed which I too might not have committed." Dr. Samuel Johnson commented, "Every man knows that of himself which he dares not tell to his dearest friends," and Count de Maistre said, "I do not know what the heart of a villain may be—I only know that of a virtuous man, and that is frightful." The novelist Thackeray had no heroes as paragons of virtue to cross the pages of his novels, and George Eliot had all of her characters act from mixed motives.[5] They were attempting to picture human nature accurately. Some men have declared that they live free from sin, but the facts of their lives have proven otherwise. Rousseau, in his *Confessions*, uttered a prayer in which he said, "Eternal Spirit, the soul that I am going to give thee back is as pure at this moment as it was when it proceeded from thee." Yet virtually all, if not all, of his children were illegitimate, and he sent them all off to a foundling hospital.

All these corroborate the assertion of Scripture: "All have sinned, and come short of the glory of God" (Rom. 3:23).

2. *The intent of sin.* It is the full intention of sin to destroy the entire race. It is fully capable of doing just that. Sin is responsible for every heartache, pain, gray hair, stoop in the shoulder, totter in the step, wrecked life and broken home; and, finally, it will bring death, "for the wages of sin is death" (Rom. 6:23). The practice of sin is fatal to man.

3. *The content of sin.* Sin has within it that element

---

[5]*Ibid.*, p. 575.

which makes it utterly impossible for man to cope with it. Man has no remedy which he can concoct for sin. He cannot close Pandora's box. If it were possible for him to get rid of sin, would it not be sensible for the whole race to get up some morning, bright and early, eat a hearty breakfast, and then set out in dead earnest to drive sin from the universe by sunset? Man could not do this in a day nor in an eternity.

The effect of sin upon God reveals something of a far-reaching nature. Sin has hung the crepe on the door of heaven. It has wounded the heart of God, marred His creation, and intruded on His very presence. The effect of sin upon God will likewise be treated under a threefold division.

1. *Sin has caused God to lose His fellowship with man* (temporarily, at least). God created man for fellowship and came down to enjoy that relationship with Adam. It can be said reverently that on the afternoon in which Adam ran away, God was lonesome. There is no way for us to measure the yearning in the heart of God for that man. Sin disrupted the relationship in such a way that man's state makes it impossible for God to see any merit in him that might be offered to make amends.

2. *Sin has caused God to punish the sinner.* There was no other alternative; the sinner must die. God banished Adam from the Garden and imputed sin to all his posterity. The race from Adam stood guilty before God and deserved the death penalty. All this brought anguish to the heart of God, for He is "not willing that any should perish" (2 Pet. 3:9). "As I live, saith the Lord GOD, I have no pleasure in the death of the wicked" (Ezek. 33:11). This does not mean that God

apologizes for punishing sin. He declares freely that
He will punish it, for it not only is contrary to His
nature, but it is rebellion against His character, and of
Him it is declared: "...in righteousness he doth
judge and make war" (Rev. 19:11).

3. *The presence of sin prompted God to make the supreme
sacrifice to redeem the sinner.* To know something about
the depths of sin, it is necessary to stand at the Cross.
The suffering of Christ attests the heinousness of sin,
although it is beyond the ability of man fully to
evaluate the extent of His Passion. Man can stand at
the foot of the Cross in awe and say with the apostle,
"He was made sin for us." The Cross is God's answer
to the sin question. In the light of the Cross, the
question is not why He permitted sin to enter the
universe. The inscrutable mystery is, Why did He pay
such a price for the sinner? The answer is hushed in
the heart of God. Jerusalem never knew the meaning
of the cross He bore through her streets and out
through her gate, and even the New Jerusalem will
only be able to sing:

> Amazing grace! how sweet the sound,
> That saved a wretch like me!
> I once was lost, but now am found,
> Was blind, but now I see.

Sin is a flagrant insult against God for which man is
guilty and over which he has no power. Redemption
is the answer of God to the presence of sin. Sometimes the question is asked, "Why did God permit
sin?" There is another question which is parallel to it
and which must be asked at the same time, if fairness

is intended to God in this matter: "Why did God permit redemption?" The answer to the second question is found in the first question. Immediately, at the first appearance of sin, God was there developing the doctrine of redemption and making it available for sinners. We wish now to follow the development of the doctrine of redemption in Scripture from the Old Testament into the New.

At first, redemption meant deliverance from any calamity that might befall one in this life.

> The Angel which redeemed me from evil, bless the lads; and let my name be named on them, and the name of my fathers Abraham and Isaac; and let them grow into a multitude in the midst of the earth (Gen. 48:16).

In his old age, Jacob recognized that he had been kept from evil by a power greater than himself. Jacob's innate tendency, as history demonstrates, was an inclination to sin. The angel of God had kept him from evil, and in this sense he had been redeemed from it. He was delivered from evil, in a redemption that was on the human plane.

Eliphaz spoke of a redemption from death in the time of famine and of a deliverance from the sword in time of war: "In famine he shall redeem thee from death: and in war from the power of the sword" (Job 5:20). Job spoke of a redemption from the hand of the enemy. "Or, Deliver me from the enemy's hand? or, Redeem me from the hand of the mighty?" (Job 6:23).

Anyone could act as redeemer in the matters of this life. However, there was a strong insistence that God was the Redeemer in the deliverance from the bondage of Egypt. Although Moses was the human instrument used, it was Jehovah who declared:

> I will bring you out from under the burdens of the Egyptians, and I will rid you out of their bondage, and I will redeem you with a stretched out arm, and with great judgments (Ex. 6:6).

Moses had a rod in his hand that he used, but he was the rod in God's hand. *God* intervened when Israel was hopelessly shackled in the chains of Egypt. After the deliverance from Egypt, God was called the Redeemer of Israel. Psalm 78, which recounts the Egyptian episode, speaks of God in this way: "And they remembered that God was their rock, and the high God their redeemer" (v. 35). The prophet Isaiah used the title "Redeemer" more times than it occurs in the remainder of the Bible. The term was used exclusively of Jehovah in the prophet's time.

> Thou shalt also suck the milk of the Gentiles, and shalt suck the breast of kings: and thou shalt know that I the LORD am thy Saviour and thy Redeemer [*Goel*], the mighty One of Jacob (Is. 60:16).

Finally, redemption was applied specifically to the deliverance of the soul from sin, and as the term became restricted to this, God alone became the Redeemer. By the time of the kingdom, it was revealed that God alone could act in the capacity of a Redeemer from sin.

> None of them can by any means redeem his brother, nor give to God a ransom for him: (for the redemption of their soul is precious, and it ceaseth for ever) (Ps. 49:7,8).

The explanation of why man could not redeem his brother is found in the further statement: "But God will redeem my soul from the power of the grave" (v. 15). The full-flowered development of the doctrine of redemption in the Old Testament is made by one of the pre-exilic prophets:

> I will ransom them from the power of the grave; I will redeem them from death: O death, I will be thy plagues; O grave, I will be thy destruction: repentance shall be hid from mine eyes (Hos. 13:14).

This is a prophecy that reaches into the kingdom for its final fulfillment. It found a partial and basic fulfillment in the resurrection of Christ, and Paul so interpreted it in 1 Corinthians 15. However, the important feature here is that Jehovah is seen in His unique position of a Redeemer from sin. A redemption from the grave and death was to the Hebrew a redemption from sin.

Not until we come to the New Testament do we find the doctrine of redemption fully developed. Here it is restricted to the deliverance purchased by the Redeemer on behalf of the sinner in the payment of the penalty of sin. The blood of Christ was the medium of exchange used to make this tremendous transaction. Redemption in the New Testament is a progressive work based upon the redemptive act of the shedding of Christ's blood. The blood is the basis for the redemptive work of God. Redemption is, first of all, a deliverance from the *penalty* of sin. This was accomplished by Christ shedding His blood on the cross. In the next place, redemption is a deliverance from the *power* of sin. This is accomplished by the indwelling Holy Spirit. Finally, redemption is a deliverance from the *presence* of sin. This is accomplished by the *parousia* of Christ. Paul made this threefold division of the redemption made by Christ:

> Who delivered us from so great a death, and doth deliver: in whom we trust that he will yet deliver us (2 Cor. 1:10).

The death of Christ accomplished one great thing: the salvation of man; but in its relationship to time, it touches all phases of man's life. It is past, present and future. It moves out of time and reaches back into eternity past where it was in the mind of God and found the basis of the covenant in the Godhead of redemption. It reaches forth into the future and lays hold of eternity to come where in anticipation the redeemed are seen in heaven. There are several Greek words translated by our word *redeem*, but each one of these conveys the thought as expressed in one of the time periods. (1) *Agorazo* refers to the past. (2) *Exagorazo* refers to the present. (3) *Lutroo* or *apolutrosis* refers to the future. We shall now take occasion to examine each one of these phases of redemption as they are related to the saved today.

1. *Redemption is a deliverance from the penalty of sin.* This has particular reference to the redemption purchased by Christ through the shedding of His own blood on the cross. The blood of Christ is full payment for sin. It is an account settled in the past. The question of the penalty of sin for the redeemed will never be raised again in this life or in eternity.

> Verily, verily, I say unto you, He that heareth my word, and believeth on him that sent me, hath everlasting

life, and shall not come into condemnation [judgment];
but is passed from death unto life (John 5:24).

This phase of redemption is seen in the meaning and use of the first word which is translated "redeem," *agorazo*. This word means "to do business in the marketplace," such as buying and selling. This word suggests the Oriental agora where everything was displayed for sale, including human beings. Slaves were as common there as any vegetable or meat. Edward Gibbon, in the *Decline and Fall of the Roman Empire*, estimated at least one half the population of the Roman Empire were slaves. This means that about sixty million people were slaves. Human life was cheap, and the traffic in human lives was tremendous. Both Gibbon and John Lord gave slavery as one of the basic reasons for the undermining and corruption of the Roman Empire and that which ultimately led to its downfall.

The New Testament, which was written in these surroundings, sees man as a slave to sin. The whole human family is in the shackles of sin and in dire need of a Redeemer. Paul speaks of himself in inspired language: "I am carnal, sold under sin" (Rom. 7:14). This is a miniature picture of the race. Again, he tells the Ephesians of their condition before deliverance was wrought: "Wherein in time past ye walked according to the course of this world, according to the prince of the power of the air, the spirit that now worketh in the children of disobedience" (Eph. 2:2). They were slaves of sin, and because of that, they did the will of Satan. This does not even suggest that Satan was the owner of these slaves exposed in the marketplace for sale. This would mean that Christ paid the ransom to the Devil. This is not the intent of the apostle. Nowhere does Scripture intimate that the redemptive price paid by Christ, even His own blood, was to the Devil.

The patristic theory of the Atonement, or the military theory of the Atonement, as it has been popularly labeled, taught that sinners were held as captives of war by Satan and that they could be bought by a ransom paid to him. Justin Martyr was the perpetrator of this theory, and it was taken up by Irenaeus and Origen. It is stated briefly in the words of Peter Lombard: "What did the Redeemer to our captor? He held out to him His Cross as a mouse-trap; in it he set, as a bait, His Blood."[6]

This heresy was also called the "mousetrap" theory. Accordingly, Christ paid a ransom to Satan with His blood. This appears highly preposterous and blasphemous, but the theory was held by many able men in the church during its early history, and today some border on this theory, even if they do not embrace it. Anselm in the eleventh century was the first to successfully refute this heresy. He pointed out that whatever man owed, he owed to God and not to Satan. Man cannot render any payment to God because of original sin, or as he stated, "A sinner cannot justify a sinner." Only God could satisfy the claims of God. Therefore, as he further stated: "If then none can make it but God, and none owes it but man, it must needs be wrought out by God, made man."[7]

Satan is a usurper here in the world, and man owes

---

[6]*Ibid.*, p. 747.
[7]*Ibid.*, p. 748.

nothing to him. God does not recognize as an eternal matter Satan's claims to this earth. He treats him as a rebel who by a *coup d'etat* temporarily has overthrown man's dominion in the universe of God and usurped God's authority. Christ's death was not an overture to Satan, and certainly Christ was making no payment to him. Christ did not buy us from Satan, but He did redeem us from the penalty of sin and the power of Satan. We no longer have to serve the usurper. In *Cur Deus Homo*, Anselm made the death of Christ and the shedding of His blood a transaction conducted entirely within the Godhead. Paul said: "...God was in Christ, reconciling the world unto himself..." (2 Cor. 5:19). The price was made to satisfy the demands of His own holiness.

Philip Mauro, it seems to me, fell into the error of the military theory of the Atonement. I quote at length from him to have his exact language. In commenting on Leviticus 25:47–49, he wrote:

> For men, instead of occupying in the world that place of dominion and supreme authority for which God intended them, have become slaves to a foreign despot, namely, that great being who has 'the power of death, that is, the devil' (Heb. 2:14); and have become subject to 'the law of sin and death' (Rom. 8:2). For we may regard the Devil as being that 'stranger' to whom the human race has been sold by the head of the race (Adam) and 'the stock of the stranger's family' to be the evil powers, vices and passions, by which men are, one and all, enslaved.[8]

The stranger in the Leviticus passage, which we have

---

[8]*Ibid.*

examined beforehand, could not be Satan. The Christ did not pay one iota to Satan. The stranger was the one who received the price of redemption, and it is a dangerous practice to make him a figure of Satan. Christ paid the penalty of sin to satisfy the justice of God so that we might not have to pay it. Sin, not Satan, prompted Christ to go into the marketplace and ransom us from the penalty of it. The sacrifice of Christ was not satisfactory to Satan. Satan was not a party in the transaction of redemption.

Christ died a penal death. He went into the marketplace and saw us exposed as slaves of sin. In such a condition, we were subject to death. Christ paid the price of the penalty of our sin and lifted the terrible load of sin that was on the slave's back.

2. *Redemption is a deliverance from the power of sin.* The entire plan of redemption rests upon the foundation of the death of Christ. In view of this, the Holy Spirit came on the Day of Pentecost to make this phase of redemption available to man. Not only is the sinner delivered from the penalty of sin, but he can be delivered from the power of sin in this life. There is a way. This has to do with the everyday walk of the believer. The Greek word which applies particularly to this phrase is *exagorazo.*

Liddell and Scott gave the meaning of *exagorazo* "to buy from" and "to redeem." It is the same word as *agorazo,* but with the addition of the preposition *ex,* meaning "out of." The word means, therefore, "to buy out of the marketplace." Dr. Scofield, who has called attention to this threefold division, made this enlightening comment: "Our adorable Kinsman-

Redeemer is no slave trader."[9] He not only bought us in the marketplace of sin, that shameful Oriental bazaar, but He took us off the market so that we might never be sold again. There is no danger of the redeemed sinner ever going on the slave block again. This refers to the security of redemption because it makes it possible for a sinning saint to come back to God and find power, never to fall again into the same heinous sin. John expressed it in this way:

> But if we walk in the light, as he is in the light, we have fellowship one with another, and the blood of Jesus Christ his Son cleanseth us from all sin (1 John 1:7).

The present tense is used here in reference to the cleansing of the blood of Christ. That it keeps on cleansing us from all sin is the thought. This refers to the present walk of the believer here on earth. There is redemption from the power of sin in the daily life.

The Holy Spirit furnishes deliverance from the power of present sin. If the Christian is not producing the fruit of the Spirit, he is doing the works of the flesh. There is no such thing as a "no-man's land" in between. The works of the flesh are sin and are so identified in the Word of God: "For I know that in me (that is, in my flesh,) dwelleth no good thing... (Rom. 7:18). If a Christian produces no fruit of the Spirit but lives in the flesh, can he expect to be saved? This is a pertinent question that baffles, because a great many so-called Christians are living in the flesh. If it is admitted that these so-called Christians have been

---

[9]Scofield, p. 490.

redeemed by the blood of the Lamb, then we may dismiss any question regarding the certainty of their salvation. They are saved. If they have not been redeemed from the penalty of sin, then they cannot figure in the discussion under this section. They have not been delivered from the penalty of sin. They need to accept the redemption that is offered by grace; and they can if they trust Christ. In this section we are discussing genuine Christians who have been redeemed by the blood of the Lamb. We are not considering their future redemption and eternal welfare, but we are confined in our discussion to the narrow limits of their present lives. How a Christian may be delivered from the power of sin right *now* is the cogent question before us. Does God have a present redemption available for saved sinners, by which they can live for Him?

This is peculiarly the age of the Holy Spirit. His most peculiar ministry, in contrast to other ages, is that He indwells every believer.

> But ye are not in the flesh, but in the Spirit, if so be that the Spirit of God dwell in you. Now if any man have not the Spirit of Christ, he is none of his (Rom. 8:9).
> What? know ye not that your body is the temple of the Holy Ghost which is in you, which ye have of God, and ye are not your own (1 Cor. 6:19).

The indwelling of believers is the grand identification of this age. The Day of Pentecost marks the transition from the Old Testament, where the Holy Spirit came and went in a sovereign way, to the New Testament, where He has come on a specific ministry. One phase of this ministry is to indwell believers. The Day of

Pentecost was the line of demarcation between the old and new, law and grace, Israel and the church. Pentecost was the Bethlehem of the Holy Spirit. He became incarnate in the body of believers on that day. To read over the Day of Pentecost as an incident in the development of the gospel story is to miss the significance and import of the tremendous transaction of that day. There was a difference after Pentecost. There would have been no church, no evangel, no testimony, no epistles, and no apostle Paul if there had not been that day. Christ carefully instructed His disciples to abide in Jerusalem after His ascension: "But ye shall receive power after that the Holy Ghost is come upon you: and ye shall be witnesses unto me . . ." (Acts 1:8). He warned them that " . . . they should not depart from Jerusalem, but wait for the promise of the Father . . . (Acts 1:4). The church was born in Jerusalem. The New Jerusalem had its inception in the earthly city, but Jerusalem was not long to be the center of the Christian movement, for it was soon shifted to the gentile city of Antioch, and from there to the four corners of the earth.

Ten days after the ascension of Christ, the disciples were gathered together in some place. Was it the upper room, the temple, or some other place? They had just had an election of an apostle to take Judas' place, conducted by the incomparable but "wrong way" Simon Peter. This election proved that they needed divine light and leading. Perhaps Matthias was a devout and faithful saint in Christ Jesus, but the Holy Spirit was not there to choose him as an apostle and apparently did not use him in that capacity afterwards. Then the Holy Spirit came. There was no star, no angel voices, and no wise men, but His advent was marked by tangible and vital evidence. There were two evidences that He had come. First of all, there was a "sound from heaven as of a rushing mighty wind" (Acts 2:2). There was no wind, but that was the effect produced; that was what the witnesses heard. Secondly, there were "cloven tongues like as of fire" (Acts 2:3). There was no fire, but that was the effect produced; that was what the witnesses saw.

There are two avenues through which man comes into possession of most of his knowledge. One is the eye gate, and the other is the ear gate. The Holy Spirit confirmed His entrance into the believer by an appeal to both, by sight and by sound. Those present both saw and heard. That day was never repeated in the life of the church, for the Holy Spirit came to indwell. There is no necessity for a repetition as He is already here, and He will not come again because He has not left since the Day of Pentecost. As long as the church is here, He will be here.

He indwells every believer and is the power for Christian living. Christian living is permitting Him to work through the believer's life. This was never true under the Old Testament arrangement. The ideal of Christian living is, therefore, much higher than that under law. "Rejoice evermore" was not a commandment under law but is a production of the indwelling Holy Spirit in the life of a Spirit-filled child of God. The great commandment for the age of grace is: "Be filled with the Spirit" or "Walk in the Spirit."

Christian living is not keeping law or following some scheme of conduct. It might be possible for a Christian to keep certain laws and rules that would make him feel as if he were doing a good job of Christian living when in reality he would be making a horrible mess of it. Christian living is yielding to the operation of the Holy Spirit in order that He might produce "the fruit of the Spirit."

Just as a peach tree yields itself to the sweet influence of the sun, rain, and gentle breezes, so the Christian is to yield to the Holy Spirit. Just as the peach tree produces sweet fruit as it yields, thus the Christian will produce the fruit of the Spirit. This fruit is not an unknown quantity but is outlined distinctly: "love, joy, peace, longsuffering, gentleness, goodness, faith, meekness, temperance: against such there is no law" (Gal. 5:22,23).

These graces cannot be produced by human effort or resolution but are distinctly declared to be fruit. A peach is not the product of the effort of the peach tree but represents what a Power greater than the peach tree can produce. A Christian may know by examining his own life if these things are being produced. If these things are absent from the life of the Christian, he is falling short of God's ideal for him. His salvation is secure, but he is missing the blessing of living for God and the prospect of a future reward.

The Holy Spirit is the power for Christian living today. When our Great Redeemer bought us in the marketplace of sin, He led us out from under the power of sin and bade us live by the new power that He had provided for us. He does not wish to sell us back under sin, but has led us out from the old life. We have been redeemed from the law to the new life under grace.

3. *Redemption is a deliverance from the presence of sin.*

Christ being come an high priest of good things to
come...entered in once into the holy place, having
obtained eternal redemption for us (Heb. 9:11,12).

The final word in this study of redemption has an
origin different from the other two. The word is *lutroo*,
which occurs also in the noun form *apolutrosis*. The
prefix and suffix do not add meaning to the word but
merely intensify what is communicated. Both words
mean "to release by payment of ransom." Simply
stated, they mean "to set free." "As our Kinsman-
Redeemer is no slave trader, so also, He is not a slave
owner."[10] The slave has not only been removed from
the slave block forever; but he also has been removed
from the position of slave. He has been removed that
he might be set free. Redemption is the "Proclamation of Emancipation" for sinners, written in the
blood of Christ.

If the Son therefore shall make you free, ye shall be
free indeed (John 8:36).
For, brethren, ye have been called into liberty; only use
not liberty for an occasion to the flesh, but by love
serve one another (Gal. 5:13).

Redemption removes a sinner from the death cell,
brings him into the Father's house, and establishes
him in the position of sonship.

For ye have not received the spirit of bondage again to
fear; but ye have received the Spirit of adoption, whereby we cry, Abba Father (Rom. 8:15).

Redemption, as expressed by the word *lutroo*, covers
the entire field and sees the sinner at last delivered

---

[10]*Ibid.*

from the presence of sin and brought into the presence of God. Christ is the One who brings us all the
way. He is our redemption, for He "is made unto
us...redemption" (1 Cor. 1:30). Twice over we are
told: "In whom we have redemption through his
blood" (Eph. 1:7; Col. 1:14). This word, therefore,
deals definitely with the future aspect of redemption.
Sin will be removed from the presence of the redeemed
and from this earth. There are two features of future
redemption which must await the coming of Christ
before they can be fulfilled. These are: the redemption of our bodies and the redemption of creation.

Paul speaks of the redemption of the body as future.

> And not only they, but ourselves also, which have the
> firstfruits of the Spirit, even we ourselves groan within
> ourselves, waiting for the adoption, to wit, the re-
> demption of our body (Rom. 8:23).

We will not be completely redeemed until we have a
body redeemed from sin and death. Although the
redeemed are at present indwelt by the Holy Spirit,
they do not have a body that is delivered from sin
and death. The old Adamic nature lives on until
death or until Christ translates the living believers in
His second coming. The resurrection of believers com-
prehends a new body: "For this corruptible must put
on incorruption, and this mortal must put on immor-
tality" (1 Cor. 15:53). This old Adamic, dying body
"is sown in corruption; it is raised in incorruption"
(1 Cor. 15:42). The modern method is to diffuse the
physical resurrection of the body into thin air by
substituting for the Christian doctrine of resurrection

Buddhist or Platonic philosophies, which deny the actual resurrection of the body by making it spiritual. Paul defended the Christian doctrine against that very system when he wrote, "It is sown a natural body; it is raised a spiritual body. There is a natural body, and there is a spiritual body" (1 Cor. 15:44).

The body will be retained in resurrection. Instead of having a body dominated by the fallen, Adamic nature, we will possess a body dominated by the Spirit of God and motivated by the Spirit of God breathed anew into it. It is impossible to dismiss the resurrection of the body from Christian doctrine. Redemption will not be complete until the bodies of the redeemed are raised in newness of life. Paul contemplated that day when he wrote, "And grieve not the holy Spirit of God, whereby ye are sealed unto the day of redemption" (Eph. 4:30). The "day of redemption" is the time of the resurrection of the saints who have died, and the translation of the living saints at the *parousia* of Christ.

The second prospect of future redemption is the lifting of the curse from physical creation. When Adam sinned, there was a curse pronounced upon the earth: "Cursed is the ground for thy sake; in sorrow shalt thou eat of it all the days of thy life; thorns also and thistles shall it bring forth to thee" (Gen. 3:17,18). *A blasted earth* fittingly describes the continued condition of our planet down to the present hour, a phenomenon Paul recognized in Romans 8:22: "The whole creation groaneth and travaileth in pain together until now."

The poet may speak of communing with nature and of the sweetness of that process, but the farmer who has wrestled with Johnson grass and cockleburs in fertile bottomland in the afternoon of a sultry July day does not call it communion, nor does he find any particular sweetness in it. The earth does not respond readily to the efforts of man but it must be compelled, by persistent effort, to yield her increase. Only by the sweat of the brow does man eke out a living from the ground (see Gen. 3:19). Still, there are times when the earth overcomes the handicap of the curse and yields bountifully, filling her cornucopia to overflowing. It is, however, a figment of the imagination and an oratorical gesture to say that man has conquered the forces of nature and has made them subservient to his beck and call.

There is a golden day in the future for this earth, for the One who created it will be here to make nature respond with her hidden treasures and possibilities, as He did when He made the fish bring a coin to Simon Peter in order for him to pay the temple tax. The curse will be lifted from the earth during the Millennium, and then man will have his first glimpse of this planet in her original beauty. The mind cannot conceive of the desert rejoicing and blossoming as the rose; yet this is the happy anticipation of the earth.

If it were possible for man today to bring the kingdom of heaven to earth, which is the modern delusion of the church, this important task of restoring the fecundity of the earth and lifting the curse would be a difficulty that even the most optimistic "kingdom builder" could not handle. The many improvements man has developed are no substitute for the ideal conditions outlined in Scripture. At present, many Bible students, filled with zeal and ardor, are speaking with rapture of the wonders that the returning Jews have wrought in Palestine by modern methods of farming. They imply that this is at least a partial fulfillment of Scripture. These changes, however, are hardly commensurate with what is spoken in Isaiah 11:6–8; 30:26; and chapter 35. The entire face of the earth will be transformed into a scene of placid beauty and verdant landscape.

Christ is the great Kinsman-Redeemer who will deliver the bodies of believers in a physical resurrection and will deliver the physical creation from the bondage of the curse. Boaz delivered both the person of Ruth and the property of Elimelech. Christ will deliver the person of the church and the property of the Jew and Gentile—this earth. Future redemption contemplates the resurrection of redeemed persons and the restoration of a sin-cursed earth. Then there will be freedom.

There may be some objection to the inclusion of a love story like Ruth in the canon of Scripture. This objection may be intensified when it is concluded that the Book of Ruth teaches the great doctrine of redemption by a Kinsman-Redeemer. Nevertheless, the story stands, and the fact remains that redemption is a love story. The love of our Kinsman-Redeemer, as He saw us plunged in the slavery of sin, prompted Him to pay with His own blood the price of our release, and He has brought us into His heart and home because He loved us.

· BOOK TWO ·

Esther

· 17 ·

The Strange Providences of God

Providence is the hand of God in the glove of history.

Providence is a theological term. Dr. Strong, in his ponderous tome, defines it like this: "Providence is that continuous agency of God by which He makes all events of the physical and moral universe fulfill the original design with which He created it."

To explain it in layman's terms, there are three words that describe the work of God as it affects His physical universe.

1. There is *creation*, which explains the existence of the universe. By God's fiat He created all things. "In the beginning God created the heaven and the earth" (Gen. 1:1). We have only two alternatives today: We either accept revelation or we choose speculation. These are the only two explanations. And regardless of what you may believe, evolution is speculation. "Science" has no scientific explanation for the origin of the universe; it has to speculate. I accept revelation because it explains the origin of the universe without resorting to the speculations of men.

2. The second word is *preservation*, which explains the continuance of the universe. In other words, God not only created the cosmos, He holds it together. The Lord Jesus Christ is the Creator. He is also the Preserver. We are told in Hebrews 1:3, ". . . upholding all things by the word of his power. . . ." All things are held together by Him. Colossians 1:17 says, ". . . by him all things consist." Everything would come unglued today if it were not for Him. God Himself is holding together the atoms which are the building blocks of this universe.

3. The third word is *providence*, which explains the progress and development of the universe. Creation explains its origin, and preservation explains its continuance; but providence explains the progress and development of the universe. Providence is the means by which God directs all things—animate and inanimate, seen and unseen, good and evil—toward a worthy purpose, which means that *His will must ultimately prevail.*

The Word of God teaches this. For instance, Psalm 103:19 says, ". . . his kingdom ruleth over all." And notice Psalm 135:6: "Whatsoever the LORD pleased, that did he in heaven, and in earth, in the seas, and all deep places." God is running this universe to please Himself, not to please you or me. We are creatures; He is the Creator. We ought to get this straight in our thinking. The only freedom of speech that you and I have is that which *He* gives us. He is the Creator. We are creatures.

Also notice verses 7–10 of Psalm 135:

He causeth the vapours to ascend from the ends of the earth; he maketh lightnings for the rain; he bringeth the wind out of his treasuries. Who smote the firstborn of Egypt, both of man and beast. Who sent tokens and wonders into the midst of thee, O Egypt, upon Pharaoh, and upon all his servants. Who smote great nations, and slew mighty kings.

God takes the responsibility for doing those things. In Daniel 4:35 it is written:

And all the inhabitants of the earth are reputed as nothing: and he doeth according to his will in the army of heaven, and among the inhabitants of the earth: and none can stay his hand, or say unto him, What doest thou?

In other words, God does not have to report to anyone concerning His conduct. God runs this universe and He runs it His own way. That is what providence means. Paul, in Ephesians 1:11, expresses it thus, ". . . who worketh all things after the counsel of his own will."

You may think that is too theological, so let me put it like this: Providence is God at the steering wheel of this universe. It is the way God coaches the man who is on second base. Providence means that God is behind the scenes, shifting and directing the happenings of the world. Or, as we have had it expressed, God stands in the shadows, keeping watch over His own. Or, again, providence is the hand of God in the glove of history, and that glove will never move until He moves it.

The Book of Esther teaches the providence of God. Actually, the name of God is not mentioned in the Book of Esther, and for this reason there were those who did not want it included in the canon of Scripture. However, the Book of Esther is a revelation of the

people of God out of the will of God. They are walking
in a willful pathway; no appeal is made to Him by
name in the entire Book of Esther. But God will overrule their attitude, and He will protect them.

The word *providence* means "to provide." God will
provide. Providence means that God is back of His
creation today, back of the human race, back of those
who are His own by redemption. And God is giving
men and women direction in the world today.

In the Book of Esther we see that this is how God
works. The young Jewish girl Esther was chosen by
King Ahasuerus to be queen of Persia. She was not
queen for a day; she was queen for a lifetime. Furthermore, she was chosen by means of a beauty contest. Many people simply would call her lucky. But
God was behind these events. Her cousin Mordecai
happened to overhear a plot to slay the king. Yes, he
was "lucky" to have overheard it. But God was overruling. Mordecai reported the plot, but his loyalty
went unrewarded. The king didn't recognize him at
all. (Say was that unlucky!) Then to make matters
worse, Mordecai incurred the wrath of Haman (whom
the king had promoted to a very influential office) by
refusing to bow to him. In revenge, Haman determined to destroy not only Mordecai but all his people
throughout the kingdom.

Then one night the king could not sleep. Since no
sleeping pill was available, he called for the book of
records of the kingdom, the chronicles—what we
would call the "minutes" of the kingdom. Believe me,
minutes are boring, I don't care whose they are. And
these minutes were boring, too. They had a few exciting items in them, like accounts of occasional murders,

but when nothing else would put the king to sleep, those minutes would do the trick. Yet on this night he was alerted because the servant read the particular page that recorded what Mordecai had done to save the king's life. The king asked the question, "Was he rewarded?" "No," the servant said, "he wasn't rewarded." And the king said, "Well, we are going to reward him." King Ahasuerus made that decision at exactly the right psychological moment. The entire sequence of events sounds like luck—it was luck on the human plane—but God was directing. And God saved an entire people from extermination because of it.

Now providence is not confined to the Book of Esther. You will find it running as a bright thread all the way through the Word of God.

Joseph is an example (see Gen. 37–45). This man Joseph, without doubt, was the champion hard luck boy. At seventeen years of age, this young fellow, the favorite of his father, was given a coat of many colors. He had a wonderful advantage at home, but his brothers plotted against him. They wanted to murder him. Worse than that, they sold him into slavery, and he was carried down into the land of Egypt. For a seventeen-year-old boy, that was terrible. However, he recognized the hand of God in his life and he began to advance, for he had been sold to an Egyptian official. Just as he got to the top, the rug was pulled out from under him, and he found himself thrown into prison. We would expect him to give up, but he didn't. He interpreted dreams for Pharaoh's baker and butler, who were also in prison. When the butler was released, Joseph said to him, "Now, be sure to tell Pharaoh about me, because I'm down here and I'm not guilty. I would like to get out." But the butler forgot all about him, and Joseph spent at least a couple of years more in prison. In two years you can become very discouraged in prison when you are not guilty! This boy—I marvel at him—seems to have ridden on top of the waves all the time. The hand of God was in his life. God by His providence was directing him. One day Pharaoh had a dream and the butler said, "I remember my sins today—I forgot all about that boy. I know somebody who can interpret your dreams." Actually, it would have been the worst thing in the world if the butler had told Pharaoh about Joseph two years earlier. Joseph would have gone back home, and he would not have been available to interpret the dreams of Pharaoh. God kept Joseph in prison, for God was preserving His people. Later on, Joseph could look back on his life and say, even to the brothers who sold him as a slave, ". . . ye thought evil against me; but God meant it unto good . . ." (Gen. 50:20).

God has put in your life enemies, and He has done so for your good. Oh, we cry and we go to the wailing wall, complaining and whining, but God permits trying situations in our lives for a purpose.

David Harum had some very old-fashioned wisdom to dish out years ago. He said that God permits a dog to have a reasonable amount of fleas and it is a good thing, for it enables the dog to take his mind off the fact that he is a dog!

God permits an enemy or trouble to come into our lives so we will turn to Him. The only way He can get the attention of a great many folk is by sending them trouble! Perhaps you have had that experience: You turned to God when trouble came to you, but you would not have come otherwise. God permits this to happen.

Shakespeare put it like this: "There is a divinity which shapes our ends, rough-hew them how we will." Someone else has suggested that disappointment should be spelled with a capital "H"—"His appointment." God permits disappointments, enemies, and even tragedies to come to us. He does so for a purpose.

Another book in the Bible, Ruth, has the romance of redemption for its theme, but it also illustrates the providential dealings of God. One morning Ruth went out from the town of Bethlehem to find a field in which to glean. She knew nothing of the surrounding countryside. I walked down that road purposely during my travels to Israel, and I looked on every side. I'll be honest with you, I wouldn't have known which field to choose. It was very important which field Ruth chose, because if she had not gone into the right field, the prophecy that Micah gave (5:2) would have been wrong—Christ would not have been born in Bethlehem. (Send word to the wise men not to come; they will not find Jesus in Bethlehem!) But Ruth did go into the right field, and we are told, ". . . her hap was to light on a part of the field belonging unto Boaz" (Ruth 2:3). From her standpoint it was chance, but God by His providence was directing.

The writer of the Proverbs made this very arresting statement:

The lot is cast into the lap, but the whole disposing thereof is of the LORD (Prov. 16:33).

God is saying that you cannot even go to Las Vegas and throw the dice but what He is there seeing how they come up. "The lot is cast into the lap." And the Greeks had a saying like this, "The dice of the gods are loaded!" God says to you and me, "Don't gamble with Me—I'll win. *I* know how it is coming up. You don't." So many people gamble with their lives at stake today. My friend, you don't gamble with God.

Ruth looked to God. I know she prayed. Yet God never revealed His will to her. He guided her by His providence, as He will guide any willing soul today.

One of the most interesting cases of God's providential dealings concerns old Ahab, king of Israel. He was a man far from God. First Kings 22 records the alliance between Ahab and Jehoshaphat (which Jehoshaphat should never have made) to go to war against Syria. Ahab pulled a good one. He went into battle in the uniform of a common soldier so that only Jehoshaphat could be identified as a king—and Jehoshaphat almost got killed because the Syrians took out after him. They were looking for the top man, the king of Israel, and Jehoshaphat was dressed as royalty. Ahab was chuckling, "They won't get me. I'm well protected by my disguise." When they took out after Jehoshaphat, Ahab probably wiped his brow and said, "I made it." But in the Syrian army there "happened" to be a trigger-happy soldier. We are told, "And a certain man drew a bow at a venture, and smote the king of Israel between the joints of the harness [armor]: wherefore he said unto the driver of his chariot, Turn thine hand, and carry me out of the host; for I am wounded" (1 Kin. 22:34).

Ahab was fatally wounded. You see, that arrow had

Ahab's name on it. That soldier put an arrow in his bow, pulled it back, and let it go. He wasn't aiming at anything.

A little boy got a B B gun for Christmas. After the boy had tried it out, a friend asked him, "What did you hit?" He said, "Nothin'." "Well," asked the friend, "what did you shoot at?" "Nothin'," said the little boy.

My friend, this soldier aimed at nothing, but he hit Ahab. And the king was killed because God had said through Micaiah the prophet that this would happen (see 1 Kin. 22:13–17).

By the providence of God, Caesar Augustus signed a tax bill. If you had leaned over his shoulder and said, "That's interesting! This bill will cause a prophecy given by Micah over seven hundred years ago to be fulfilled," he would have laughed and said, "I know nothing about that. I need taxes. I have a huge army to maintain, and I need to carry on the poverty program here in Rome." So he signed the tax bill that moved Mary and Joseph to Bethlehem in fulfillment of Micah 5:2.

The psalmist wrote long ago, "For the kingdom is the LORD's; and he is the governor among the nations" (Ps. 22:28). Yes, God was and is in control.

One day a young man was arrested. His name was Stephen; the verdict was handed in; and they stoned him to death. We are told that in the midst of all the trouble,

He [Stephen], being full of the Holy Ghost, looked up stedfastly into heaven, and saw the glory of God, and Jesus standing on the right hand of God, and said, Behold, I see the heavens opened, and the Son of man

standing on the right hand of God. Then they cried out
with a loud voice, and stopped their ears, and ran upon
him with one accord, and cast him out of the city, and
stoned him: and the witnesses laid down their clothes
at a young man's feet, whose name was Saul (Acts
7:55–58).

When that young man looked up and said, "I see
the heavens opened and the Son of man standing on
the right hand of God," the crowd all cried out, "This
is blasphemy." And Saul of Tarsus, a brilliant young
Pharisee and the biggest skeptic of all, led the group.
They put their coats at his feet, and he directed the
stoning of Stephen. After he looked down at the
bloody body of that boy lying there, he looked into the
heavens, realizing that Stephen had something he did
not have. And a few days later, on the way to Damascus, Saul spiritually was prepared for what happened
(see Acts 9). There was a blinding light, and the Lord
Jesus Christ Himself spoke to him. God by His providential dealings used Stephen's testimony to prepare
Saul for the appearance of Jesus on the Damascus
Road.

The examples of God's providence are not confined
to the Bible. They are evident in secular history. All
you have to do is open your eyes.

God stopped Xerxes. God had said through Daniel
(see Dan. 8) that He was going to move the center of
world power out of the East, from Asia and Africa, to
Europe. He did so when Xerxes lost the Battle of Thermopylae. How could Xerxes lose? The Greeks were
masters on the ocean; yet they could not match the
three hundred vessels of Xerxes. But God could. In my
travels in Greece we stopped by the Bay of Salamis,

and I took several pictures of the site of the battle. As I looked out over Thermopylae, a modern port today, I thought of the storm that destroyed three hundred of Xerxes' vessels. A single storm shifted the power from the East to the West and changed the entire destiny of the world. God moves in the affairs of men.

Napoleon said that God is on the side of the biggest battalions, but he was wrong. He had the biggest battalions at Waterloo, and he lost.

The Spanish Armada was anchored off the coast of England. The next day England would have gone down in defeat, but that night a storm came. When the morning broke, the Spanish Armada was wrecked, and Great Britain became the proud leader of the seas for three hundred years. The destiny of the world was changed.

The hand of God has been in our own nation. You cannot read our history without recognizing the fact that God has moved in the history of this nation. When Columbus was coming to the Western Hemisphere the first time, he was headed directly to either the coast of Virginia or the Carolinas. A flight of pigeons went by and he followed them. Consequently, the Spanish flag went up on South America and the West Indies, while Protestantism came to this country. South America has more natural resources than North America has ever had, yet it has lagged and the story is told in religion. May I say to you, God was directing the affairs of this nation.

During the Revolutionary War, Benedict Arnold betrayed his country. He gave the entire blueprint of West Point to Major André of the British forces. Major André was riding on horseback toward the British lines with those blueprints in his boot. He came to a crossroad and did not know which road to take—but God knew. Down the road he chose were Revolutionary soldiers. If he had not made the big mistake of saying the wrong thing, they never would have searched him. But he spoke, and they searched him, and they discovered the awful betrayal and saved our country.

In the early days of America the colonists stayed too close to the eastern seaboard. They were afraid to penetrate the vast expanse of the Middle West. Eventually God waved a little gold, and the Gold Rush was underway. A lot of people came to California. They didn't all find gold, but they've been coming ever since. That was one way God moved.

You may be saying, "Yes, God guides nations—I can see that—but what about people today? What about the individual who has turned his or her back on God? Is there any hope?"

Certainly there is. That is the kind of people I am interested in. In the forty-second chapter of Isaiah, verse 16, there is an arresting statement. After presenting "my servant" (the Lord Jesus Christ) and talking about the nation Israel, God says:

> And I will bring the blind by a way that they knew not; I will lead them in paths that they have not known: I will make darkness light before them, and crooked things straight. These things will I do unto them, and not forsake them.

God says the person who does not know, who cannot see the way, or who has ruled Him out is still under His care. God will lead such a person by a way that he or she knows not.

May I use a personal example? The first time I preached in Los Angeles was a Sunday evening. I had come to California as a tourist. Apparently, very few people knew that a "famous" preacher from a little town in Texas was preaching, because not many folk were in attendance that evening. However there was a lady in the congregation—a very distinguished looking lady—who, when an invitation to accept Christ was given, raised her hand. The one who talked with her after the service related her story to me. This woman had come to California from the Chicago area in search of one of her children. A daughter, movie crazy and hoping to crash into stardom, had headed for Hollywood, and the mother had lost contact with her. Of course the woman was frantic. She had been unsuccessful in her search, and finally had gone to the railroad station to return home. With five hours to wait for her train, terribly disturbed in her own mind and heart, she began to walk. She heard chimes playing and finally located the source, the church where I was preaching. Years later, the counselor told me that she had received letters from the woman, telling how those few hours had been the turning point in her life. She had come into the church that night in a suicidal frame of mind, for she thought everything had gone black for her. Accepting Christ was the greatest moment in her life.

Do you know how she found that church? By the providence of God.

A doctor was attending a medical convention in a downtown hotel. From what he told me, it had been a pretty rough Saturday night. He was far from God. He got up in the morning, looked out his window, and saw the sign, "Jesus Saves." And he came to the church where I was preaching that morning. He said later, when he told me about the experience, "I knew the message was for me from the beginning. When you gave the invitation, not a hand went up and I knew for sure that you preached this one for me. I went back to my room and got down on my knees." "Thru the Bible" is on the radio station in Yakima, Washington, today because of that doctor. Do you know why he came to church? Because of the providence of God.

I would quit preaching if it were not for the providence of God. His providence is what makes life thrilling and exciting. Neither you nor I know what is around the corner, but God by His providence is leading.

Look at the plight of this "now" generation. The philosophy being taught in a majority of our colleges today is one of the aimlessness of life, the purposelessness of life, and the meaninglessness of life. Yet God by His providence had an aim, a purpose, a meaning for you in mind millions of years ago. Today He wants to direct you. Why don't you let Him?

Every day is a new adventure for a child of God. He brings into our lives enemies and trouble, but He also brings sweetness and love, blessings, light and abundant life. He alone is the One who can do that today, and He wants to do it for you.

Abraham took his son Isaac to the top of Mt. Moriah (which today lies within the walls of Jerusalem). He built the altar, he arranged the wood, the fire was ready, and his son said, "Dad, here is the altar, the wood, and the fire, but where is the lamb?" Listen to Abraham: ". . . God will provide himself a lamb . . ."

(Gen. 22:8). "God will provide . . . ." *Provide* is my word; *providence* means "to provide." "God will provide Himself a Lamb."

Now do not be confused about the ram that got caught in a bush. That was a *ram*, not a lamb. Abraham and Isaac looked around and there was no lamb; there was a ram caught in the thicket. Nineteen hundred years later a Man walked into that area where Abraham had offered Isaac and of Him John the Baptist said, ". . . Behold the Lamb of God, which taketh away the sin of the world" (John 1:29).

God has provided a Lamb of sacrifice for you, friend. I do not know what the specific needs of your life are today, but I know this: You need the Lamb of God to take away your sin. You need Jesus. He can save you and He can make your life meaningful and purposeful.

The oil fields of east Texas were probably the last rough and tumble oil fields that this country had. In that area was a dirt farmer, a man who was uneducated but very shrewd. Oil was discovered on his land, and he was sharp enough not to sell. He became an independent oil operator and grew immensely wealthy. He built a magnificent home. He had a lovely wife and two little boys. This man was as godless, as wicked, as vile and profane as any person who has walked this earth.

Then a flu epidemic hit east Texas. His wife and one of the little boys died.

Two friends who were pastors in that area told me the story. One of them pastored a church nearby and went to visit the man that evening. The pastor was ushered into this lovely, spacious home. There were the two caskets, and there sat the man. The pastor went over to sit beside the man and started to put his arm around him to comfort him. The man shrugged him off and began to curse him. "I had never heard language like that," the pastor told me. "He cursed me as I had never been cursed before, and he cursed God. 'What right had God to take my wife and my little boy?' he said."

A few short years went by. Then early one morning, as I was waiting to air my program at the radio station in Dallas, the news commentator who preceded me announced that an explosion had occurred at the New London school in east Texas. Five hundred children and teachers were killed, I learned later. It was one of the greatest tragedies this country has ever had.

The oil man knew his little boy was at the school. He rushed to the scene of the explosion and, not seeing his child anywhere, began to dig like a madman in the debris and rubble. Finally, someone called to him. His son had been found—dead. The father gathered the little boy into his arms and paced up and down the school yard as if he were insane. Finally, the man was taken home, and the little body was placed in a casket.

My pastor friend knew he had to go through the ordeal again. He drove to the mansion, knocked on the door, and was ushered in. Over against the wall was one small casket, and there sat the father huddled over, crushed and broken. The pastor steeled himself for what he was sure would come. Not daring to put his arm around the man or even to touch him, he simply said, "I have come to comfort you the best I can." The man looked up, tears coursing down his cheeks, and said, "I have known all along that God was after me, but I didn't know He would have to do this to get me." That man came to Christ.

The providence of God can be tender, as it was with Abraham, or it can be severe, as it was with the oil executive and with Joseph. By His providence God moves in lives today, and He wants to move in your life, freely. Let us take a good, long look at how God moved in the lives of those who lived in a godless land—as seen in the account of Esther—and see what lessons there are for us, living in our world today.

· 18 ·

The Wife Who Refused To Obey Her Husband

Esther, Chapter 1

Now it came to pass in the days of Ahasuerus, (this is Ahasuerus which reigned, from India even unto Ethiopia, over an hundred and seven and twenty provinces:) that in those days, when the king Ahasuerus sat on the throne of his kingdom, which was in Shushan the palace, in the third year of his reign, he made a feast unto all his princes and his servants; the power of Persia and Media, the nobles and princes of the provinces, being before him: when he shewed the riches of his glorious kingdom and the honour of his excellent majesty many days, even an hundred and four-score days. And when these days were expired, the king made a feast unto all the people that were present in Shushan the palace, both unto great and small, seven days, in the court of the garden of the king's palace; where were white, green, and blue, hangings, fastened with cords of fine linen and purple to silver rings and pillars of marble: the

beds were of gold and silver, upon a pavement of
red, and blue, and white, and black, marble. And
they gave them drink in vessels of gold (the vessels being diverse one from another,) and royal
wine in abundance, according to the state of the
king. And the drinking was according to the law;
none did compel: for so the king had appointed to
all the officers of his house, that they should do
according to every man's pleasure. Also Vashti
the queen made a feast for the women in the royal
house which belonged to king Ahasuerus.

On the seventh day, when the heart of the king
was merry with wine, he commanded Mehuman,
Biztha, Harbona, Bigtha, and Abagtha, Zethar,
and Carcas, the seven chamberlains that served in
the presence of Ahasuerus the king, to bring
Vashti the queen before the king with the crown
royal, to shew the people and the princes her
beauty: for she was fair to look on. But the queen
Vashti refused to come at the king's commandment by his chamberlains: therefore was the king
very wroth, and his anger burned in him.

Then the king said to the wise men, which
knew the times, (for so was the king's manner
toward all that knew law and judgment: and the
next unto him was Carshena, Shethar, Admatha,
Tarshish, Meres, Marsena, and Memucan, the
seven princes of Persia and Media, which saw the
king's face, and which sat the first in the kingdom;) What shall we do unto the queen Vashti
according to law because she hath not performed
the commandment of the king Ahasuerus by the
chamberlains? And Memucan answered before

the king and the princes, Vashti the queen hath
not done wrong to the king only, but also to all the
princes, and to all the people that are in all the
provinces of the king Ahasuerus. For this deed of
the queen shall come abroad unto all women, so
that they shall despise their husbands in their
eyes, when it shall be reported, The king Ahasuerus commanded Vashti the queen to be brought
in before him, but she came not. Likewise shall
the ladies of Persia and Media say this day unto all
the king's princes, which have heard of the deed
of the queen. Thus shall there arise too much
contempt and wrath. If it please the king, let there
go a royal commandment from him, and let it be
written among the laws of the Persians and the
Medes, that it be not altered, that Vashti come no
more before king Ahasuerus; and let the king give
her royal estate unto another that is better than
she. And when the king's decree which he shall
make be published throughout all his empire, (for
it is great,) all the wives shall give to their husbands honour, both to great and small. And the
saying pleased the king and the princes; and the
king did according to the word of Memucan: for
he sent letters into all the king's provinces, into
every province according to the writing thereof,
and to every people after their language, that every man should bear rule in his own house, and
that it should be published according to the language of every people.

This chapter out of the history of a pagan nation is
inserted in the Word of God for a very definite pur-

pose: to teach the providence of God, as we shall see as we turn the pages of this book.

The story begins with the law of a heathen kingdom and a difficulty—a matrimonial difficulty. It was a very personal affair that arose in this kingdom, but it had international repercussions.

In order to relieve any anxiety that might be in the hearts of some, I digress to say that if you wish to know how Christians ought to get along in marriage, you should read the fifth chapter of the Epistle to the Ephesians. In fact, you should read the entire epistle. When you come to the passage that reads, "Wives, submit yourselves unto your own husbands, as unto the Lord" (Eph. 5:22), you must continue to read, because Paul adds, "Husbands, love your wives, even as Christ also loved the church, and gave himself for it" (Eph. 5:25). Women, if you are married to a godless husband, God never asks you to be obedient to him. In speaking of the married life of Spirit-filled believers, God does say that if you are married to a man who is willing to die for you because of his love for you, then you ought to be submissive to that man. Where there is perfect love there should be perfect happiness in submission. Certainly that is the Christian ideal, for it is used by God to illustrate the relationship between Christ and His church. However, the events of the Book of Esther took place in a pagan culture, where God's instructions were not considered.

The first thing we shall attempt to do is to identify Ahasuerus. As previously suggested, this king is probably the Xerxes of secular history. Understand that *Ahasuerus* was not the name of the man but his title. The word means "high father" or "ruler." As the word

Caesar is a title and does not identify the man, so *Ahasuerus* does not identify this Persian king in secular history. Archaeological discoveries have confirmed the belief of many scholars that *Darius* (which means "maintainer"), *Ahasuerus* (which means "venerable king," "high father," or "a king worthy of reverence") and *Artaxerxes* ("great king"—"great" as to character, rule, and empire) were titles, and may have referred to the same person at different periods of his life as his greatness increased.

There is quite a divergence of opinion concerning the identity of the Ahasuerus of the Book of Esther. The viewpoint that I hold is that he was Xerxes the Great of Persia, because that man was the one who actually brought the Medo-Persian Empire to its zenith. Xerxes was the man who made the last great effort of the East to overcome the West, and it was a tremendous effort. Evidently the banquet referred to in the Book of Esther was the one in which he brought together the leaders of his entire kingdom, to sell them, if you please, on the idea of making a great campaign against Greece. From the time the forces of Xerxes came to Thermopylae until Japan's attack on Pearl Harbor in the twentieth century, no Eastern power had made a bid for world domination. Xerxes—Ahasuerus—was a man of tremendous ability and probably one of the greatest of the world rulers.

The banquet recounted in the Book of Esther causes anything that humans might attempt in these days to pale into insignificance. We are told that ". . . in the third year of his reign, he made a feast unto all his princes and his servants. . ." (1:3). We have already been told that there were 127 provinces, and out of each of these he brought a delegation (how many, I don't know), so that he had present probably one thousand or two thousand people for this banquet! You can see that it was no little private supper that he was having.

The record continues, "When he shewed the riches of his glorious kingdom and the honour of his excellent majesty many days, even an hundred and fourscore days" (1:4). For 180 days he boarded these fellows! He had a perpetual smorgasbord for six months! The father of Louis XV of France is said to have talked with the preceptor and the exchequer of his kingdom about this banquet, and he said that he did not see how the king had the patience to have that kind of a banquet. The exchequer, who was handling the finances for Louis XV, said that he did not see how he financed it. When you have just a few friends in for Christmas dinner, you know what it costs you for turkey and all the trimmings. It's an expensive sort of an affair. Well, you can imagine the expense that this man incurred. He brought the feast to a climax in the last seven days: "And when these days were expired, the king made a feast unto all the people that were present in Shushan the palace, both unto great and small, seven days, in the court of the garden of the king's palace" (1:5). Apparently Ahasuerus brought in a tremendous population of people for the final seven days in the court of the garden.

The description of Shushan in verse 6 has always interested expositors of the Word. There are those who find in it all kinds of spiritual meaning. I must confess that I have to agree with Dr. Ironside and other men who, when they get into this maze, can find

no spiritual meaning whatsoever. You will notice that
the colors are a little different from what we are accustomed to seeing in the Bible as pertaining to God's
people. The colors in the tabernacle were largely red
and blue and purple. There was white, of course, and
gold and silver. But here you find two other colors
introduced, green and black, that did not appear in
any word that God gave concerning the tabernacle or
concerning the New Jerusalem.

This banquet revealed the wealth, the luxury, and
the regal character of this Oriental court. The reason
for it is obvious. Ahasuerus had called in all of his
princes and all of his rulers from every corner of his
kingdom that he might win their wholehearted support for the military campaign to capture Greece. He
intended to make himself the supreme ruler of the
world. And, of course, Ahasuerus almost succeeded in
that attempt. I am confident he would have succeeded
had God not already determined that the operation
would end in failure and that the center of world
dominance would be shifted from the East to the West.

We have seen Ahasuerus' method of strategy used
on a comparably small scale in our day. Several years
ago, when one of the great automobile concerns came
out with a new model, they brought all of their dealers
from all over the world to Detroit for a convention. The
convention was made up of drinking parties and banquets, with the idea of selling the dealers on the new
model before it came out.

So it was with Ahasuerus, only he was bidding for
support of a new model campaign. He was going to
attempt something never before done by the East:
domination of the West.

Ahasuerus' banquet, a pagan event from the beginning, ended in a drunken orgy. However, we are told
that "the drinking was according to law; none did
compel" (1:8). Even these pagan Oriental rulers who
had absolute sovereignty never forced anyone to
drink, although they themselves were given to it. Today we are more "civilized": A person either has to
drink or get out!

One evening a lumberman in Tacoma, Washington,
came into a hotel lobby where I was sitting, waiting for
someone to pick me up for a meeting. The man sat
down with me and began to talk, and I discovered that
he was a fine Christian. I asked, "Aren't you going to
the banquet they are having here?" He said, "Yes, but
this is the cocktail hour, and I never attend it." I asked,
"How do you get by, not attending it?" And he said,
"I just happen to own the lumber company." Then he
added, "But I'll have to go in there in thirty minutes
and listen to some of the silliest conversation that
you've ever heard! When you are sober, you don't like
to listen to it." There was a man of high caliber who
had to put up with that sort of thing.

Back in the days of the Persian kingdom the law was
that a man did not have to put up with it—"none did
compel."

"Also Vashti the queen made a feast for the women
in the royal house which belonged to king Ahasuerus"
(1:9). She made a feast for the women's auxiliary. The
men who had come had brought their wives, but
women couldn't go to the main banquet—which
makes it different from some present-day banquets, by
the way. Women were kept in separate quarters, so
Vashti held a separate banquet for them.

"On the seventh day, when the heart of the king was merry with wine" (1:10) means, in the language of the street, the king was "high" on the seventh day. The question arises concerning not only this king but any king or ruler: Is he a fit ruler if he is engaged in drunkenness? It is said that the Oriental people today are asking if America with all of her drunkenness is in a position to be the leader of the nations of the world. This is a question that America must answer within the next few years. Drunkenness, and not the neutron bomb, could be the thing that would take us under. If drunkenness continues as it is today, it will ultimately destroy our land.

Under the influence of alcohol, Ahasuerus did something that he would never have done if he had been sober. He commanded the chamberlains who served in his presence to bring Vashti to the banquet. He had displayed his wealth and his luxury, and he had demonstrated to the princes and rulers his ability to carry on the campaign he had in mind. Under the influence of alcohol, he attempted to make a display that was contrary to the proprieties of that day. He tried to display Vashti, who was a beautiful woman to look at. Ahasuerus decided that he would bring her into the banquet court before that convention of men. He would never have done so had he not been drunk.

This queen (she is going to be put aside—moved off the stage, so to speak—and we will not see her again) was a noble woman of a pagan culture. She refused to go. "But the queen Vashti refused to come at the king's commandment by his chamberlains. . ." (1:12). Believe me, that revealed a scandal in the kingdom: The king was having trouble with his queen! She refused to come, and I admire her for her decision.

Perhaps you thought I was going to say that she made a grave mistake. I will come to that conclusion in a minute, but let me first say that Vashti was absolutely right, or justified, in not coming; she did not have to come. According to the etiquette of that day, she did not belong in such a gathering of men, so this queen refused her king's commandment. She stood instead under the protection of her rights, and I admire her for that. There was no law at that time that would compel her to come; therefore she stood and said that she would not.

You can imagine the king getting up at the banquet and announcing, "Now, gentlemen, I have a real treat for you. I have sent for my queen. I want you to see her. She's a beauty. I want to introduce her to you so that you can see all the wealth and the wonder of this kingdom." And then in a few moments a chamberlain walks up behind him and whispers, "She won't come." Imagine having to get up and say, "I'm very sorry, gentlemen, but we've had to change the program of the evening. Our main attraction didn't arrive; we'll not be having the queen this evening."

Well, that started the buzzing throughout the banquet. The thousand or more guests probably began to say, "Is he a king, or is he not a king? What kind of king cannot even command his queen?" Although Vashti was perfectly justified in refusing to come, I think she should have thought the situation over in this manner: *I can refuse and I probably ought to refuse. But this is a scandal that will get out and this will hurt my king, my husband. I think, under the circumstances, I'll go.* On that basis, she should have gone to the banquet. She should have obeyed.

There is a spiritual application for us here. The body

of believers, the church, is called the bride of Christ. And the church's task in this age is to display her beauty to the world. But are we fulfilling our responsibility? We the church are wrapped up in our own little programs. We are not too concerned about the lost, are we? Do you know there is a world outside that is going to hell? How much do we really care? The church has been called upon to obey our husband, Jesus Christ.

There is a lovely picture presented in the Song of Solomon of a husband and his bride. This is the bride speaking:

> I sleep, but my heart waketh: it is the voice of my beloved that knocketh, saying, Open to me, my sister, my love, my dove, my undefiled: for my head is filled with dew, and my locks with drops of the night (Song 5:2).

The husband, the bridegroom, has been out witnessing, looking for lost sheep, and he wants her to join him in this. He is a picture of Christ.

But where is the bride, the church? She says,

> I have put off my coat; how shall I put it on? I have washed my feet; how shall I defile them? (Song 5:3).

The home has a dirt floor, and the bride says, "I'm in bed; I am comfortable; I have already washed my feet. I don't intend to get up and soil them again." That is the position of the church in our day. We have come to the place of comfort; we do not want to go out after the lost.

> My beloved put in his hand by the hole [latch] of the door, and my bowels were moved for him. I rose up to open to my beloved; and my hands dropped with myrrh, and my fingers with sweet smelling myrrh, upon the handles of the lock (Song 5:4,5).

It was a lovely custom of that day that when the bridegroom came to the house and could not get in, he would reach inside and put myrrh on the handle of the door. This was like sending a bottle of perfume to the bride. Finally when the bride in the Song came to open the door for him, she found there only the myrrh, the sweet fragrance of his presence.

It is wonderful today to study the Word of God; it is good to have our groups for fellowship, but outside our comfortable lives is a world that has not heard the gospel. Let me ask you this question: What are you doing now to get the gospel out to this lost world? Honestly, what are you doing? Lots of folks in our churches are busy as termites, but the activity is all on the inside of the church. They are not obeying their King who said, ". . . Go ye into all the world, and preach the gospel to every creature" (Mark 16:15). The Lord Jesus has said that we are the light of the world. His command is, "Let your light so shine before men, that they may see your good works, and glorify your Father which is in heaven" (Matt. 5:16). The church today is like Queen Vashti, saying that she will not go.

This brings to mind the tremendous story told by Dr. J. Wilbur Chapman many years ago. It illustrates the great love of our Shepherd, the One whom we should represent today. He told of one of the great sheep dogs in the Swiss Alps. One cold night when heavy snow was falling, the shepherd brought in the sheep but three of them were missing. He looked down at this great dog, warmly bedded down with her little puppies for the night, and said to her, "Go get the three sheep." This intelligent dog looked up, then put her head down again, for she did not want to go. The shepherd gave the command again. Then this great shepherd dog got up, left her puppies, and went out into the snow. She was gone for several hours. When she returned with two of the sheep, she was torn and bloody. She settled herself with her puppies. The shepherd looked at her and said, "There is still one missing. Go, get the sheep." And the dog again got up and went out into the dark, stormy night. After a period of several hours the dog returned; this time she could hardly walk, but she had the last sheep. What a picture this is of our Savior. What a picture it should be of His church!

Let us look again at Queen Vashti and her refusal to do the king's bidding. It called for a crisis meeting of the cabinet. The king's advisors talked over this new development, for it was no incidental matter. They were preparing for a great campaign, and suddenly the queen would not obey the command of the king. What should be done with her?

One member of this cabinet was a henpecked husband by the name of Memucan. How do I know he is henpecked? Look at this fellow! "And Memucan answered before the king and the princes, Vashti the queen hath not done wrong to the king only, but also to all the princes, and to all the people that are in all the provinces of the king Ahasuerus. For this deed of the queen shall come abroad unto all women, so that they shall despise their husbands in their eyes, when it shall be reported, The king Ahasuerus commanded Vashti the queen to be brought in before him, but she came not" (1:16,17). In other words, he was saying, "Something must be done about this, because I don't dare go home!"

Perhaps you have heard of the henpecked husband

who came to the office one morning and boasted, "Last night my wife was down on her knees before me." One of the fellows, knowing the situation, was a little skeptical. He said, "What were the circumstances, and what exactly did she say to you?" The husband looked a little embarrassed and admitted, "Well, she was down on her knees, looking under the bed, and she said, 'Come out from under there, you coward!' "

That's Memucan. He was a henpecked Mr. Milquetoast. He was saying, "Something must be done to protect our homes in this matter." Actually this was a real crisis, because the king and the queen set an example for the kingdom. Notice Memucan's proposal. "If it please the king, let there go a royal commandment from him, and let it be written among the laws of the Persians and the Medes, that it be not altered, That Vashti come no more before king Ahasuerus; and let the king give her royal estate unto another that is better than she" (1:19). Memucan's recommendation was radical surgery: "Let's eliminate this woman who refuses to obey."

You may be thinking, "Doesn't the Bible teach that a wife is to obey her husband?" No, it does not. You cannot find that in the Word of God. Obedience was imposed upon wives in Oriental and other pagan cultures, but this never has been true among Christians. You may challenge that statement because in the fifth chapter of Ephesians Paul says, "Wives, submit yourselves unto your own husbands, as unto the Lord" (Eph. 5:22). But let's look at what that command really means.

To begin with, Paul speaks here of the Spirit-filled

life. He commands us to be filled with the Spirit and mentions the things that will result from being filled with the Spirit. And I do not think there can be a right husband-wife relationship without a filling of the Spirit on the part of both. Actually I don't believe you can even sing to God unless you are filled with the Spirit of God; I don't believe you can preach a sermon or teach a Sunday school class unless you are filled with the Spirit of God. And I do not think you can have a right husband-wife relationship unless you are filled with the Spirit of God.

When Paul says, "Wives, submit," he is not saying to obey, but to respond to your husband. God has made man and woman in such a way that the wife is a responder and the husband a leader. The husband always takes the lead—or at least he should. All God is saying to the woman is, "Respond to your husband." When the man says to the woman, "I love you," she is to respond by saying, "I love you." But suppose the husband doesn't love; suppose the husband does not say, "I love you." Then God does not ask her to say that she loves him. Suppose the husband is brutal. The wife will respond in kind. Anytime a man comes to me and says, "My wife is cold," he gives himself away. She is responding to the kind of husband he is. God never asks any woman to obey a godless man. You cannot find that in the Word of God. "Wives, submit yourselves unto your own husbands" speaks of a Spirit-filled relationship; God says to the wife, "Respond to your husband," and to the husband, "Love your [wife], even as Christ also loved the church, and gave himself for it" (Eph. 5:25).

Understanding these truths only throws the setting

for the Book of Esther—a pagan court—into sharper relief. The pagan law enacted had nothing to do with the Mosaic Law and was not Christian by any means. Ahasuerus and his council made a new law, but it was the law of the Medes and the Persians: ". . . That Vashti come no more before king Ahasuerus; and let the king give her royal estate unto another that is better than she.

"And when the king's decree which he shall make shall be published throughout all his empire, (for it is great,) all the wives shall give to their husbands honour, both to great and small. And the saying pleased the king and the princes; and the king did according to the word of Memucan: For he sent letters into all the king's provinces, into every province according to the writing thereof, and to every people after their language, that every man should bear rule in his own house, and that it should be published according to the language of every people" (1:19–22).

The law concerning Vashti reveals to us today the character of Ahasuerus, who I believe was Xerxes in secular history. You will recall that he took his army, the largest that ever had been marshalled, as far as Thermopylae, and led a fleet of three hundred ships, which were destroyed at Salamis. After that defeat, in a fit of madness Xerxes went down to the sea and beat the waves with a belt for destroying his fleet. Now a man who would do that evidently has something radically wrong with him. Apparently he was a man who suffered from some form of abnormality, as many rulers have—and still do. Julius Caesar, Napoleon, Hitler were men of abnormal mental processes. Nebuchadnezzar, great man that he was, represented in Daniel (see 2:38) by the head of gold, suffered from an abnormality known as hysteria (see Dan. 4:33). Any man today who even wants to be a world ruler ought to be examined by a psychiatrist! However, forms of abnormality have not kept men from achieving greatness in the history of the world. And this was true of Ahasuerus. He was a man of tremendous ability. Yet in unreasoning anger he allowed this banishment of his lovely queen. It became the law of the Medes and the Persians, an edict which could not be altered. Although later the king himself wanted to break the law, he could not. The law of the Medes and the Persians could not be broken.

Here was a man's law that could not be changed or altered in any way whatsoever, nor could it be revoked. Even the king himself had to bow to this law. Then what about the laws of God? God has laws whether you like them or not. He has said, "The soul that sinneth, it shall die . . ." (Ezek. 18:20). That law cannot be changed. The "new morality" and our changing culture cannot alter it. Sin is still sin, and God says, "The soul that sinneth, it shall die." The law has not been changed today. God will not change it. God cannot Himself change it. Do you know why? Because He would be untrue to His own nature. He would deny His own attributes and His own character. Of course He would never do that. "The soul that sinneth, it shall die" stands at this moment. "Well," someone says, "that leaves the human race in a terrible plight because God also says, 'All have sinned, and come short of the glory of God' " (Rom. 3:23). That's correct. But, you see, these laws of God have been superseded by a higher law, the law of a Savior who came down to this earth to die upon a cross. Jesus

Himself gave His reason for coming to this earth. ", , ,
the Son of man came not to be ministered unto, but to
minister, and to give his life a ransom for many" (Mark
10:45). God, without changing His law one iota, sent
His Son to take your place and my place. Since He
could not change His law, "The soul that sinneth it
shall die," Jesus Christ was made sin for us and He
died in our stead.

The Lord Jesus also said, "I came not to call the
righteous, but sinners to repentance" (Luke 5:32).
Why? There is none righteous to call. But He has come
for *sinners*. Those are the only ones He saves. You see,
we must be willing to accept God's estimate of us: We
are sinners. Dr. Hudson Taylor made that statement to
a man one day, and the man objected, "I don't feel like
a sinner." Dr. Taylor said, "If you don't feel like one,
then believe God: You are." God says we are sinners,
Take God's word for it.

In San Francisco during World War II, I saw a ship at
the dock that was loaded and ready to sail. One of the
officers told me, "We have to wait for the tide to come
in. That ship is so loaded that nothing in the world can
lift it but the tide." When the tide came in, the ship
went out. I crossed the Atlantic on the *Queen Mary*
once. We boarded her about seven o'clock in the evening, but the announcement was made that we would
not sail until morning. The ship had been delayed
coming in because of a storm in the Atlantic, and she
could not go out because the tide was out. But when
the tide came in, the water lifted that great ship. At
four o'clock in the morning we felt our vessel moving
out to sea. The law of the tide overcame the law of
gravity.

It is still true that "The wages of sin is death" (Rom.

6:23). It is still true that "The soul that sinneth, it shall die." But, thank God, there is another law in operation. There is a Savior who, because of His vicarious death, can reach down and in His marvelous grace receive you and take you home to glory.

· 19 ·

The First Beauty Contest To Choose a Queen

Esther, Chapter 2

After these things, when the wrath of King Ahasuerus was appeased, he remembered Vashti, and what she had done, and what was decreed against her. Then said the king's servants that ministered unto him, Let there be fair young virgins sought for the king: and let the king appoint officers in all the provinces of his kingdom, that they may gather together all the fair young virgins unto Shushan the palace, to the house of the women, unto the custody of Hege the king's chamberlain, keeper of the women; and let their things for purification be given them: And let the maiden which pleaseth the king be queen instead of Vashti. And the thing pleased the king; and he did so.

Now in Shushan the palace there was a certain Jew, whose name was Mordecai, the son of Jair, the son of Shimei, the son of Kish, a Benjamite; who had been carried away from Jerusalem with

the captivity which had been carried away with
Jeconiah king of Judah, whom Nebuchadnezzar
the king of Babylon had carried away. And he
brought up Hadassah, that is, Esther, his uncle's
daughter: for she had neither father nor mother,
and the maid was fair and beautiful; whom Mordecai, when her father and mother were dead,
took for his own daughter.

So it came to pass, when the king's commandment and his decree was heard, and when many
maidens were gathered together unto Shushan
the palace, to the custody of Hegai, that Esther
was brought also unto the king's house, to the
custody of Hegai, keeper of the women. And the
maiden pleased him, and she obtained kindness
of him; and he speedily gave her her things for
purification, with such things as belonged to her,
and seven maidens, which were meet to be given
her, out of the king's house: and he preferred her
and her maids unto the best place of the house of
the women. Esther had not shewed her people
nor her kindred: for Mordecai had charged her
that she should not shew it. And Mordecai walked
every day before the court of the women's house,
to know how Esther did, and what should become
of her.

Now when every maid's turn was come to go in
to king Ahasuerus, after that she had been twelve
months, according to the manner for the women,
(for so were the days of their purifications accomplished, to wit, six months with oil of myrrh, and
six months with sweet odours, and with other
things for the purifying of the women;) then thus

came every maiden unto the king; whatsoever she desired was given her to go with her out of the house of the women unto the king's house. In the evening she went, and on the morrow she returned into the second house of the women, to the custody of Shaashgaz, the king's chamberlain, which kept the concubines: she came in unto the king no more, except the king delighted in her, and that she were called by name.

Now when the turn of Esther, the daughter of Abihail the uncle of Mordecai, who had taken her for his daughter, was come to go in unto the king, she required nothing but what Hegai the king's chamberlain, the keeper of the women, appointed. And Esther obtained favour in the sight of all them that looked upon her. So Esther was taken unto king Ahasuerus into his house royal in the tenth month, which is the month Tebeth, in the seventh year of his reign. And the king loved Esther above all the women, and she obtained grace and favour in his sight more than all the virgins; so that he set the royal crown upon her head, and made her queen instead of Vashti. Then the king made a great feast unto all his princes and his servants, even Esther's feast; and he made a release to the provinces, and gave gifts, according to the state of the king. And when the virgins were gathered together the second time, then Mordecai sat in the king's gate. Esther had not yet shewed her kindred nor her people; as Mordecai had charged her: for Esther did the commandment of Mordecai, like as when she was brought up with him.

In those days, while Mordecai sat in the king's gate, two of the king's chamberlains, Bigthan and Teresh, of those which kept the door, were wroth, and sought to lay hand on the king Ahasuerus. And the thing was known to Mordecai, who told it unto Esther the queen; and Esther certified the king thereof in Mordecai's name. And when inquisition was made of the matter, it was found out; therefore they were both hanged on a tree: and it was written in the book of the chronicles before the king.

The second chapter of the Book of Esther opens with the phrase "after these things." After Ahasuerus returned to his palace without Vashti, he recognized how lonely he was. The record tells us, ". . . he remembered Vashti, and what she had done, and what was decreed against her" (2:1). According to the law of the Medes and the Persians, Ahasuerus himself, though he was the supreme ruler, was not able to change his own law—although by this time I am sure he wanted to do so. Vashti had been set aside forever. The law of the Medes and the Persians could not be altered.

Those who were around the king—his cabinet, those who were ruling with him or who occupied high positions—noticed how moody he was and how lonely, and they made a suggestion. The suggestion was, very candidly, that there be conducted a beauty contest the like of which Atlantic City and Long Beach never have seen or heard. The entire kingdom was searched for beautiful women, and they were brought in from that wide kingdom, near and far. You can well imagine the number that were brought in—I'm sure it was in the hundreds. The king was to be the judge, the sole judge, of this contest.

Esther's story begins with verse 5 of chapter 2. "Now in Shushan the palace there was a certain Jew, whose name was Mordecai, the son of Jair, the son of Shimei, the son of Kish, a Benjamite [of the tribe of Benjamin]." The question that immediately arises is: What is *he* doing here? God had permitted His people to return to their own land, as He had prophesied (see 2 Chr. 36:22,23). Cyrus was to give a decree to permit them to return, and those who were in the will of God did return to Palestine. However, very few returned to their homeland—less than sixty thousand. The greater number of them had made a place for themselves in the land of their captivity. They had learned shop-keeping from the Gentiles and had elected to remain.

Have you ever noticed that the Jew, when he is in Palestine, is a farmer, but when he is out of Palestine, he's a shopkeeper (or anything but a farmer)? This is true today. When I was in Palestine, guides pointed this out with delight: Here was a man who had been a brilliant scientist in Germany, who was now living in a kibbutz and working with his hands out in the field. I was amazed to see how the Jews have gone back to the soil in Palestine. But the Jews of Esther's day had learned shopkeeping from the Gentiles in Babylon and they liked it. When they were free to go, they did not want to return to Jerusalem. Many of them, out of the will of God, chose to remain in a pagan culture, and Mordecai happened to be one of them.

Mordecai should have been back in his homeland, but notice where he was of all places: in the palace of

Persia. He had a political job. You may remember that
Joseph also had a political job in Egypt, yet he was in
the will of God directly; Daniel in the court of Babylon
was in the will of God; but Mordecai was not in the
direct will of God. You will see that Esther is the book
of the providence of God. As I have said, if you want a
popular definition of providence: Providence is how
God coaches the man on second base. And this man
Mordecai was brought to home base, although he was
out of the will of God and although he was not looking
to God for help. Even at a time when you think he and
his people would have turned to God, they did not.
There is no mention of God or of prayer in this book at
all, because these people were out of the will of God.

Both Mordecai and Esther come on the page of
Scripture in a poor light, although they prove to be
very noble individuals, as we shall see later in the
story. Mordecai had been taken captive, probably at a
young age, in Nebuchadnezzar's second deportation
of captives from Jerusalem. That was during the reign
of Jeconiah (better known as Jehoiachin). The first
deportation that had left Jerusalem was made up of the
princes, the nobility, and the upper class. Daniel was
with that group. The second captivity had taken those,
shall we say, of the upper middle class. And this man
Mordecai was in that group. After the third deportation, when Jerusalem was finally destroyed, only the
poorest class was left in the land.

Mordecai had a young cousin, whose parents may
have been slain in Nebuchadnezzar's taking the city,
for multitudes were slain. Her Hebrew name was
Hadassah, and he adopted her as his own daughter. If
you go back to Palestine today, you will see one of the

finest hospitals in the world. A great deal of research is being done there. It is the Hadassah Hospital, named for this young Hebrew woman.

Notice what is said concerning her. "And he brought up Hadassah, that is, Esther, his uncle's daughter: for she had neither father nor mother, and the maid was fair and beautiful; whom Mordecai, when her father and mother were dead, took for his own daughter" (2:7). She had one asset (and it is an asset), and that was beauty. Beauty is God's handiwork, and it is wonderful to see that it can be dedicated to Him. I wish today that the devil did not get so much that is beautiful in this world, but he does. If God has blessed you with good looks, offer that to Him for He can use it.

When the announcement was made that there was to be a choice of another queen for Ahasuerus, immediately Mordecai was interested. He took his young cousin Esther and entered her in the beauty contest. "So it came to pass, when the king's commandment and his decree was heard, and when many maidens were gathered together unto Shushan the palace, to the custody of Hegai, that Esther was brought also unto the king's house, to the custody of Hegai, keeper of the women" (2:8). You see the providence of God moving into this situation. "And the maiden pleased him [that's no accident], and she obtained kindness of him; and he speedily gave her her things for purification, with such things as belonged to her . . ."(2:9).

An interesting fact comes to light in verse 10: "Esther had not shewed her people nor her kindred: for Mordecai had charged her that she should not shew it." Remember that Mordecai and Esther were a part of a captive people, and anti-Semitism always has been a curse in the nations of the world. And it had been in Babylon. You cannot read the account of Nebuchadnezzar's destruction of Jerusalem without realizing his hatred for these people. He was the first to bring them to Babylon, but by Esther's time a new nation—Persia—was in charge. Yet the anti-Semitic feeling remained, and Mordecai, being very sensitive to that, warned Esther not to reveal her nationality. That silence was tantamount to a denial of her religion, and religion is the very thing that had identified God's chosen people down through the years. The moment Mordecai and Esther denied their nationality, that moment they denied their religion.

You remember that Jonah did the same thing on board ship. He had revealed neither his nationality nor the fact that he believed in and worshipped the living and true God. In going to Tarshish he was out of the will of God. Mordecai and Esther, by remaining in the land of captivity, were out of the will of God. Because of this they had no witness for God. It is of interest to note that today, when men and women are out of the will of God, they have very little to say about their faith in Christ.

Mordecai is not resting upon God at all. He doesn't turn to Him in prayer, and we read, "Mordecai walked every day before the court of the women's house, to know how Esther did, and what should become of her" (2:11). This man, out of God's will, paces up and down, nervously biting his fingernails, wondering how the contest will come out. He has not, nor can he, put his worries into God's hands. I'm not sure that he knows anything about the providence of God. But

God is overruling in this. May I remind you of our definition of providence? Providence is the way that God leads the man who will not be led. We see Him beginning to move at this particular point in the story of Esther. It is no accident that Esther is given the most prominent place, or that she is shown every favor and is given every consideration. There are no accidents with God.

Notice the type of beautification (called "purification") that went on. "Now when every maid's turn was come to go in to king Ahasuerus, after that she had been twelve months, according to the manner of the women, (for so were the days of their purifications accomplished, to wit, six months with oil of myrrh, and six months with sweet odours, and with other things for the purifying of the women)" (2:12). May I say to you, men, that if your wife takes a few hours in the beauty salon, you ought not to complain. These girls spent a whole year there! The first six months they went to the spa for reducing and for oil treatments. Then the next six months they went to the perfumers. I suppose they even swam in cologne in order to be prepared to go into the presence of the king. You can see the tremendous emphasis that was placed on physical beauty, and this is typical of pagan cultures. The farther away America gets from God, the more counters we have in our department stores for beauty aids. Have you noticed that? (And with the multiplicity of beautifying treatments, it is rather disappointing that we don't have more beauty than we do today.) But these girls went through an entire year of beauty conditioning for the contest.

Notice the awful chance that Esther takes. "In the

evening she went, and on the morrow she returned into the second house of the women, to the custody of Shaashgaz, the king's chamberlain, which kept the concubines . . ." (2:14). If she does not win, she becomes a concubine of the king of Persia, which certainly would have been a horrible thing for this Jewish maiden. That is the reason Mordecai is biting his fingernails. Out of the will of God, he knows the awful chance this girl is taking.

Yet, God is going to overrule. Notice: "Now when the turn of Esther, the daughter of Abihail the uncle of Mordecai, who had taken her for his daughter, was come to go in unto the king, she required nothing but what Hegai the king's chamberlain, the keeper of the women, appointed . . ." (2:15). When her time comes she requires no more than is appointed for a contestant to wear. She goes in her natural beauty and stands before the king. ". . . And Esther obtained favour in the sight of all them that looked upon her" (2:15). God, you see, is overruling. Esther has not yet let anyone know her background and her race.

"So Esther was taken unto King Ahasuerus into his house royal in the tenth month, which is the month Tebeth, in the seventh year of his reign. And the king loved Esther above all the women, and she obtained grace and favour in his sight more than all the virgins; so that he set the royal crown upon her head, and made her queen instead of Vashti" (2:16,17). He does not have to look any further; the contest is over as far as he is concerned. He has found the one to take Vashti's place, and Esther is made queen.

We are told that the king loved Esther. I must confess that I am not impressed by that statement at all.

Those of you who have read my book on Ruth know the emphasis put upon the romance of Boaz and Ruth, the loveliest love story, I think, that has ever been told. It is a picture of Christ's love for His church. But I have to say that I do not find that quality here. This was an old, disappointed king who almost had reached the end of the road. I am reminded of the story of a foreigner who came to this country. He asked, "What are these 'three R's' that I keep hearing about in this country?" Some wiseacre gave him this answer: "At twenty it's romance; at thirty it's rent; and at fifty it's rheumatism." Well, it was rheumatism with this man here. Ahasuerus was an old king, and Esther was a lovely young girl. He was an old pagan with no knowledge at all of what real love in God might mean to a couple. I must say that I cannot see anything in the text to wax eloquent about or to say, as some have done, that this is a picture of Christ and His church. I do not see that at all.

However, the event was of utmost significance. It is thrilling to hear how this girl, belonging to a captive people, suddenly became queen over one of the greatest gentile empires the world has ever seen. The wave of anti-Semitism that was imminent would have blotted out these people, and God's entire purpose with Israel would have been frustrated. But when the wave hit, Esther was in a unique position. How did she get there? By the providence of God. *God* moved her into that place.

Esther was not in God's direct will. The Mosaic Law was clear: Neither she nor any one of her people were to marry a Gentile. But Esther had stooped in order to conquer. In this lies another great lesson for God's children. There are many things in this world that God's people do, and in the doing are out of His will. In spite of it all, God will overrule and make circumstances work out for His glory and the fulfillment of His purpose. I have in mind a very clear example of this. Repeatedly people ask me the question: Do you believe that women preachers are scriptural? No, I do not believe that women preachers are scriptural. There are many passages in the Bible to support my statement. The next question usually is: How then do you explain the fact that many women preachers have been and are being wonderfully blessed by God? May I say to you that in spite of the fact that women preachers are not God's direct will, God will always bless His Word when it is given out. There are many things today that are not in accordance with God's will, but He overrules them for His glory. Esther was disobeying God absolutely, but that did not mean that she was out from under the control and care of almighty God.

You will remember that this book opened with a feast. Now Ahasuerus held another feast: Esther's feast. "Then the king made a great feast unto all his princes and his servants, even Esther's feast; and he made a release to the provinces, and gave gifts, according to the state of the king" (2:18). With a lovely queen to take Vashti's place, Ahasuerus was so jubilant he suspended taxes for one year. If such a decree were made in our day, it would rock the world! But it is interesting to see that the king did have that authority to suspend taxes for a year.

"And when the virgins were gathered together the second time, then Mordecai sat in the king's gate"

(2:19). "Sitting in the king's gate" means that Mordecai had a new position—not a job, a position. It means he was a judge, for the courthouse of the ancient world was the gate of the city. Most of the cities were walled, and sooner or later all the citizens would pass through the gate. Court convened at the city gate, not at the courthouse in the town square. The city gate was the place Boaz went to have a legal matter taken care of. Lot sat in the gate, which meant that he had gotten into politics in Sodom and had a judgeship.

Isn't it interesting that when Esther became queen, the next thing you know Mordecai was a judge, sitting in the gate? That was nepotism—getting your kinfolk into office. I do not know whether Mordecai was made judge because of his ability or because Esther whispered in the ear of the king, "This man Mordecai has been just like a father to me. He is a man of remarkable ability, and I think you ought to give him a good position." The king may have said, "Well, that's interesting. We've just had an opening for a judge here at the east gate, and I'll give him that position." Esther is a very human book, you see, and politics haven't changed a bit, have they?

"Esther had not yet shewed her kindred nor her people; as Mordecai had charged her: for Esther did the commandment of Mordecai, like as when she was brought up with him" (2:20).

Esther was a rather remarkable person. Even married to the king, she took instructions from the man who reared her! And probably Mordecai is one of the outstanding men in Scripture to whom we have paid very little attention. Apparently he was a man of remarkable ability.

At this point in the story something takes place that seems extraneous; yet it is upon this incident that the whole book hinges. As someone has said, "God swings big doors on little hinges." Again we see the providence of God; He was moving behind the scene. "In those days, while Mordecai sat in the king's gate, two of the king's chamberlains, Bigthan and Teresh, of those which kept the door, were wroth, and sought to lay hand on the king Ahasuerus" (2:21). This is a very familiar scenario: an Oriental potentate, and fellows with long mustachios, hiding behind pillars, plotting against the king. Actually, intrigue in an Oriental court was common; there seemed always to be someone who was after the king's job. Mordecai's new position gained him a vantage point so that he was able to overhear the plot. "And the thing was known to Mordecai, who told it unto Esther, the queen; and Esther certified the king thereof in Mordecai's name" (2:22).

I suppose that Esther said to the king, "You remember that I recommended Mordecai as a judge, and you can see that he is already doing a very excellent job. He has discovered a plot against your life!" The "FBI" investigated and found it to be true. "And when inquisition was made of the matter, it was found out; therefore they were both hanged on a tree. . . ." There wasn't even a trial. All Ahasuerus had to do was give the word. And the incident ". . . was written in the book of the chronicles before the king" (2:23).

It is interesting to see that Mordecai was not rewarded for what he had done. That omission is important. I suppose he brooded over it many times, wondering why in the world he had been ignored. God is overruling. Chapter 2 of Esther in a very special way reveals the theme of the book: the providence of God.

There is abroad in our midst today the notion that if circumstances are not favorable, God is not in them. A young student once came to me for counseling. He said that he felt that perhaps he was out of the will of God. When I inquired why he felt so, he replied that circumstances were growing difficult for him, and his subjects in school were becoming harder than he had anticipated. In short, he was finding so many obstacles that he felt he was not in accord with the purposes of God for his life. I find that many folk reach this decision through just such reasoning. However, circumstances are no indication at all, for God was moving in Esther's affairs, and He was moving in the affairs of Mordecai.

God is moving today by providence. I love the story of Vaughn Shoemaker, the Christian cartoonist. God in His providence chose this boy. He was a poor boy, but he had a wonderful mother of prayer. He grew up with an older brother who felt that prayer and religion generally were for sissies. Instead of finishing his education, Vaughn took odd jobs, and in the course of time he met a young woman with whom he fell in love. When he proposed to her, she startled him by saying that she would not let him ruin her life, as well as his own, by not having a definite occupation and purpose in life. If he would prove that he wanted to establish himself under the guidance of God, then she, as a Christian girl, would be interested.

He went to his older brother and asked for the necessary financial assistance to enter the Chicago Art Institute. The loan was made, but the Art Institute dismissed him, saying they did not think he would ever become a cartoonist. Shortly afterwards he was able to secure a position with the *Chicago Daily News*. Then came the "break"—some call it luck, but he calls it providence. The head cartoonist was given a position in New York City; the second in charge went to Features; the third had to leave because of illness in his family, and Vaughn was the only one left in the office. The editor called him in and said, "Vaughn, draw something until I can get another cartoonist." The editor never did secure another cartoonist, for Vaughn Shoemaker proved his abilities and soon his drawings went into syndication.

Vaughn tells the story of how he was called to the hospital where his elder brother was desperately ill. Realizing that this brother who had helped him so much could not live much longer, he asked, "Roger, do you know Christ as your Savior?" Roger smiled and said, "Yes, I do," and he was gone. Vaughn left that place of parting, went to his own room, and upon his knees gave his life to God. From that moment he has never drawn a cartoon without first kneeling to ask God to direct him. His cartoons reveal deep insight and imagination and often carry a Christian message of intrinsic value. God has led that man through the years. Long before he knew Him, God was leading, bringing him to Himself.

Finally, let me tell the story of a man who began listening to our radio program in the San Francisco Bay area. He was a contractor and a Roman Catholic. I was teaching the Book of Romans at the time, and he has since told me, "If I could have gotten to you, I would have punched you in the nose for the things you were saying." God, in His providence, tuned him in; he would get angry and tune out. "But the next morning," he said, "I always was right there waiting for you." In the providence of God, the man was transferred from the San Francisco Bay area to Los Angeles, where he is now. For about three months, he came to the church that I was pastoring on Thursday night for Bible Study, going down the street to confession beforehand. Finally one night, after three months, he gave his heart to the Lord. How did it happen? By God's providence.

To me the most thrilling thing in the world is to give out the Word of God and to know that by His providence God will bring this one and that one to Himself.

How we should thank God for His providential dealings in the affairs of men! We can take this little Book of Esther and trace His hand through it all, although He is not visible in Person. The participants in this drama were totally unaware that God was directing; yet in every turn of events He was leading and guiding.

God has not taken His hand off this earth. It may seem as though He has, but He has not. Nor has He taken His hand off your life and mine. Whoever you are, God is moving in your life. I pray that you will recognize this, and that you will trust Christ as your Savior and your Guide.

· 20 ·

Haman and Anti-Semitism

Esther, Chapter 3

After these things did king Ahasuerus promote
Haman the son of Hammedatha the Agagite, and
advanced him, and set his seat above all the
princes that were with him. And all the king's
servants, that were in king's gate, bowed, and
reverenced Haman: for the king had so commanded concerning him. But Mordecai bowed
not, nor did him reverence. Then the king's servants, which were in the king's gate, said unto
Mordecai, Why transgressest thou the king's commandment? Now it came to pass, when they
spake daily unto him, and he hearkened not unto
them, that they told Haman, to see whether Mordecai's matters would stand: for he had told them
that he was a Jew. And when Haman saw that
Mordecai bowed not, nor did him reverence, then
was Haman full of wrath. And he thought scorn to
lay hands on Mordecai alone; for they had shewed
him the people of Mordecai: wherefore Haman

sought to destroy all the Jews that were throughout the whole kingdom of Ahasuerus, even the
people of Mordecai.

In the first month, that is, the month Nisan, in
the twelfth year of King Ahasuerus, they cast Pur,
that is, the lot, before Haman from day to day,
and from month to month, to the twelfth month,
that is, the month Adar.

And Haman said unto king Ahasuerus, There is
a certain people scattered abroad and dispersed
among the people in all the provinces of thy kingdom; and their laws are diverse from all people;
neither keep they the king's laws: therefore it is
not for the king's profit to suffer them. If it please
the king, let it be written that they may be destroyed: and I will pay ten thousand talents of
silver to the hands of those that have the charge of
the business, to bring it into the king's treasuries.
And the king took his ring from his hand, and
gave it unto Haman the son of Hammedatha the
Agagite, the Jews' enemy. And the king said unto
Haman, The silver is given to thee, the people
also, to do with them as it seemeth good to thee.
Then were the king's scribes called on the thirteenth day of the first month, and there was written according to all that Haman had commanded
unto the king's lieutenants, and to the governors
that were over every province, and to the rulers of
every people of every province according to the
writing thereof, and to every people after their
language; in the name of king Ahasuerus was it
written, and sealed with the king's ring. And the
letters were sent by posts into all the king's pro-

vinces, to destroy, to kill, and to cause to perish, all Jews, both young and old, little children and women, in one day, even upon the thirteenth day of the twelfth month, which is the month Adar, and to take the spoil of them for a prey. The copy of the writing for a commandment to be given in every province was published unto all people, that they should be ready against that day. The posts went out, being hastened by the king's commandment, and the decree was given in Shushan the palace. And the king and Haman sat down to drink; but the city Shushan was perplexed.

Chapter 3 introduces us to the man who truly is the villain of the Book of Esther: Haman. He had a bitterness and a hatred in his heart. He was identified as an Agagite. Does that suggest anything to you? In 1 Samuel 15 you'll find that Samuel told Saul that he was to exterminate the Amalekites (known also as Agagites). And you remember the disobedience of this man Saul; he did not do so. If Saul had done what God had commanded him to do, God's people would not have been threatened by Haman because the Agagites would have long before disappeared. God could see down through history and He knew what was coming. Saul's failure to exterminate the Agagites would have led to the extermination of his own people, but for the providence of God. Again, God is behind the scenes, keeping watch over His own.

Haman, apparently a very wealthy man, was promoted to a place next to Ahasuerus himself, the king of Persia. He was given a "blank check" signed by the king. He could have anything he wanted. He had free

rein. And one of the things he required of the officials
of the kingdom was to recognize his position and do
obeisance to him. That is, they were to bow down to
him.

As we have already seen, Mordecai was a judge at
the gate. He had a political job, which meant he was
one of the officials of the kingdom and he had to bow
to Haman. However, Mordecai refused to bow. And
for the first time, we see the hand of God beginning to
move in the life of Mordecai. You may say, But he was
out of the will of God. He should have returned to his
own land. How could God move in a case like that?

These questions are appropriate. For reasons of his
own, Mordecai did not return to Palestine, although
that was his place. Clearly, he was out of the will of
God; yet he still recognized God. Though Mordecai
made no appeal to Him anywhere in the Book of
Esther, it is evident he recognized God. How do I
come to this conclusion? God's law to the Jews was
explicit. They were not to bow to anything but God
Himself. They were not to make an image, nor ever
bow to an image. They were not to bow down to
anything or anyone. So when Haman came by after his
promotion, everybody who had a political job went
down on their faces before him—except one man,
Mordecai. Believe me, his lack of homage was obvious
when he was the only one left standing!

The other officials ask him why he doesn't bow, and
for the first time Mordecai reveals that he is a Jew. Up
to this time he has told no one. You will remember that
he had instructed Esther, when she entered the beauty
contest, not to let anyone know her race. She did not
even tell the king after they married.

But with Haman's promotion, Mordecai has to "let the cat out of the bag," so to speak. He says flatly, "The reason I'm not bowing is because I'm a Jew." The minute he says that he also reveals his religion. He worships only the true and living God; therefore he bows to no idol, no image, no man. At this point in the story I'm ready to throw my hat in the air and say, "Hurrah for Mordecai!" For the first time, he is taking a stand for God, and it is going to cost him a great deal. I do not think he has any idea that the effects of his declaration would be so far-reaching as to touch all of his people, but he probably recognizes that it might cost him his job and even his life.

As Mordecai began to stand out as a man of God, Haman began to stand out in all his ugliness as a man of Satan. The first thing we notice is his littleness. We are going to note all the way through our study that Haman is a little man. You'll hear him later on crying on his wife's shoulder. He will say something like this: "I've got everything in the world I want, and I can have anything in the kingdom. But that little Jew won't bow to me." Only a small man will let that sort of thing bother him, and Haman permitted it to disturb him a great deal.

In his agitation, Haman decided to do a terrible thing. "And he thought scorn to lay hands on Mordecai alone; for they had shewed him the people of Mordecai: wherefore Haman sought to destroy all the Jews that were throughout the whole kingdom of Ahasuerus, even the people of Mordecai" (3:6).

Haman did not know, I am sure, anything about the promise that God had made to Abraham. When God called Abraham, He said to him:

And I will make of thee a great nation, and I will bless
thee, and make thy name great; and thou shalt be a
blessing: And I will bless them that bless thee, and
curse him that curseth thee: and in thee shall all families
of the earth be blessed (Gen. 12:2,3).

God has made that promise good. Whether you and
I like it or not, all we have to do is turn back the pages
of history, and we'll find that every great nation has
persecuted the descendants of Abraham—the Jews—
and has tried to exterminate them. Yet the Jews have
attended the funeral of every one of these great nations. More recently, Hitler tried to exterminate them
in the ovens and in the camps of the Gestapo. He
thought he would get rid of them; yet today Hitler and
his group are gone, and the Jews are still with us.

It is not likely that either Hitler or Haman—or contemporary anti-Semites—are cognizant of or pay much
attention to Isaiah 54:17. But anyone who is tinctured
with anti-Semitism ought to read this:

No weapon that is formed against thee shall prosper;
and every tongue that shall rise against thee in judgment thou shalt condemn. This is the heritage of the
servants of the LORD, and their righteousness is of me,
saith the LORD.

God says that He will take care of every instrument
that is formed to destroy this people. No people have
ever been abused by the nations of the world as have
the Jews. That they have not been exterminated is in
itself miraculous. God has preserved them. And we
will see Him do it in the Book of Esther.

Haman's irritation grows every time he goes
through the gate. All the people go down on their face

except that little Jew Mordecai, and it disturbs him. He resolves to do something about it. Finally, he takes the liberty of going to Ahasuerus himself. He says, "There is a people in your kingdom who are different, and they are causing trouble." And Ahasuerus has so little regard for life, as most of the potentates of that day did, that he does not even inquire who the people happen to be. Haman does not know that Esther the queen happens to belong to that nationality. Even Ahasuerus himself does not know that his queen is Jewish, nor does he know that he is signing away her life at this time. He takes a ring off his finger, and he gives it to Haman. It is his signet ring. The signet on the ring, pressed down in soft wax, becomes the signature of the king. An order that had that signet stamped on it would become the law of the kingdom. So Ahasuerus carelessly takes off his ring, hands it to Haman, and says in effect, "I don't know who they are and I don't care who they are, but if you feel they ought to be exterminated, then go ahead and take care of the matter." What little regard Ahasuerus has for human life!

The decree now goes out as a law of the Medes and Persians. "Then were the king's scribes called on the thirteenth day of the first month, and there was written according to all that Haman had commanded unto the king's lieutenants, and to the governors that were over every province, and to the rulers of every people of every province according to the writing thereof, and to every people after their language; in the name of king Ahasuerus was it written, and sealed with the king's ring" (3:12).

And this was the content of the message that went

out: "And the letters were sent by posts into all the king's provinces, to destroy, to kill, and to cause to perish, all Jews, both young and old, little children and women, in one day, even upon the thirteenth day of the twelfth month, which is the month Adar, and to take the spoil of them for a prey" (3:13).

On a certain day the Jews were to be exterminated. Haman was giving anti-Semitism full rein and permitting a great many to do what apparently was in their hearts. On this designated day murdering Jews would be legal.

Haman's decree is a chapter in the life of the Jew that has been duplicated many, many times. When you read this chapter, you can almost substitute the name of Pharaoh or Hitler or Nasser for Haman. In fact, there are many names that would fit here. There never has been a time since the Israelites became a nation down in the land of Egypt that there has not been a movement somewhere to exterminate them. As I write this, the Jews in Russia are under awful persecution. Russia will permit only certain ones to come out and return to Palestine; there are actually ample funds available for this purpose.

Notice that Haman's decree was to go out into all the provinces, which means that the Jews were scattered all over the Medo-Persian Empire. That empire covered two continents and had even penetrated into Europe. The Jews had been scattered throughout the civilized world because of the Babylonian captivity.

Evidently there was a wave of anti-Semitism throughout the entire Persian kingdom. And the thing that precipitated it as far as Haman was concerned was one Jew, Mordecai.

The decree went out as a law of the Medes and Persians. We were told again and again at the very beginning of this book that a law once made was irrevocable. The law could not be changed, nor could it be repealed. The law had to stand on the books. "The posts went out, being hastened by the king's commandment, and the decree was given in Shushan the palace. And the king and Haman sat down to drink; but the city Shushan was perplexed" (3:15). The people in the city could not understand what was happening. Although they may not have liked the Jews, and although they considered them foreigners with differing customs in their midst, most of them did not want to exterminate them. They were perplexed. They could not understand Ahasuerus permitting a decree like this to go out. But Ahasuerus and Haman sat down to drink over it.

Outside Shushan the palace late that evening you could see the riders getting their orders. Literally hundreds of them must have been pressed into service because this was a great kingdom with many provinces. The different riders were given copies of the new decree that had become law. One company started riding down the road to the south; one went to the north; another to the west; a fourth to the east. They rode all night. When they came to a little town, they nailed on the bulletin board of that town the decree for the people to read the next morning. Then the riders pressed on. When their horses tired, fresh horses were there to carry on. All over the kingdom, the decree was posted, the decree that the Jews were to perish. The messengers hastened, we are told, at the king's commandment.

Anti-Semitism is an awful thing—and it's with us today. Certainly no Christian should have any part in it.

Anti-Semitism had its origin down in the brickyards of Egypt, under the cruel hands of Pharaoh, where the Jews became a nation. From that time on the great nations of the world have moved against them. It was the story of Assyria and it was the story of Babylon, the nations that took them into captivity. In the Book of Esther we see how the Jews fared in Persia. Rome also must plead guilty, and the Spanish Inquisition was leveled largely at the Jews. Under Hitler in Germany it is estimated that six million Jews perished.

What is the reason for this persecution that we call anti-Semitism? Let's analyze it briefly. There are two things that are back of it. The first reason is a natural one; the second, supernatural.

The natural reason is simply this: The Jews are unlovely. Now do not misunderstand me. There was a Christian Jew in Memphis, Tennessee, who was a very personal friend of mine. Some years ago as I was holding a series of meetings there, he came to me and said, "Mac, there is a spirit of anti-Semitism rising in Memphis and throughout this part of America. I find it on every hand. Some people are attempting to foment it and stir it up in this country." Then he added, with bowed head, "My people give cause for it. They are so unlovely at times." Before agreeing with him, let's face the fact: Any godless person, Jew or Gentile, is unlovely. I know of no person more unlovely than a godless Gentile, nor do I know a lovelier person than a Christian Jew. God sees us unlovely, undone, and unattractive, but by His sovereign grace He makes us new creatures in Christ. That same grace reached down and called the Israelites God's chosen people.

There is also a supernatural reason that the Jews are hated. In the providence and design of God, the people of this race have been designated the custodians of His written Word. The Bible has come to us through them. God chose them for that. They transmitted the Scriptures. Satan hates them because they have been the repository of the Scriptures and because the Lord Jesus Christ, after the flesh, came from them—as Paul put it: "Whose are the fathers, and of whom as concerning the flesh Christ came . . ." (Rom. 9:5). There is no way of escaping the fact that there is a supernatural hatred of them, in part because Jesus was born a Jew. This is certainly clear in Scripture. And we know that God has chosen the Jewish race as His people, as His nation. Several years ago a wag wrote the following words on a bulletin board:

> It is odd
> That God
> Should choose
> The Jew.

A Jew came and wrote underneath it:

> God chose,
> Which shows
> God knew
> His Jew.

A Christian came along and wrote beneath that:

> This Jew
> Spoke true.
> God knew
> His Jew

As King
Would bring
To earth
New birth.

God chose them for that purpose, and because of that they are hated. They are hated by Satan, and as a result the nations of the world are fanned into fury at times against these people.

There is, by the way, a very subtle form of anti-Semitism in our midst today: Denying that all of the promises made to the nation Israel by God will be fulfilled. A very eminent scholar said to me recently, "I do not like your Judaistic eschatology." He also used another term for it, namely "Scofieldism." He continued, "I do not like this idea that God has yet to deal with the nation of Israel." I told him that I consider that the very heart of the Bible. Then I asked him what he did with the promises made to Israel. He said, "They are for the church." Immediately I asked, "What about the curses that were pronounced on the nation Israel?" "Well," he said, "I don't worry with those." Never yet have I found anyone who takes the promises away from Israel that ever takes the curses also! They always leave the curses for the Jews. Beloved, they have the curses, but they have the promises too.

Here is one of the promises concerning the Jews:

Thus saith the LORD, which giveth the sun for a light by day, and the ordinances of the moon and of the stars for a light by night, which divideth the sea when the waves thereof roar; The LORD of hosts is his name: If those ordinances depart from before me, saith the LORD, then the seed of Israel also shall cease from being a nation before me for ever (Jer. 31:35,36).

Think of that! God says that if you can blot the sun out of the sky, if you can wipe the moon out of existence, then you can get rid of the nation of Israel. But as long as the sun shines and the moon is in the heavens, God says that He is not through with these people. They are His chosen instrument.

Had it not been for God's faithfulness to His promises, these people would have been obliterated from the face of the earth at the time of Queen Esther. God ever stands in the shadows, keeping watch over His own.

· 21 ·

For Such a Time as This

Esther, Chapter 4

When Mordecai perceived all that was done,
Mordecai rent his clothes, and put on sackcloth
with ashes, and went out into the midst of the
city, and cried with a loud and a bitter cry; and
came even before the king's gate: for none might
enter into the king's gate clothed with sackcloth.
And in every province, whithersoever the king's
commandment and his decree came, there was
great mourning among the Jews, and fasting, and
weeping, and wailing; and many lay in sackcloth
and ashes.

So Esther's maids and her chamberlains came
and told it her. Then was the queen exceedingly
grieved; and she sent raiment to clothe Mordecai,
and to take away his sackcloth from him, but he
received it not. Then called Esther for Hatach, one
of the king's chamberlains, whom he had
appointed to attend upon her, and gave him a
commandment to Mordecai, to know what it was,

and why it was. So Hatach went forth to Mordecai unto the street of the city, which was before the king's gate. And Mordecai told him of all that had happened unto him, and of the sum of the money that Haman had promised to pay to the king's treasuries for the Jews, to destroy them. Also he gave him the copy of the writing of the decree that was given at Shushan to destroy them, to shew it unto Esther, and to declare it unto her, and to charge her that she should go in unto the king, to make supplication unto him, and to make request before him for her people. And Hatach came and told Esther the words of Mordecai.

Again Esther spoke unto Hatach, and gave him commandment unto Mordecai; All the king's servants, and the people of the king's provinces, do know, that whosoever, whether man or woman, shall come unto the king into the inner court, who is not called, there is one law of his to put him to death, except such to whom the king shall hold out the golden sceptre, that he may live: but I have not been called to come in unto the king these thirty days. And they told to Mordecai Esther's words. Then Mordecai commanded to answer Esther, Think not with thyself that thou shalt escape in the king's house, more than all the Jews. For if thou altogether holdest thy peace at this time, then shall there enlargement and deliverance arise to the Jews from another place; but thou and thy father's house shall be destroyed: and who knoweth whether thou art come to the kingdom for such a time as this?

Then Esther bade them return to Mordecai this

answer, Go, gather together all the Jews that are present in Shushan, and fast ye for me, and neither eat nor drink three days, night or day: I also and my maidens will fast likewise; and so will I go in unto the king, which is not according to the law: and if I perish, I perish. So Mordecai went his way, and did according to all that Esther had commanded him.

Chapter 4 of Esther opens with the reaction of Mordecai to what had happened, along with the reaction in every province. "And in every province, whithersoever the king's commandment and his decree came, there was great mourning among the Jews, and fasting, and weeping, and wailing; and many lay in sackcloth and ashes" (4:3). Do you notice that there was no call to prayer? These people were out of the will of God. As was said earlier, the decree of Cyrus, prophesied by Isaiah, had permitted them to return to Israel, but these folk did not return. They were out of God's will, and consequently they made no call to prayer whatsoever. Yet they went through the remainder of the ritual: fasting, putting on the sackcloth and ashes, and mourning greatly.

The Jews *believed* the decree that had gone out from Ahasuerus. It was the law of the Medes and the Persians, which was unalterable according to these historical books and also according to the Book of Daniel. And you remember that even Xerxes himself, when he had put aside his beautiful queen Vashti, could never take her again because the decree had been made that she was to come no more before the king. Even he could not change his own law after it had been made.

So when this decree of death came throughout the empire, the Jews believed it and mourned in sackcloth and ashes.

It is a strange and sad commentary upon the human race that, although from the throne of God, there had to come a decree to this world that "All have sinned, and come short of the glory of God" (Rom. 3:23) and "The wages of sin is death" (Rom. 6:23), there are those today who treat this as if it were not true at all. The average person you meet on the street will tell you that he does not believe this. How foolish it would have been if the Jews in that day had not believed that the decree of death would be enforced. Yet almighty God says that ". . . death passed upon all men, for that all have sinned" (Rom. 5:12). He also says, "It is appointed unto men once to die, but after this the judgment" (Heb. 9:27).

Conspicuously absent today (and the church, I think, is responsible) is conviction concerning sin—not only in the hearts and lives of the unsaved but also in the hearts and lives of believers. The average believer says, "Yes, I trust Christ," but he has no real conviction of sin in his life at all. It is absent in contemporary church life. When is the last time you heard a sinner, either a saved sinner or a lost sinner, cry out to God for mercy? At the beginning of my ministry I used to see a great many tears, and I used to see people cry out to God. I do not see that today. Even in evangelistic crusades there is a great deal of "coming forward," but there is that lack of weeping over sin in the lives of folk. Why? They just don't believe God means it. They do not believe that sin merits punishment. They do not believe that God intends to enforce judgment against sin and against the sinner who holds to it and will not turn to Christ.

Mordecai knew and believed the seriousness of the decree. "When Mordecai perceived all that was done, Mordecai rent his clothes, and put on sackcloth with ashes, and went out into the midst of the city, and cried with a loud and bitter cry" (4:1).

However, Esther, living in safety and seclusion in the queen's quarters, knew nothing of the decree. She did not realize what was taking place until her maids and her chamberlains came to tell her that her cousin Mordecai was in sackcloth and ashes. Perhaps she thought, *That's not a very nice way to show his appreciation for my getting him this very excellent position as judge—by mourning in sackcloth and ashes!*

". . . Then was the queen exceedingly grieved; and she sent raiment to clothe Mordecai, and to take away his sackcloth from him: but he received it not" (4:4). She thought, *I don't know what the trouble is, but I'm going to send him some colorful clothes.* She sent a sporty new suit, something very ornate. But he turned it away. Why? Because it wasn't new clothes that he needed. Esther, secure in the palace, thought that all in the world Mordecai needed was a new suit of clothes to make him take off the sackcloth and ashes. But gaudy clothes could not destroy the terrible edict of death. Mordecai did not regard the clothes as having any part in the grave crisis, so he refused them.

Today there are a great many folk who are wearing gaudy garments. They refuse to believe that we are all sinners, although God has declared that we are. They reach out for any garment that might hide from them the reality of sin.

The fact of the matter is, there are those today who take the position that sin is actually only a mistake or an error. There is one word in the Bible for that, *hamartano*, meaning "to miss the mark." It means, actually, to take an arrow, put it in a bow, pull it back, let the arrow fly, but come short of the bull's-eye. A great many people today think that is the extent of sin. It is just to miss the mark. It is a mistake, an error. You just say, "Pardon me," and go on. That's all in the world that sin is, and God has no right to hold us responsible for our mistakes. If we say, "Pardon me," He ought to say, "I pardon you." And that ends it.

There are also those today who take that position and think all the human family needs is reformation. There are a great many religions today—a great many cults—that go in for reformation. As I write, members of the Hollywood movie colony are falling over each other to get to these Indian gurus. They go to them because they are trying to find some program whereby they can improve themselves, reform themselves, or change themselves. They argue that sinning man has only blundered and needs nothing but the gaudy garments of a few reformation programs. Oh, for the understanding of Mordecai! He knew that only the garments of sackcloth and ashes are proper raiment when facing the reality of sin.

There is another type of garment in which people take refuge: education. In the 1920s that was the method. Shaler Matthews, who in that day was connected with the University of Chicago's School of Religion, gave this definition of sin: "Sin is the backward pull of an outworn good." Think that one over for a while. Take away the modifiers and what you have left is "Sin is good." Some readers can remember the twenties, when it was taught that all we had to do was educate folk. If we would educate them right, we would get rid of this thing called sin, since it was nothing but selfishness.

I had such an experience when a Christian day school was begun in the church where I served as pastor. The principal came into my study one day and said, "Dr. McGee, I have a case that I don't know what to do with."

I asked, "What in the world is it?"

"Well," she said, "a mother from one of the liberal churches has brought over a child. She wants to get him out of the public school and into a Christian school, but apparently she has misunderstood what a Christian school is."

The mother had talked to the principal in the presence of the child. When she came to the word *sin* she did not pronounce it; instead she spelled it out. The same thing occurred when she came to the word D-e-v-i-l. She insisted that she did not want the little fellow to hear those words, as they belonged to the Dark Ages.

The principal asked me what she should do. I said, "Well, I think I'd tell the mother that it's better for the little boy to find out about s-i-n and D-e-v-i-l in a Christian day school than to find out about them written on the back fence in an alley. I don't think that is the best way to be educated. If she thinks that her little Willy is going to grow up in this world without knowing what sin is and who the Devil is, then she certainly is living in a dream world herself and needs to move into a world of reality."

We need more than education. People cannot be educated away from sin. Right now some of the biggest sinners abroad are carrying Ph.D. degrees.

There are those who have attempted to define sin as ignorance. That is, since people don't know the way and must find the way, they must "discover" God. There is a great deal of that going on right now. People are attempting to discover God. When I was speaking in the San Francisco Bay area several months ago, a young man told me one evening, "I have been interested in what you have had to say tonight because I am trying to discover God. I heard that you were over here, and I thought I might get a new angle."

"Did you get a new angle tonight?" I asked him.

"Yes, I got a new angle."

And that is about all he got, because he was attempting to *find* a way. People become religious today because of that. They say they are turning to God.

I have come to the conclusion that the increase in church membership after World War II was merely an escape mechanism for a great many folk. It was like a life insurance policy; joining the church was an escape from God. You may say to me, "That is strange reasoning." I don't think so. People found that if they joined the church, they became insulated from any type of evangelism. If anyone asked them if they were a Christian, they could immediately say, "I'm a Presbyterian," or "I'm a Methodist," or "I'm a Baptist," or "I'm a member of such-and-such a church." You can be all of that and not be saved, my beloved. These are garments that people have attempted to put on— gaudy garments—but they do not cancel the edict that has gone out from the throne of God that we are all sinners and that sin must be dealt with.

Although the great difference between liberal and conservative theology has been on the doctrine of the Lord Jesus Christ and His deity, the final test is attitude toward sin. Let a person tell you what he or she thinks about sin, and you know what that person thinks about Christ. Because of the impact and influence of liberalism, many people have lost a consciousness of sin. The average definition of a Christian today is one who lives a respectable life in the community and stays out of jail. (By this definition the apostle Paul would not qualify because he saw the jails from the inside throughout the Roman Empire!) No, just to be moralists does not mean that we are Christians. All have sinned; all stand in His presence as lost sinners.

Samuel Johnson, England's great literary critic of the eighteenth century, made this observation: "Every man knows that of himself which he dares not tell his dearest friend." Goethe, the German author, said: "I never read of a crime that has been committed but that I, too, might have committed." Remember this: You and I have the same kind of nature as every other individual walking the face of the earth. "But," you say, "I would not commit that crime!" Of course you would not, but do you know why? It is because of the grace of God. We are all sinners in the sight of God. That is His condemnation. And no one has anything to present to God for salvation.

Others complain, "You always emphasize that we are all sinners." The reason I emphasize that fact is because I find that it is not being emphasized in our society. A young man in my own congregation once was very resentful. In fact, he was angry.

"Dr. McGee," he said, "I resent your saying that we

all are sinners. I take it that you are referring to my mother as a sinner."

"Yes," I said, "you inferred correctly."

"Well," he said, "I want you to know that I have the loveliest mother, the most wonderful mother . . ." and tears rolled down the boy's cheeks. "My mother is not a sinner."

"Have you ever stopped to think about this," I replied. "David thought a great deal of his mother, but in Psalm 51:5 David said, 'In sin did my mother conceive me.' Have you turned that over in your mind?" He turned and walked out.

All of us have sinned and come short of the glory of God. This morning a beautiful young lady came to my associate pastor and demanded, "Why is Dr. McGee so negative? Why does he emphasize our being sinners?" She did not like it. "Why doesn't he talk about the good and the beautiful? Why does he emphasize sin?" She agreed to have an interview with the pastor, and I hope she will find that the reason I emphasize sin is that sin is common to the human family and that she is a sinner and needs a Savior.

Some folk ask me, "Are people worse today than they were years ago?" Frankly, I do not think so. There is not more sin in the world today, there is just no consciousness of sin so that sin is out in the open. A man on television the other night frankly said that he was a homosexual. Twenty years ago, that man never would have opened his mouth on that subject. You see, what used to be done in the back yard is now done in the front yard. What used to be done undercover is now being done out in the open. People have been sinners right down through the ages, but it is the consciousness of sin that we have lost today.

Mordecai could have put on the gaudy garments Esther sent to him and ignored the decree that had gone out, but that would not have changed the fact that he was a Jew and that on a certain date he was to die. He and the rest of the Jews would have been absolutely stupid not to believe it.

The gaudy garments of religion or reformation or education will not cover our nakedness before the holy presence of God. The fig leaves were not adequate for our first parents; they had to be clothed with that which God provided. Not only will Christ forgive our sins, but He will clothe us in the robe of His righteousness, giving us an eternal standing before God (see Rev. 19:8). Do not take the garments which the world offers. Only the robe of righteousness can cover your sin before a holy and just God.

Mordecai sends a message back to Queen Esther saying to her in effect, "The reason that I'm in sackcloth and ashes is that our people, you and I, have come under an awful decree of death." And Esther sends back a message to him to this effect, "That's too bad. I'm sorry to hear it. I didn't know about it before." And she adds, ". . . but I have not been called to come in unto the king these thirty days" (4:11). That is to say, "I do not know his attitude toward me—and you know what the law is."

As was the case in every kingdom of that day, anyone who dared go into the presence of the king without being summoned would be summarily and automatically put to death, unless the king extended his sceptre to him. Ahasuerus was noted for his fits of temper; he could have put his queen to death if she had gone in without being called. So Esther sends word back to Mordecai, "If I go in, it may mean death to me." Then Mordecai returns to her this memorable message: ". . . Think not with thyself that thou shalt escape in the king's house, more than all the Jews" (4:13). "Just because you happen to be the queen does not exempt you from the execution, because it will reach every Jew in the kingdom, and it'll reach the queen."

Mordecai goes on to say, "For if thou altogether holdest thy peace at this time, then shall there enlargement and deliverance arise to the Jews from another place . . ." (4:14). Someday when I see Mordecai (and I do expect to see him), I'd like to ask him what he had in mind when he said that deliverance would arise from another place. I've thought this over, and I ask you the question: What other place was there to which they could turn? Where could deliverance have come to them except from God? He was their only hope at this time, and I'm confident that Mordecai had that in mind when he said, "If *you* don't move, then deliverance will come from another place." God would move in another direction. Mordecai must have known that deliverance would come because he was acquainted with the promises that God had made to Abraham. So he challenges his cousin, ". . . who knoweth whether thou art come to the kingdom for such a time as this?" (4:14).

We begin to see God by His providence moving now in the affairs of the nation. It is obvious that Esther did not accidentally win the beauty contest. She was not accidentally the one who became queen. She was in her position for a very definite purpose, and God had been arranging this all the time. "Who knoweth whether thou art come to the kingdom for such a time as this?" What a challenge was given to this young woman, and God used her. If she had not moved, God would have moved in a different direction. But she was placed there for a purpose.

Have you ever noticed how the hand of God has moved in the affairs of this world and that "at such a time as this" God has brought certain ones to the kingdom? Let me remind you of several. Abraham was called of God in a day when the whole world seemed to be departing from God as it had in the days of Noah. God called this man to move out, and through him He brought the Savior into the world. He came to the kingdom for such a time as that. Moses was a man who stood in the gap. He was the one God raised up at a particular time to be the deliverer of his people. Then there was David. While Saul, Satan's man, was plunging the nation into sin and idolatry, God was training a shepherd boy to be the king. David came to the kingdom for such a time as that.

John the Baptist, a solo voice crying in the wilderness, the first voice lifted in God's behalf after a silence of four hundred years, was called to the kingdom for such a time as that.

Saul of Tarsus was a brilliant young man who hated Christ and the church, but God all the time was training him, for he was to come to the kingdom for such a time.

Luther, Calvin, John Knox, John Wesley were raised up by God. Lloyd George said that Wesley was the greatest man who ever lived. He made the greatest contribution to England. These were men whom God raised up.

Let's move to the secular realm. I noticed in World

War II that God seemed to be moving. Can you re-member the day when Hitler was coming to power? Can you remember when he was having victory after victory, and he overran France? He was moving into Russia; he was moving through North Africa. But God raised up a Christian general by the name of Mont-gomery. He is the one who started the wave that halted the progress of this awful Nazi horde. Isn't it interesting that God also raised up in the Far East General Douglas MacArthur at the right time?

Isn't it interesting that God has *not* raised up a man in this day? That ought to make America come alert. During my entire ministry I have been looking for God to raise up somebody to lead America back to God. The first time Billy Graham ever spoke in Los Angeles, I said, "Maybe this is the man." Now God has used him marvelously, but Billy himself says he has not seen revival. I'm wondering if somewhere God may be training some young boy, some young man. Wouldn't it be wonderful if God would raise up some young person today through whom He could bring real re-vival to America?

You may say, "You're a premillennialist, and you believe the apostasy is on us, so it's impossible to have a revival!" Nothing is impossible with God. I believe that God, by His providence, could be training and bringing up someone for such a time as this.

Oh, beloved, this is an hour when God's people must pray that He will set apart a man for clear and powerful leadership in a revival, for revival will come through a human instrument. Ask God for this man.

Naturally, some are going to say, "Yes, but you are speaking of great folk. We are little people, and God does not move in our affairs like that." Oh, but you can be great in prayer and faithful in giving out the Word in your small sphere. Think of the Scottish minister (whose name we do not even know) who gave his report to the elders at the end of one year. They had prayer and great heart-searching and concluded that the year had been a complete failure. There had been only one conversion: wee Bobby Moffat. Can you imagine having the privilege of humbly leading to Christ such a man as Robert Moffat, the great missionary to Africa? That was the greatest work for God that minister ever did; yet he confessed it as his greatest failure.

God moves strangely in the affairs of this world. Let us take a hypothetical case in examining ourselves with reference to this fact. You may be a young person who has heard a soul-stirring message by a missionary from the mountains of Kentucky. Perhaps you are much impressed; you feel the call of God to go to Kentucky, while the person sitting next to you is not interested. Suppose in those mountains there is a little boy who, in the economy of God, is going to be President of these United States. Suppose you refuse the call of God and stay home instead. Suppose that little fellow grows up, becomes a godless young man, and when he is elected to the presidency of the United States, he brings this nation to destruction and defeat. I ask you, without answering the question, because I don't know the answer: Who is responsible? Too few of us are concerned about fitting our lives into God's great plan and purpose. "Thou art come to the kingdom for such a time as this."

Watch Esther. She is a queen now, every inch a

queen. She says simply, ". . . if I perish, I perish" (4:16). What a statement! How noble she becomes.

Her statement reminds us of Another who said, "For even the Son of man came not to be ministered unto, but to minister, and to give his life a ransom for many" (Mark 10:45). Christ also said, ". . . I lay down my life, that I might take it again. No man taketh it from me, but I lay it down of myself. I have power to lay it down, and I have power to take it again . . ." (John 10:17,18). This One came to our earth; He gave His life a ransom for many. He came from heaven's glory to perish—to die upon the cross so that you and I might be saved.

During the Civil War the last and the bloodiest battle occurred when Grant surrounded Richmond. The two armies moved back and forth over the battlements all day long. At times it looked as if the boys in gray would win, and then all odds seemed to be in favor of the boys in blue. The battlefield was strewn with the wounded, the dying, the dead. In the intense heat of the afternoon the cry began to go up, "Water . . . water . . . water." Finally, a young lieutenant could stand it no longer, and he went to his commanding officer for permission to carry water to those men. He filled his canteen from the canteens of the others around him, and he crawled across the battlefield between the firing lines. He went first to one man and then to another giving them water. Finally the boys in blue as well as the boys in gray saw him. The commanders on both sides called for a halt, there was a cease-fire, and a shout went up from both sides as this young lieutenant went from man to man bringing water.

That was a brave act.

Beloved, there is One more noble than that. He vaulted the battlements of heaven, came down to earth, and took upon Himself our human flesh. He didn't say, "If I perish, I perish." He said, "I came to *give* my life a ransom for many."

· 22 ·

When a King Could Not Sleep

Esther, Chapters 5:1-6:4

Now it came to pass on the third day, that
Esther put on her royal apparel, and stood in the
inner court of the king's house, over against the
king's house: and the king sat upon his royal
throne in the royal house, over against the gate of
the house. And it was so, when the king saw
Esther the queen standing in the court, that she
obtained favour in his sight: and the king held out
to Esther the golden sceptre that was in his hand.
So Esther drew near, and touched the top of the
sceptre. Then said the king unto her, What wilt
thou, Queen Esther? and what is thy request? it
shall be even given thee to the half of the kingdom. And Esther answered, If it seem good unto
the king, let the king and Haman come this day
unto the banquet that I have prepared for him.
Then the king said, Cause Haman to make haste,
that he may do as Esther hath said. So the king
and Haman came to the banquet that Esther had
prepared.

And the king said unto Esther at the banquet of wine, What is thy petition? and it shall be granted thee: and what is thy request? even to the half of the kingdom it shall be performed. Then answered Esther, and said, My petition and my request is; If I have found favour in the sight of the king, and if it please the king to grant my petition, and to perform my request, let the king and Haman come to the banquet that I shall prepare for them, and I will do to-morrow as the king hath said.

Then went Haman forth that day joyful and with a glad heart: but when Haman saw Mordecai in the king's gate, that he stood not up, nor moved for him, he was full of indignation against Mordecai. Nevertheless Haman refrained himself: and when he came home, he sent and called for his friends, and Zeresh his wife. And Haman told them of the glory of his riches, and the multitude of his children, and all the things wherein the king had promoted him, and how he had advanced him above the princes and servants of the king. Haman said moreover, Yea, Esther the queen did let no man come in with the king unto the banquet that she had prepared but myself; and to-morrow am I invited unto her also with the king. Yet all this availeth me nothing, so long as I see Mordecai the Jew sitting at the king's gate.

Then said Zeresh his wife and all his friends unto him, Let a gallows be made of fifty cubits high, and to-morrow speak thou unto the king that Mordecai may be hanged thereon: then go thou in merrily with the king unto the banquet. And the thing pleased Haman; and he caused the gallows to be made.

On that night could not the king sleep, and he commanded to bring the book of records of the chronicles; and they were read before the king. And it was found written, that Mordecai had told of Bigthana and Teresh, two of the king's chamberlains, the keepers of the door, who sought to lay hand on the king Ahasuerus. And the king said, What honour and dignity hath been done to Mordecai for this? Then said the king's servants that ministered unto him, There is nothing done for him.

And the king said, Who is in the court? Now Haman was come into the outward court of the king's house, to speak unto the king to hang Mordecai on the gallows that he had prepared for him.

Picking up the narrative where the preceding chapter ended, we see that the brave Queen Esther agreed that, for the sake of her people, she would go into the presence of the king to plead for them. You understand that when she entered the beauty contest Mordecai had instructed her not to tell anything about her nationality—that she was a Jewess. Her race was still unknown to the king when he signed the decree, having been paid a large sum of money by Haman to exterminate the Jews in the kingdom of Persia. And of course, practically all of the Jews were in that kingdom in that day so that it would have meant the total extermination of these people. Esther's mission was a most important one.

The custom of the day was that no one could come into the presence of the king unless the king asked for him or her. If a person dared to come into his presence uninvited, and he did not extend to him or her his sceptre, it would mean death. Ahasuerus did not even have to move. If he simply sat without lifting his sceptre, the person who had entered would be taken out and summarily executed with neither trial nor questions asked. The king was supreme, of course.

Notice that in this hour of crisis Esther did not ask that her people be in prayer. She asked for the Jews to fast (4:16), but she did not mention prayer. After all, they were out of the will of God, and God's name is not even mentioned in this book. But God is standing in the shadows here, keeping watch over His own. This is my reason for believing that the purpose of this book in the canon of Scripture is to teach the providence of God. The hand of God is in the glove of history. Though men may neither recognize Him nor acknowledge Him, He is moving in the affairs of the world.

Esther turned to preparing herself for appearing before the king. You will remember that the first time she had come before the king and had won the beauty contest, she had required none of the fine clothing or elaborate accessories that the other contestants had used. By her natural beauty she had won, and the king had fallen in love with her. But this time I'm sure that she spent a great deal of time on her dress. We are told that "Esther put on her royal apparel" (5:1), which meant that she put on the finest that she had. It meant that she looked the best that she could. In fact, if I may use the language of the street, she knocked the king's eye out! I tell you, she was lovely.

"And it was so, when the king saw Esther the queen standing in the court, that she obtained favour in his

sight: and the king held out to Esther the golden sceptre that was in his hand. So Esther drew near, and
touched the top of the sceptre" (5:2).

When she steps into that royal court and waits—it is
certainly a dramatic moment—the king looks at her.
Will he raise the sceptre or will he not? In this moment
I'm confident this Hebrew girl prays, although there is
no record of it. She must recognize how helpless and
hopeless she really is. Then the king holds out the
golden sceptre to her, and possibly smiles. She ad-
vances and places her hand on the sceptre, as was the
custom of the day.

What a picture we have here! In this book I have
been emphasizing the law of the Medes and Persians
and comparing their law to the law of God. God's law
says, "The soul that sinneth, it shall die" (Ezek. 18:20).
God has never changed that. It is as true now as it ever
was that the soul that sins shall die. That's God's law.
It is immutable. He cannot change that without changing His character.

There is another side to the story. Just as the king
held out the sceptre to Queen Esther, our God holds
out the sceptre to humanity today. It is true that "All
have sinned and come short of the glory of God"
(Rom. 3:23). It is true we are "dead in trespasses and
sins" (Eph. 2:1). It is true that "The soul that sinneth, it
shall die." But our God overcame that tremendous
law, and the only way in the world He could overcome
it was for Him to come to this earth Himself, take upon
Himself our sins, and pay that penalty. The law was
not abrogated, and it is not abrogated today. When
God saves you, it is because Somebody else paid the
penalty for your sins. Jesus died a substitutionary

death upon that cross for you and me. As a result of that, God holds out to the earth the sceptre of grace, and He says to an individual, "You can come to Me. You can touch that sceptre of grace. You can receive from Me salvation because I am reconciled to you."

When Adam sinned in the Garden of Eden, he lost his fellowship with God. I do not mean to be irreverent, but I think God lost more than Adam lost. God lost His fellowship also with this creature whom He evidently had created for fellowship. They were together at the beginning; God came down and had fellowship with Adam. Then Adam rebelled against God and sinned. When Adam sinned, he turned his back on God, and a holy God must turn His back on a sinner.

But when Christ died on the cross, God turned around. Paul said to the Corinthian believers, "We are ambassadors for Christ" (2 Cor. 5:20), and you never have an ambassador unless there is peace between the two countries. The embassy is closed when there is war, and the ambassador goes home. God is not at war with this world today. Let me paraphrase what Paul said: "We are His ambassadors down here, and we are saying, 'Be ye reconciled to God' " (2 Cor. 5:20).

The gospel is simply this: God is favorable; His sceptre of grace is extended to you, and He's asking you simply to turn around. Will you turn around? God holds out the sceptre of grace to a lost world. The message of His ambassador is, "Be ye reconciled to God." Notice that you don't have to reconcile God; He is already reconciled. That happened when Christ died on the cross.

When Esther comes into the presence of the king, he

recognizes immediately that she never would have been so bold if an emergency had not arisen. Notice how he speaks to her: "Then said the king unto her, What wilt thou, queen Esther? and what is thy request?" (5:3). He uses the expression "It shall be even given thee to the half of the kingdom" (5:3). This is no idle expression. He means that he sees she is greatly distressed, and he wants to make her feel comfortable. So he puts into her hand a blank check. "Whatever your request is, up to half the kingdom, it's yours. You fill out the check."

"And Esther answered, If it seem good unto the king, let the king and Haman come this day unto the banquet that I have prepared for him" (5:4). This is a remarkable verse in several respects. Notice a technical detail that may be important. As you have seen, the name of God is not in the Book of Esther, but this verse in the Hebrew forms an acrostic, and that acrostic is the name of God, which is quite interesting indeed. There are those who believe it was put here for that very reason. I do not know.

The verse also tells us something about Esther. This girl did not make her request known at first. She wanted Haman present when she let the king know that what he had demanded was not only the death of the Jews but her death also. "Then the king said, Cause Haman to make haste, that he may do as Esther hath said. . ." (5:5). In other words, "You tell Haman that Esther has invited us to dinner and that he is to come." And notice: "That he may do as Esther hath said."

The feeling of the king is evident here. He had been very generous to Haman. He had made him prime

minister; he had given him his ring; he had let him
send out the edict to slay the Jews; but when the
comparison was made with Queen Esther, Haman had
to obey her. Esther was queen, and she was in a very
favorable light indeed.

". . . So the king and Haman came to the banquet
that Esther had prepared" (5:5). At the banquet Esther
obviously is anxious, so that Ahasuerus can see that
something is troubling her a great deal. "And the king
said unto Esther at the banquet of wine, What is thy
petition? and it shall be granted thee: and what is thy
request? even to the half of the kingdom it shall be
performed" (5:6). As we have seen, this idiomatic expression means Esther can have anything she wants.
You would think this carte blanche put in her hand
would encourage her to say what is on her heart. But
she is still anxious. Esther's anxiety is only more evidence that the Jews are far from God; yet God by His
providence is overruling. So notice how gingerly she
moves.

"Then answered Esther, and said, My petition and
my request is; If I have found favour in the sight of the
king, and if it please the king to grant my petition, and
to perform my request, let the king and Haman come
to the banquet that I shall prepare for them, and I will
do to-morrow as the king hath said" (5:7,8). Esther
does not have the courage yet to express her request,
so she says, "I'm making another banquet tomorrow.
We have had only a smorgasbord today, but come
back tomorrow and I'll prepare a real banquet. Then
I'll let you know my request." You can see the fear that
is in the heart of this girl.

"Then went Haman forth that day joyful and with a

glad heart. . ." We really get acquainted with Haman now. ". . . but when Haman saw Mordecai in the king's gate, that he stood not up, nor moved for him, he was full of indignation against Mordecai" (5:9). This man Haman comes out from the banquet pleased with himself that only *he* has been the guest of the king and queen (you'll hear him brag in a moment). His ego has been greatly expanded. As he leaves the palace all the functionaries of the kingdom are there, and they all bow before him—except one, Mordecai the judge, who stands erect. You would think that a man in the position of Haman would ignore a little thing like that, but he is not ignoring anything. He is full of indignation against Mordecai and only restrains himself by thinking, *Well, I'll get even with you in a few days!*

". . . and when he came home, he sent and called for his friends, and Zeresh his wife" (5:10). Listen to Haman. "And Haman told them of the glory of his riches, and the multitude of his children . . ." (5:11). (Have you ever noticed that when a man starts bragging, he will tell you how much money he has made and about what fine children he has? Those are the two things a man of the world will brag about. And here was the man of the world, Haman.) ". . . and all the things wherein the king had promoted him, and how he had advanced him above the princes and servants of the king. Haman said moreover, Yea, Esther the queen did let no man come in with the king unto the banquet that she had prepared but myself; and tomorrow am I invited unto her also with the king" (5:11,12).

Listen to him brag! There is a Greek proverb that says, "Whom the gods would destroy they first make mad." This was the position of Haman exactly. Or, as the Scriptures put it, "Pride goeth before destruction, and an haughty spirit before a fall" (Prov. 16:18).

This fellow Haman, walking up and down bragging, calling in his friends, telling them how rich he is, telling about his children, then telling about the important position he holds—does he sound like anyone you know? Unfortunately, sometimes you hear Christians bragging like this, and they ought not.

Haman boasts, "And just think of it—I had lunch today with the queen, and not only that, I'm having dinner there tomorrow night." Well, he doesn't know what is in store for him. He would do well to turn down *that* invitation, but not this man.

There is, however, a fly in the ointment. He adds, "Yet all this availeth me nothing, so long as I see Mordecai the Jew sitting at the king's gate" (5:13). *"He won't bow to me!"* Someone has said that you can always tell the size of a man by the things that irritate him. If little things irritate him, he is a little man. If it takes big things to irritate him, he is a big man.

My friend, what bothers you? Do little things annoy you? In the church today how many people say, "Mrs. Jones didn't speak to me today" or "I was at the morning service and the minister looked right at me, but later he did not shake my hand; I feel so miserable about it." Don't let insignificant things mar your life. That is the mark of littleness. Yet most of us must confess that it is the small things, the "little foxes that spoil the vines" as far as our own lives are concerned.

Haman revealed himself to be a little man. After all, Mordecai was only a judge, a petty judge, in the kingdom. Haman was prime minister. He could have ignored the fellow! But not Haman. "All this availeth me nothing, so long as I see Mordecai the Jew sitting at the king's gate" (5:13).

Haman's "lovely" wife offered a solution. "Then said Zeresh his wife and all his friends unto him, Let a gallows be made of fifty cubits high, and to-morrow speak thou unto the king that Mordecai may be hanged thereon: then go thou in merrily with the king unto the banquet. And the thing pleased Haman; and he caused the gallows to be made" (5:14).

Late that evening workmen constructed a gallows fifty cubits high (that's about seventy-five feet). Think of that! Consider it in light of the meaning of the name *Mordecai*. It means "little man"—Mordecai was a short fellow. To erect a gallows seventy-five feet high on which to hang a short fellow reveals the extent of the resentment, the hatred, and the bitterness in Haman's heart. So with his happy solution he went to bed.

Night came, which brings us to the most fateful night, the most eventful night in the history of the Medo-Persian Empire, the night which is the turning point of the Book of Esther. That night the king could not sleep. It was a little thing, you may say, a trivial incident. Most of us have missed a night's sleep at one time or another.

Have you noticed that God uses the little things to carry out His program? At one time God brought together a woman's heart and a baby's cry to change the destiny of a people. That baby's cry was what drew Pharaoh's daughter to the water's edge. As she looked down into the puckered face of the baby alone in the basket, her woman's heart went out to him. She took Moses and reared him as her own. God used a baby's cry.

Coming to the New Testament, we find examples of God's use of little things. On Easter we talk at length about the tomb being sealed and the stone rolled away, but do you know the greatest proof of the resurrection of Jesus Christ? It was the evidence that convinced Peter and John. They saw the linen wrappings lying flat. The body of Jesus had been prepared for burial like a mummy, wrapped around and around with a linen cloth and sealed with myrrh. The apostles knew Jesus could not get out unless He was unwound, but He was out—and there remained the grave clothes, still wound. They saw and they believed! God used the simple medium of grave clothes to prove the resurrection of Jesus.

A supposedly unimportant situation developed at the palace of Shushan: the king could not sleep. "On that night could not the king sleep, and he commanded to bring the book of records of the chronicles; and they were read before the king" (6:1). This proved to be an epochal night in that kingdom; the fatal hour had come, and the hand of God was moving. The king had insomnia, I suspect. After all, in his position the sword of Damocles was over his head all the time. As it has been said, "Uneasy lies the head that wears the crown" as well as "A good conscience is a luxury that only a righteous man can enjoy."

Ahasuerus, we happen to know from secular history, was not a righteous man. When he couldn't sleep that night, he wasn't able to call for an array of sleeping pills or tranquilizers like we have today, but he did have something to induce sleep which apparently he had used before. It was the book of records of the chronicles, that is, the detailed records of the kingdom. A servant was summoned to drone off this record, which was like a log or the minutes of the kingdom.

I do not mean to be unlovely, but to me the most boring thing in the world is to listen to minutes. Have you ever heard any minutes that were interesting? I never have. I've been on mission boards, I've been on church boards, I've been on all kinds of boards, and I've gotten off every board I can get off. You know why? I don't like to listen to minutes. They're boring. I can understand that this king went to sleep many a night with them being read to him. "Bring them in. Let's read them again."

On that particular night the reader happened to turn. . . . Did I say "happened" to turn? Yes, from his viewpoint. If you had been there with this servant and said, "Do you know that you turned to the right page?" he would have answered, "I don't know anything about that. I just opened the book, and I'm going to begin reading right here." But the hand of God was moving, because what he read began a chain of reactions that changed the course of history. Here it is: "And it was found written, that Mordecai had told of Bigthana and Teresh, two of the king's chamberlains, the keepers of the door, who sought to lay hand on the king Ahasuerus" (6:2).

Talk about the Mafia—these two fellows had belonged to the Mafia of that day. Mordecai had overheard them plotting, the kind of plotting that we always think of in connection with the Persian Empire: shadowy figures behind pillars, talking in low tones of how, when the king comes in, they'll put a dagger in him. Mordecai had passed that word on to Queen Esther, and Queen Esther had notified the king. The

incident was entered in the records of the kingdom.
When the chamberlain read this, the king was alerted,
and he rose up in bed. He said, "By the way, you
didn't read there—or I must have missed it—was this
man Mordecai rewarded?" The servant looked down,
read the next set of minutes, and said, "No, he was
never rewarded." The king said, "The man who saved
my life must be rewarded!"

At that moment there is a noise outside the king's
chambers—a gate opening and closing, and someone coming in. "And the king said, Who is in the
court? . . ." Somebody else can not sleep this night.
". . . Now Haman was come into the outer court of the
king's house, to speak unto the king to hang Mordecai
on the gallows that he had prepared for him" (6:4).
Haman's appearance is no accident. The providence of
God is moving in that kingdom as the providence of
God moves in the lives and hearts of many today.

One evening a young man attended a service where
I was preaching. He held the doubtful distinction of
being a most successful gambler at the Las Vegas casi-
nos. His wife had left him and had taken the children
with her. He did not know where they were, and it
was breaking his heart. On this particular evening he
had come to our city and was eating at a restaurant
where one of our church members was having dinner.
Seeing this young man and sensing that he was in
deep sorrow of some nature, she ventured over and
quietly sat down beside him. During the conversation
she extended an invitation to our evening worship. He
accepted and sat at the rear of the church. At the close
of the service when we asked those who wished to
accept Christ to come forward, he was one of the

number who came. He had come to the church that
night by the providence of God, and the sceptre of
grace was extended to him.

Out of the long ago comes this story of Esther. It
speaks to our twentieth century of the sceptre of grace
that is extended to a lost world. People today are
sinners; people today deserve the judgment of God;
people today are dead in trespasses and sins. But
people today can come to God on one basis alone, by
receiving Christ who said, ". . . I am the way, the
truth, and the life: no man cometh unto the Father, but
by me" (John 14:6).

· 23 ·

The Man Who Came to Dinner
but Died on the Gallows

Esther, Chapters 6:4–7:10

And the king said, Who is in the court? Now
Haman was come into the outward court of the
king's house, to speak unto the king to hang Mordecai on the gallows that he had prepared for him.
And the king's servants said unto him, Behold,
Haman standeth in the court. And the king said,
Let him come in. So Haman came in. And the king
said unto him, What shall be done unto the man
whom the king delighteth to honour? Now Haman thought in his heart, To whom would the
king delight to do honour more than to myself?
And Haman answered the king, For the man
whom the king delighteth to honour, let the royal
apparel be brought which the king useth to wear,
and the horse that the king rideth upon, and the
crown royal which is set upon his head: and let
this apparel and horse be delivered to the hand of
one of the king's most noble princes, that they
may array the man withal whom the king delighteth to honour, and bring him on horseback

through the street of the city, and proclaim before
him, Thus shall it be done to the man whom the
king delighteth to honour. Then the king said to
Haman, Make haste, and take the apparel and the
horse, as thou hast said, and do even so to Mordecai the Jew, that sitteth at the king's gate: let
nothing fail of all that thou hast spoken. Then
took Haman the apparel and the horse, and
arrayed Mordecai, and brought him on horseback
through the street of the city, and proclaimed
before him, Thus shall it be done unto the man
whom the king delighteth to honour.

And Mordecai came again to the king's gate.
But Haman hastened to his house mourning, and
having his head covered. And Haman told Zeresh
his wife and all his friends every thing that had
befallen him. Then said his wise men and Zeresh
his wife unto him, If Mordecai be of the seed of
the Jews, before whom thou hast begun to fall,
thou shalt not prevail against him, but shalt surely
fall before him. And while they were yet talking
with him, came the king's chamberlains, and
hasted to bring Haman unto the banquet that
Esther had prepared.

So the king and Haman came to banquet with
Esther the queen. And the king said again unto
Esther on the second day at the banquet of wine,
What is thy petition, queen Esther? and it shall be
granted thee: and what is thy request? and it shall
be performed, even to the half of the kingdom.
Then Esther the queen answered and said, If I
have found favour in thy sight, O king, and if it
please the king, let my life be given me at my
petition, and my people at my request: For we are

sold, I and my people, to be destroyed, to be slain, and to perish. But if we had been sold for bondmen and bondwomen, I had held my tongue, although the enemy could not countervail the king's damage.

Then the king Ahasuerus answered and said unto Esther the queen, Who is he, and where is he, that durst presume in his heart to do so? And Esther said, The adversary and enemy is this wicked Haman. Then Haman was afraid before the king and the queen.

And the king arising from the banquet of wine in his wrath went into the palace garden: and Haman stood up to make request for his life to Esther the queen; for he saw that there was evil determined against him by the king. Then the king returned out of the palace garden into the place of the banquet of wine; and Haman was fallen upon the bed whereon Esther was. Then said the king, Will he force the queen also before me in the house? As the word went out of the king's mouth, they covered Haman's face. And Harbonah, one of the chamberlains, said before the king, Behold also, the gallows fifty cubits high, which Haman had made for Mordecai, who had spoken good for the king, standeth in the house of Haman. Then the king said, Hang him thereon. So they hanged Haman on the gallows that he had prepared for Mordecai. Then was the king's wrath pacified.

Early morning had come to the palace at Shushan, but sleep had not come to the king. There was another man also who had not slept that night, but for a different reason. You will recall that the king had been listening to the chronicles of his kingdom being read, hoping it would put him to sleep. But the servant had turned to the section that recorded the service Mordecai had performed in discovering the plot to put the king to death. The king, who was probably half asleep until he heard this, asked, ". . . What honour and dignity hath been done to Mordecai for this? Then said the king's servants that ministered unto him, There is nothing done for him" (6:3).

At that moment Haman is heard coming into the outer court. The king wants to know who has come so early. "And the king said, Who is in the court? Now Haman was come into the outward court of the king's house, to speak unto the king to hang Mordecai on the gallows that he had prepared for him" (6:4). The king is informed that it is Haman, and Haman comes in. Apparently he has entrée to the king at any time. When he comes in, the king brings him into the conversation without giving him any background. Haman has come to ask for the life of Mordecai at the same moment the king is preparing to reward Mordecai!·

These circumstances continue to reveal the providence of God. In the shadows God is keeping watch over His own. Although these people were out of the will of God, in the land far away from where God wanted them, they were still not out from under His direct leading. These providential dealings could not have been accidental.

When Haman walks in he is greeted with the question, ". . . What shall be done unto the man whom the king delighteth to honour? Now Haman thought in his heart, To whom would the king delight to do honour

more than to myself?" (6:6). After all, Haman has been
made prime minister. He has been given the ring of
the king. He has paid the king a handsome sum of
money in order to exterminate the Jewish people, *in
toto*. Certainly, there is no one else in the kingdom that
Haman can think of that the king would delight to
honor.

The true nature of this man is revealed in his
answer. "And Haman answered the king, For the man
whom the king delighteth to honour, let the royal
apparel be brought which the king useth to wear, and
the horse that the king rideth upon, and the crown
royal which is set upon his head: and let this apparel
and horse be delivered to the hand of one of the king's
most noble princes, that they may array the man withal whom the king delighteth to honour, and bring him
on horseback through the street of the city, and proclaim before him, Thus shall it be done to the man
whom the king delighteth to honour" (6:7–9). I am
sure you can see what is in the heart of Haman. Haman has his eye upon the throne. It is his intention,
when the time is right, to eliminate the king; he wants
to destroy him.

That was the story of the Persian monarchs, anyway. It was difficult for a man to stay on the throne
very long. In Israel's history, as recorded in First and
Second Kings, if it were not tragic it would be humor-
ous to see how short a time some of the kings ruled.
Some of them only made it through two months. If a
king reigned as long as ten years in the northern kingdom, he was doing well. And when the king sat on his
throne and looked around him, he didn't know who
was his friend and who was his enemy. He realized

that any man who was lifted up would attempt to slay him in order that he might become king.

Obviously such designs were in the heart of Haman. He was thinking, *To whom would the king delight to do honor more than to myself? You let me have the apparel of the king, put the crown on my head, let me ride the king's horse, let it be announced by a herald when I go through the streets.* What was Haman doing? He was preparing the people for the day when the crown and the royal apparel would be his. Surely Ahasuerus suspected this type of scheming, for he recognized that this man was thinking of himself and certainly not of Mordecai.

"Then the king said to Haman, Make haste, and take the apparel and the horse, as thou hast said, and do even so to Mordecai the Jew, that sitteth at the king's gate: let nothing fail of all that thou hast spoken" (6:10). For Haman, the decree was mortification beyond words. "Then took Haman the apparel and the horse, and arrayed Mordecai, and brought him on horseback through the street of the city, and proclaimed before him, Thus shall it be done unto the man whom the king delighteth to honour" (6:11). The humiliation of Haman was absolutely unspeakable. You can imagine the feeling that he had as he led the horse through the street with Mordecai—the man who wouldn't bow to him—seated on it, when Haman had at home a gallows seventy-five feet high on which to hang him!

Finally the ordeal was over. "And Mordecai came again to the king's gate. But Haman hastened to his house mourning, and having his head covered" (6:12). Shame beyond shame. "And Haman told Zeresh his wife and all his friends every thing that had befallen him. Then said his wise men and Zeresh his wife unto him, If Mordecai be of the seed of the Jews, before whom thou hast begun to fall, thou shalt not prevail against him, but shalt surely fall before him" (6:13). What comforting friends to have around, and how nice to have a wife like this, who tells you that prob-ably tomorrow will be your last day! "And while they were yet talking with him, came the king's chamber-lains, and hasted to bring Haman unto the banquet that Esther had prepared" (6:14). Things began to hap-pen thick and fast. This man Haman no sooner arrived home and explained to his wife and his wise men what had happened and they cautioned him, than there was a knock at the door. The king's servants told him to hurry. The banquet was ready that he had promised to attend. Haman had looked forward to this, you re-member. He had boasted about the fact that he was the only one whom the queen had invited to attend her banquet with the king. As was said earlier, this is an illustration of the Proverb: "Pride goeth before de-struction, and an haughty spirit before a fall" (Prov, 16:18).

Esther has, if I may use the expression, screwed up her courage, after the second day, to tell what is on her heart. She could not bring herself to do it earlier, but the time has come.

"So the king and Haman came to banquet with Esther the queen. And the king said again unto Esther on the second day at the banquet of wine, What is thy petition, queen Esther? and it shall be granted thee; and what is thy request? and it shall be performed, even to the half of the kingdom" (7:1,2). For the third time Ahasuerus says to his lovely queen, "You may ask what's on your mind. Tell me because I will grant your request."

Now she is going to speak. It is a frightful thing that Esther reveals, and there are two startled men there that day because neither knows her nationality. As you remember, when Mordecai, her cousin, entered her in the beauty contest, and also when she became queen, he instructed her not to tell her nationality. Esther kept this fact to herself all this time. When Haman sent out the edict that all the Jews in the kingdom are to be destroyed, he had no idea that the queen was a Jewess.

"Then Esther the queen answered and said, If I have found favour in thy sight, O king, and if it please the king, let my life be given me at my petition, and my people at my request" (7:3). Esther finally identifies herself with her people. Once so far removed from God that she did not even want to be known as a Jewess, she finally takes her place with her people. For her to do so is to identify herself with her religion and with her God.

Her plea is eloquent. "For we are sold, I and my people, to be destroyed, to be slain, and to perish . . ." (7:4). Those are the exact words used in the proclamation that went out over the king's signature. " . . . But if we had been sold for bondmen and bondwomen, I had held my tongue, although the enemy could not countervail the king's damage" (7:4). In other words, Esther is saying, "Although the king would have suffered a great loss, I would have kept quiet if we were just going to be sold into slavery. But that isn't the case. We are to be *slain* on a certain day."

"Then the king Ahasuerus answered and said unto

Esther the queen, Who is he, and where is he, that durst presume in his heart to do so?" (7:5). Ahasuerus is startled. He is amazed. He does not dream that there is any such thing as that taking place in his kingdom. He apparently does not recognize even yet the people who are to be slain.

This only reiterated what little regard this man had for life. If you read the secular account of Xerxes' campaign which he made into Europe against Greece, you will find that he threw men about as if they all were expendable. He lost thousands and thousands of men in that campaign, but he was not disturbed one bit. Human life was very cheap in that day.

What disturbs Ahasuerus is that they are the people of Esther and that his queen is in mortal danger. He truly is asking a question, for he does not know "Who is he, and where is he, who would presume in his heart to do so?"

Remember that the man is Haman, who is there at the table, reclining on a couch. He is the prime minister, and he had the full confidence of the king. A similar situation would be going to the President of the United States to accuse the Secretary of State of some great crime against the President's wife.

Ahasuerus asks who the man is, and Esther reveals her bravery to the fullest. She is putting her life on the line by speaking the truth. "And Esther said, The adversary and enemy is this wicked Haman. Then Haman was afraid before the king and the queen" (7:6). Haman himself had not realized the extent of the decree that he has obtained against the Jews. He knew it included Mordecai, but he did not realize that it included Queen Esther! He is startled.

The king is so shocked at what he has heard that he cannot speak. "And the king arising from the banquet of wine in his wrath went into the palace garden . . ." (7:7). The sudden turn of events is so puzzling his head is swimming, and he has to go out and think his way through the sequence of events. *How in the world has it happened that a decree has gone out over my signature to slay my own queen?* he must have thought. *How could a thing like this happen in my kingdom?* After all, Ahasuerus is ultimately responsible for that decree. And so he goes out to think the matter over.

Haman is in a bad spot. ". . . and Haman stood up to make request for his life to Esther the queen; for he saw that there was evil determined against him by the king" (7:7). He begins to plead with Queen Esther, for he knows she is his only hope.

Haman, when he hears her accusation, leaps to his feet and begins pleading for his life. Seeing that he is getting nowhere, he grovels at her feet, then pulls himself up on her couch (you recall that the custom was to recline on couches while dining).

As we have noted, it is interesting that Herodotus, the Greek historian, recorded that when Xerxes returned after his defeat in the Greek campaign, the new queen whom he married was very vindictive and cold. If he was referring to Queen Esther it would be understandable that to the outside world and to the historian she would appear vindictive and cold in this situation. Haman was punished justly—but fearfully—for the thing that he had done.

"Then the king returned out of the palace garden into the place of the banquet of wine; and Haman was fallen upon the couch whereon Esther was . . ." (7:8).

Haman, coward that he is, is clawing in terror at her couch. The man is beside himself with fear. When the king comes in and sees the high sort of indignity that is taking place, he says, "Will he force the queen also before me in the house?"

This man's fate is sealed when the king sees that spectacle. " . . . As the word went out of the king's mouth, they covered Haman's face" (7:8).

Notice that Ahasuerus did not have to issue an order at all. He simply walked in, saw what was taking place, made the statement, and the servants who were standing there knew what to do. They took Haman out. Not only was he placed under palace guard and under house arrest, but he was executed that night—because the king happened to be the "Supreme Court" also. "And Harbonah, one of the chamberlains, said before the king, Behold also, the gallows fifty cubits high, which Haman had made for Mordecai, who had spoken good for the king, standeth in the house of Haman. Then the king said, Hang him thereon. So they hanged Haman on the gallows that he had prepared for Mordecai. Then was the king's wrath pacified" (7:9,10).

This is a revelation of a great truth that runs all the way through the Word of God. Paul annunciated it for believers, "Be not deceived; God is not mocked: for whatsoever a man soweth, that shall he also reap" (Gal. 6:7). Is it not interesting that the very gallows that Haman had prepared to hang an innocent man on was the gallows on which he was hanged?

You remember that Ahab was told by Elijah the prophet that right where the dogs licked the blood of Naboth, whom he brutally and cruelly murdered, there the dogs would lick his blood (see 1 Kin. 21:19). Ahab thought, *Well, I'll stay away from that place!* And he did. But after he was mortally wounded in battle, that is where his chariot was brought. The record says that one washed his chariot and his armor in the pool of Samaria and the dogs licked up his blood (see 1 Kin. 22:38).

Jacob experienced similar retribution. He deceived his father (see Gen. 27:1–29). Oh, he was a clever boy. He put on Esau's clothes; old Isaac smelled them and said, "It smells just like my son Esau." They had no lovely deodorants in that day, so when Esau came in, even if you didn't hear him, your other senses told you he had arrived. Jacob put goatskin on his hands, and blind old Isaac reached out and said, "It feels like Esau." Jacob thought he was clever. He was God's man, but God did not let him get by with sin. Years later, when he was old and the father of twelve sons, they brought to him the coat of many colors dipped in the blood of a goat (see Gen. 37:31–35). They said, "Is this your son's coat?" Old Jacob broke down and wept. He in turn was deceived about his favorite son.

This is an inexorable law of God. I believe it operates today as it has always operated, and it will operate in any field. Whatsoever a person sows, he'll reap. When you sow cotton, you reap cotton. When you sow corn, you reap corn. "For he that soweth to his flesh shall of the flesh reap corruption; but he that soweth to the Spirit shall of the Spirit reap life everlasting" (Gal. 6:8).

Paul knew a great deal about the operation of this law in his own experience. He was the man who apparently gave the orders for the stoning of Stephen (see Acts 7:57–8:1). They put their clothes at his feet, which indicates that he was in charge. But Paul didn't get by with it. You may say, "Well, he was converted. He came to Christ and his sins were forgiven." Yes, they were forgiven, but chickens always come home to roost. Whatever a man sows will be harvested. And Paul's seed did come up. On his first missionary journey he went into the Galatian country and came to Lystra, where the people stoned him and left him for dead (see Acts 14:19,20). I believe he *was* dead, and that's the reason they left him. God raised him from the dead, but Paul experienced the truth of these words: "Whatsoever a man soweth, that shall he also reap." God is not mocked.

Haman experienced the same thing. He learned this law the hard way. Here was a man who went to dinner and found out it was a necktie party. They hanged him!

May I call your attention to two Scriptures as we conclude this chapter. The first passage is a general statement.

> I have seen the wicked in great power, and spreading himself like a green bay tree. Yet he passed away, and, lo, he was not: yea, I sought him, but he could not be found (Ps. 37:35,36).

Do you remember Adolph Hitler? I heard a Presbyterian preacher in Texas years ago say, even when Hitler was going great guns, "When the time comes, God will stop him." He did. It's interesting: Mussolini, Stalin—consider any one of them—"Yet he passed away, and lo, he was not: yea, I sought him, but he could not be found."

Now the second verse of Scripture is one of the

greatest statements in the Word of God concerning the nation Israel. It is found in Isaiah's prophecy.

> No weapon that is formed against thee shall prosper; and every tongue that shall rise against thee in judgment thou shalt condemn. This is the heritage of the servants of the LORD, and their righteousness is of me, saith the LORD (Is. 54:17).

That is a tremendous statement!

Haman died on that cursed gallows because there was no one to die for him. Let us go forward in history for a moment, when there was another man in prison. His name was Barabbas, and he was condemned to die. They already had made a cross for him to die on. He waited that long night through, knowing the next morning he was to be crucified. In the morning he heard the jailer coming, and he heard the clank of the keys. He heard him turn the key in his cell door and that old door creak open. He mustered his courage, for he knew his time had come. The jailer came in and said to Barabbas, "You are free!"

"What do you mean 'You're free'?" Barabbas asked. "What are you trying to do—amuse yourself with me? Ridicule me? I'm to die."

"No, you're not to die."

"Well, why am I not to die?"

"Because last night a Man was arrested, and this morning they found Him guilty. Pilate wanted to let Him go. He offered to release Him, and he gave the people a choice: 'Jesus or Barabbas?' The crowd said, 'Release Barabbas.' Jesus is going to die on your cross, Barabbas." I do not know this, but I assume this is how it was.

Although the record does not say, I think Barabbas went out to Calvary that day, looked up, and said, "That's my cross. That is where I deserve to die." And I like to think that he found out, as the centurion found and as the thief found that the One dying there did not deserve to die (see Luke 23:39–47). Not only that, but He was dying for another. He was the Son of man who ". . . came not to be ministered unto, but to minister, and to give His life a ransom for many" (Matt. 20:28). At least Barabbas knew that Somebody else died for him. Haman had no one to die for him.

You and I stand guilty before God as sinners. We deserve exactly the condemnation of Haman. You may say, "I never committed a crime like that." Who said you did? But you have the same kind of human nature that he had, which is in rebellion against God and which is opposed to God. In that state, while you were dead in trespasses and sins, Christ died for you and took your place on the cross. That cross not only was Barabbas' cross, it was my cross, and it was your cross, if you'll have it that way and will trust Him. He died in our stead.

· 24 ·

The Message of Hope That Went Out From the King

Esther, Chapter 8

On that day did the king Ahasuerus give the house of Haman the Jews' enemy unto Esther the queen. And Mordecai came before the king; for Esther had told what he was unto her. And the king took off his ring, which he had taken from Haman, and gave it unto Mordecai. And Esther set Mordecai over the house of Haman.

And Esther spake yet again before the king, and fell down at his feet, and besought him with tears to put away the mischief of Haman the Agagite, and his device that he had devised against the Jews. Then the king held out the golden sceptre toward Esther. So Esther arose, and stood before the king, and said, If it please the king, and if I have found favour in his sight, and the thing seem right before the king, and I be pleasing in his eyes, let it be written to reverse the letters devised by Haman the son of Hammedatha the Agagite, which he wrote to destroy the Jews which are in all the king's provinces: for how can I endure to see the evil that shall come unto my people? or how can I endure to see the destruction of my kindred?

Then the king Ahasuerus said unto Esther the queen and to Mordecai the Jew, Behold, I have given Esther the house of Haman, and him they have hanged upon the gallows, because he laid his hand upon the Jews. Write ye also for the Jews, as it liketh you, in the king's name, and seal it with the king's ring: for the writing which is written in the king's name, and sealed with the king's ring, may no man reverse. Then were the king's scribes called at that time in the third month, that is, the month Sivan, on the three and twentieth day thereof; and it was written according to all that Mordecai commanded unto the Jews, and to the lieutenants, and the deputies and rulers of the provinces which are from India unto Ethiopia, an hundred twenty and seven provinces, unto every province according to the writing thereof, and unto every people after their language, and to the Jews according to their writing, and according to their language. And he wrote in the king Ahasuerus' name, and sealed it with the king's ring, and sent letters by posts on horseback, and riders on mules, camels, and young dromedaries: wherein the king granted the Jews which were in every city to gather themselves together, and to stand for their life, to destroy, to slay, and to cause to perish, all the power of the people and province that would assault them, both little ones and women, and to take the spoil of them for a prey, upon one day in all the provinces of king Ahasuerus, namely, upon the thirteenth day of the twelfth month, which is the month Adar. The copy of the writing for a commandment to be given in every province was published unto all people, and that the Jews should be ready against that day to avenge themselves on their enemies. So the posts that rode upon mules and camels went out, being hastened and pressed on by the king's commandment. And the decree was given at Shushan the palace.

And Mordecai went out from the presence of the king in royal apparel of blue and white, and with a great crown of gold, and with a garment of fine linen and purple: and the city of Shushan rejoiced and was glad. The Jews had light, and gladness, and joy, and honour. And in every province, and in every city, whithersoever the king's commandment and his decree came, the Jews had joy and gladness, a feast and a good day. And many of the people of the land became Jews; for the fear of the Jews fell upon them.

Our study closed in the previous chapter with the judgment pronounced upon Haman and the execution of that judgment. Additionally, Queen Esther was given power over all of Haman's household, who might do her or her people harm. That, however, did not alter the decree that had gone out against the Jews. The decree still stood: On a certain day the Jews in the 127 provinces, all the way from India to Ethiopia, were to be destroyed. This included even the remnant who had returned to the Promised Land. That small remnant was struggling to rebuild the walls, the city, and the temple in Jerusalem; no doubt their enemies were awaiting eagerly the day when the decree would be effective. There was to be a great slaughter: the destruction of the Jews throughout the empire.

". . . And Mordecai came before the king; for Esther had told what he was unto her. And the king took off his ring, which he had taken from Haman, and gave it unto Mordecai. And Esther set Mordecai over the house of Haman" (8:1,2). For the first time Esther let it be known that Mordecai was her adoptive father—Mordecai, the man whose refusal to bow to Haman had occasioned this terrible decree.

Evidently Ahasuerus was quite free with the use of his ring. It was a powerful and important ring. It could be pressed down into wax to seal a law that would destroy people. The ring passed on to Mordecai was the ring Ahasuerus had entrusted to Haman when Haman was prime minister. The ring came to be in good hands, but it tells us something about Ahasuerus, that he was very careless in passing his power around.

"And Esther spake yet again before the king, and fell down at his feet, and besought him with tears to put away the mischief of Haman the Agagite, and his device that he had devised against the Jews" (8:3). When Queen Esther realized for the first time that Haman's decree could not be altered, she made a plea for her people and cried for help. But the solution wasn't as simple as she had thought. The king could not sit down and cancel the previous order.

It was impossible to change the decree. Even the king could not change it. According to the law of the Medes and the Persians, Ahasuerus must bow to his own law. We had seen this already in reference to his first queen, Vashti. When he made the decree to set her aside, then later wanted to take her back, the decree said he could not. Even the king could not break his own decree, and he was powerless to change the decree concerning the destruction of the Jews.

So Queen Esther tried a different strategy. She came into the king's presence, and he was gracious once again and extended to her his golden sceptre. Then Esther said, "If it please the king, and if I have found favour in his sight, and the thing seem right before the king, and I be pleasing in his eyes, let it be written to reverse the letters devised by Haman the son of Hammedatha the Agagite, which he wrote to destroy the Jews which are in all the king's provinces: For how can I endure to see the evil that shall come unto my people? or how can I endure to see the destruction of my kindred?" (8:5,6).

Esther made it quite plain to the king that the judgment against Haman was of no avail unless her people were rescued as well. Something had to be done to save them.

"Then the king Ahasuerus said unto Esther the queen and to Mordecai the Jew, Behold, I have given Esther the house of Haman, and him they have hanged upon the gallows, because he laid his hand upon the Jews" (8:7). The king had given to Esther and to Mordecai the house of Haman, but that was still no solution to the decree of death.

Finally Ahasuerus shrugged his shoulders and said, "Write ye also for the Jews, as it liketh you, in the king's name, and seal it with the king's ring: for the writing which is written in the king's name, and sealed with the king's ring, may no man reverse" (8:8).

With that, Mordecai went into action. He could not revoke the day of slaughter for his people, but he could send out a new order, and the new order permitted the Jews to defend themselves. Under the first order, the Jews could no more have defended themselves than they could have in Hitler's gas chambers. They would have been slaughtered like animals. But under the new decree they were permitted to defend themselves.

Additionally, the government declared their support of the Jews. We read, "And all the rulers of the provinces, and the lieutenants, and the deputies, and officers of the king, helped the Jews; because the fear of Mordecai fell upon them" (9:3). The entire power of the king, as evidenced by his army and his officers, aligned themselves on the side of the Jews. That changed the entire picture. When this new decree came to the different provinces, we're told "The Jews had light, and gladness, and joy, and honour" (8:16). The first decree also had brought sadness to a great many people other than the Jews, as was the case in Nazi Germany. There were a great many German people who were saddened by the gas chambers and embarrassed by them. Many have shown evidences of real repentance since then; but at the time they could do little in the face of Hitler's decrees. Nothing was done for the Jew at that time; neither could anything be done in the time of Esther until this new decree was made.

As we read this record, we can imagine the sequence of events. It must have been late in the evening that Queen Esther went again into the presence of the king to plead for her people. Then the new decree was written and was signed with the king's ring. "Mordecai went out from the presence of the king in royal apparel of blue and white, and with a great crown of gold, and with a garment of fine linen and purple:

and the city of Shushan rejoiced and was glad" (8:15).

The royal apparel Mordecai donned certainly was different from the sackcloth and ashes he had worn only a short time earlier. His appearance in the city undoubtedly reinforced the joy produced by the king's new decree. Notice the contrast between the two decrees: Haman's decree produced sorrow, but Mordecai's decree produced joy.

Persia was a polyglot kingdom—many languages were spoken. To spread the word, amanuenses had to be summoned to write the decree in the languages of the 127 provinces, and probably there were hundreds of copies for each language.

"And he wrote in the king Ahasuerus' name, and sealed it with the king's ring, and sent letters by posts on horseback, and riders on mules, camels, and young dromedaries: Wherein the king granted the Jews which were in every city to gather themselves together, and to stand for their life, to destroy, to slay, and to cause to perish, all the power of the people and province that would assault them, both little ones and women, and to take the spoil of them for a prey,

"Upon one day in all the provinces of king Ahasuerus, namely, upon the thirteenth day of the twelfth month, which is the month Adar" (8:10–12).

The kingdom employed all the means of communication common to that day. Haste was of the essence. If the Jews heard the new decree—and believed it—they would be saved. Heralds were sent on horseback, on mules, on camels, and on dromedaries—across the Arabian Desert, up the Euphrates and Tigris rivers, down into India, and even into Africa. The heralds were riding in every direction, getting the decree out as quickly as possible to every village and hamlet in the kingdom. Because the original decree could not be altered in any way, another decree was made and sent out just as the first one was. It was signed by the king, and the entire power of the king was now on the side of the Jews.

One can picture easily the scene in any one of these little towns. The Jews, garbed in sackcloth and ashes, were hopeless and full of despair. They had been marked out and kept under the constant derision of their enemies, who doubtless were reminding them of the approaching day of their destruction. But then a rider appeared on the horizon, the first to arrive since the carrier who had born the decree of destruction. Quickly this rider approached the town bulletin board and nailed a notice there, then just as quickly mounted his steed again and was off. Everybody crowded around the bulletin board to see what was written. They read that the tables had been turned; the king was on the side of those people who formerly had been marked for death. He even urged them to band together and protect themselves. The Jews began to move gingerly into the crowd, hesitant because the last time they had gone to the bulletin board they were confronted with the terrible news that they were to be destroyed. Cautiously they came up; then as they began to read the message, they could not believe their eyes.

It was too glorious to be true! Something had happened, for now the king was on their side. They were to be spared, saved! What good news it was and what rejoicing there was among these people! The king was holding out the sceptre of grace to them. There was no longer judgment; there was grace.

· 25 ·

The Feast of Joy

Esther, Chapters 9 and 10

Now in the twelfth month, that is, the month
Adar, on the thirteenth day of the same, when the
king's commandment and his decree drew near to
be put in execution, in the day that the enemies of
the Jews hoped to have power over them, (though
it was turned to the contrary, that the Jews had
rule over them that hated them;) The Jews
gathered themselves together in their cities
throughout all the provinces of the king Ahasuerus, to lay hand on such as sought their hurt:
and no man could withstand them; for the fear of
them fell upon all people. And all the rulers of the
provinces, and the lieutenants, and the deputies,
and officers of the king, helped the Jews; because
the fear of Mordecai fell upon them. For Mordecai
was great in the king's house, and his fame went
out throughout all the provinces: for this man
Mordecai waxed greater and greater. Thus the
Jews smote all their enemies with the stroke of the

sword, and slaughter, and destruction, and did what they would unto those that hated them. And in Shushan the palace the Jews slew and destroyed five hundred men. And Parshandatha, and Dalphon, and Aspatha, and Poratha, and Adalia, and Aridatha, and Parmashta, and Arisai, and Aridai, and Vajezatha. The ten sons of Haman the son of Hammedatha, the enemy of the Jews, slew they; but on the spoil laid they not their hand. On that day the number of those that were slain in Shushan the palace was brought before the king.

And the king said unto Esther the queen, The Jews have slain and destroyed five hundred men in Shushan the palace, and the ten sons of Haman; what have they done in the rest of the king's provinces? now what is thy petition? and it shall be granted thee: or what is thy request further? and it shall be done. Then said Esther, If it please the king, let it be granted to the Jews which are in Shushan to do tomorrow also according unto this day's decree, and let Haman's ten sons be hanged upon the gallows. And the king commanded it so to be done: and the decree was given at Shushan; and they hanged Haman's ten sons. For the Jews that were in Shushan gathered themselves together on the fourteenth day also of the month Adar, and slew three hundred men at Shushan; but on the prey they laid not their hand. But the other Jews that were in the king's provinces gathered themselves together, and stood for their lives, and had rest from their enemies, and slew of their foes seventy and five thousand, but

they laid not their hands on the prey, On the
thirteenth day of the month Adar; and on the
fourteenth day of the same rested they, and made
it a day of feasting and gladness. But the Jews that
were at Shushan assembled together on the thirteenth day thereof, and on the fourteenth thereof;
and on the fifteenth day of the same they rested,
and made it a day of feasting and gladness. Therefore the Jews of the villages that dwelt in the
unwalled towns, made the fourteenth day of the
month Adar a day of gladness and feasting, and a
good day, and of sending portions one to another.

And Mordecai wrote these things, and sent letters unto all the Jews that were in all the provinces
of the king Ahasuerus, both nigh and far, to stablish this among them, that they should keep the
fourteenth day of the month Adar, and the fifteenth day of the same, yearly, as the days wherein the Jews rested from their enemies, and the
month which was turned unto them from sorrow
to joy, and from mourning into a good day: that
they should make them days of feasting and joy,
and of sending portions one to another, and gifts
to the poor. And the Jews undertook to do as they
had begun, and as Mordecai had written unto
them; because Haman the son of Hammedatha,
the Agagite, the enemy of all the Jews, had devised against the Jews to destroy them, and had
cast Pur, that is, the lot, to consume them, and to
destroy them; but when Esther came before the
king, he commanded by letters that his wicked
device, which he devised against the Jews, should
return upon his own head, and that he and his

sons should be hanged on the gallows. Wherefore they called these days Purim after the name of Pur. Therefore for all the words of this letter, and of that which they had seen concerning this matter, and which had come unto them, the Jews ordained, and took upon them, and upon their seed, and upon all such as joined themselves unto them, so as it should not fail, that they would keep these two days according to their writing, and according to their appointed time every year; and that these days should be remembered and kept throughout every generation, every family, every province, and every city; and that these days of Purim should not fail from among the Jews, nor the memorial of them perish from their seed. Then Esther the queen, the daughter of Abihail, and Mordecai the Jew, wrote with all authority, to confirm this second letter of Purim. And he sent the letters unto all the Jews, to the hundred twenty and seven provinces of the kingdom of Ahasuerus, with words of peace and truth, to confirm these days of Purim in their times appointed, according as Mordecai the Jew and Esther the queen had enjoined them, and as they had decreed for themselves and for their seed, the matters of the fastings and their cry. And the decree of Esther confirmed these matters of Purim; and it was written in the book.

And the king Ahasuerus laid a tribute upon the land, and. upon the isles of the sea. And all the acts of his power and of his might, and the declaration of the greatness of Mordecai, whereunto the king advanced him, are they not written in the

book of the chronicles of the kings of Media and
Persia? For Mordecai the Jew was next unto king
Ahasuerus, and great among the Jews, and
accepted of the multitude of his brethren, seeking
the wealth of his people, and speaking peace to all
his seed.

As we see in the ninth chapter of the Book of Esther,
the anti-Semitic element still tried to carry out their
nefarious plan. I'm of the opinion that very few of the
Jews were slain. (Scripture gives no evidence that they
were.) Instead, "the Jews smote all their enemies with
the stroke of the sword, and slaughter, and destruction, and did what they would unto those that hated
them" (9:5).

There are people who feel that it was brutal and
cruel for a court of law to sentence many of Hitler's
henchmen to prison, but those henchmen were rascals
of the first order. Their treatment of the Jews in con-
centration camps was absolutely inhuman. To many
people on the outside it did not look as if Hitler's men
should be treated with such harshness, but those who
knew the inside story knew that they were rewarded
with justice.

"And all the rulers of the provinces, and the lieutenants, and the deputies, and officers of the king,
helped the Jews; because the fear of Mordecai fell
upon them. For Mordecai was great in the king's
house, and his fame went out throughout all the provinces: for this man Mordecai waxed greater and greater" (9:3,4).

For once Mordecai, one of their own, was by the
side of the king. Haman, who would have put the

Jews to death, had been put to death. The very throne
that had once condemned the Jews protected them.

After this marvelous deliverance, a celebration was
instituted called the Feast of Purim. "And Mordecai
wrote these things, and sent letters unto all the Jews
that were in all the provinces of the king Ahasuerus,
both nigh and far, to stablish this among them, that
they should keep the fourteenth day of the month
Adar, and the fifteenth day of the same, yearly, as the
days wherein the Jews rested from their enemies, and
the month which was turned unto them from sorrow
to joy, and from mourning into a good day: that they
should make them days of feasting and joy, and of
sending portions one to another, and gifts to the poor"
(9:20–22).

The Jews still celebrate the Feast of Purim each year.
(Adar is the month of March). *Purim* comes from the
word *pur*, meaning "lots." Haman rolled the pur like
dice to determine the day of the Jews' execution. "Because Haman the son of Hammedatha, the Agagite,
the enemy of all the Jews, had devised against the
Jews to destroy them, and had cast Pur, that is, the lot,
to consume them, and to destroy them. . . . Wherefore they called these days Purim after the name of
Pur. Therefore for all the words of this letter, and of
that which they had seen concerning this matter, and
which had come unto them, the Jews ordained, and
took upon them, and upon their seed, and upon all
such as joined themselves unto them, so as it should
not fail, that they would keep these two days according to their writing, and according to their appointed
time every year" (9:24–27).

(Incidentally, the unnamed feast mentioned in the

fifth chapter of the Gospel of John could not be the Feast of Purim, as some hold, because the Jews were not required to go to Jerusalem for Purim, and no sacrifice was offered. Purim was celebrated throughout the empire of Persia.)

In our day the Feast of Purim still is commemorated by the Jews. The day preceding is the "Fast of Esther." On the first evening, the festival begins with a convocation in their synagogues, concluded by the reading of the Book of Esther. As the Scriptures are read, the listeners stamp on the floor whenever the name of Haman is mentioned, saying, "Let his name be blotted out. The name of the wicked will rot." And at the end of the reading they say, "Cursed be Haman; blessed be Mordecai!" Then the following morning they come to the synagogue again. The remainder of the festival is a time of rejoicing to celebrate the great fact that God has delivered them (they also include subsequent deliverances such as from the Nazi German atrocities) according to the promise that He made to Abraham. God said, "I will bless them that bless thee, and curse him that curseth thee . . ." (Gen. 12:3).

The Book of Esther concludes with this interesting sidelight in chapter 10: "And the king Ahasuerus laid a tribute upon the land, and upon the isles of the sea. And all the acts of his power and of his might, and the declaration of the greatness of Mordecai, whereunto the king advanced him, are they not written in the book of the chronicles of the kings of Media and Persia? For Mordecai the Jew was next unto king Ahasuerus, and great among the Jews, and accepted of the multitude of his brethren, seeking the wealth of his people, and speaking peace to all his seed (10:1–3).

Let us stop for a moment to think through the history of the world, noticing in particular the nations that have engaged in anti-Semitism and seeing where they are today. For example, consider the nations of Europe. During World War I people lamented the plight of "poor little Belgium." Do you want to know about poor little Belgium? It had instituted an awful siege of anti-Semitism. God says, "I will bless them that bless thee, and curse him that curseth thee." Look at Spain. Spain was the first nation to bring her flag into the Western Hemisphere. What happened to her greatness? Spain conducted the Inquisition. We think of the Spanish Inquisition as being against Protestants, but it was primarily against Jews. Spain lost her power. The Jews have attended the funeral of every nation that has attempted to destroy them. Babylon attempted it. Assyria attempted it. Egypt attempted it. And the glory of those nations lies in the dust. It would be well for our nation to take note of this fact.

In the end Ahasuerus celebrated the presence of the Jews in his own nation, and the Feast of Purim that the Jews celebrate each year sets forth that fact in a very vivid way.

As we conclude our study of the Book of Esther, let's draw a parallel. A decree has gone out from almighty God: "The soul that sinneth, it shall die . . ." (Ezek. 18:20). God has said also, "All have sinned, and come short of the glory of God" (Rom. 3:23). He says that the entire world stands before Him dead in trespasses and sins, waiting to be executed. He says that the world today is guilty and that the death penalty must prevail.

Now there are a great many softhearted and soft-
headed liberal theologians who have taken the position that God forgives sin simply because He is
bighearted, He has forgotten His law, He has changed
it, or He has become a weakling. Liberalism in this
century has depicted God as a senile old man sitting
on a cloud. He has no notion of carrying through any
kind of a decree that says, "The soul that sinneth, it
shall die." You hear sloppy teaching about God being
a God of "love." If the expression "God is dead"
means that the liberal god is dead, then I'll attend his
funeral. I'm glad he's dead. But the God of the Bible is
quite different. God has not changed—not one whit.
His decree about sin holds today one hundred per-
cent. The idea that we are getting by with sin is a lie.
We are getting by with nothing!

"Well," you may say, "it *looks* as if we are getting by
with it." The psalmist thought so too. He wrote (in
Psalm 73), "I was envious at the foolish, when I saw
the prosperity of the wicked. For there are no bands in
their death: but their strength is firm. They are not in
trouble as other men; neither are they plagued like
other men" (vv. 3–5). That disturbed him, and he
wondered about it. Then he said: "When I thought to
know this, it was too painful for me; until I went into
the sanctuary of God; then understood I their end"
(vv. 16,17). In other words, "In the temple I found out
that God has a whole lot of time on His hands, and He
doesn't have to move today or tomorrow, next week or
even next month. He has eternity out yonder ahead of
Him, and He moves according to His schedule. I
found out that the wicked finally are judged, that God
does deal with them."

I can remember (maybe you are old enough to remember, too) that when Hitler was going great guns, many people said, "Why doesn't God stop Hitler?" Where is Hitler today? God has plenty of time on His hands. He doesn't have to move today against the wicked, but His decree stands: "The soul that sinneth, it shall die."

However, this is not the end of the story. God has another decree that has gone out from heaven. That decree is: "For God so loved the world, that he gave his only begotten Son, that whosoever believeth in him should not perish . . ." because He bore the penalty (John 3:16). God cannot change His first decree, but He can send out another decree: a decree of grace that Another, His own Son, has paid the penalty for your sins and mine.

When God forgives today, He loves. Don't forget that He loves, but He loves in the context of the Cross. You do not find the love of God anywhere in this world but in the Cross of Christ.

You will not find God's love in nature. Within a block of my home, four teen-agers came careening down the street the other day, and their car, a little Volkswagen, went out of control. One of the passengers was killed; the others were rushed to the hospital. This world in which we live operates according to hard law. The law of gravity has not been repealed. None of God's laws have been repealed. But, thank God, the grace of God can reach down and save any sinner who will come in under the provision He has made. That is love.

That is good news. In fact, the literal meaning of the word *gospel* is "good news." The gospel, correctly interpreted, is good news for the human family. The gospel is defined for us by the apostle Paul in the fifteenth chapter of First Corinthians: "Moreover, brethren, I declare unto you the gospel which I preached unto you, which also ye have received, and wherein ye stand; by which also ye are saved . . ." (vv. 1,2). The gospel is what saves men today. The gospel is what Someone has done for us. The gospel is not a request on God's part for you and me to do something. On the contrary, the gospel is what He has done for us. Here is what Paul says the gospel is: "For I delivered unto you first of all that which I also received, how that Christ died for our sins according to the scriptures; and that he was buried, and that he rose again the third day according to the scriptures" (vv. 3,4). That is good news! That is what Christ has done for us. We may accept it and receive it now by faith, by faith alone.

Just as the throne of Ahasuerus protected the Jews when Esther and Mordecai interceded, the very throne of God protects us today. The apostle says, "Who shall lay any thing to the charge of God's elect? It is God that justifieth. Who is he that condemneth? It is Christ that died, yea rather, that is risen again, who is even at the right hand of God, who also maketh intercession for us" (Rom. 8:33,34). Notice how He justifies: (1) Christ died; (2) He is risen again; (3) He is even at the right hand of God; (4) He also makes intercession for us. These are the reasons no one can condemn a believer. How wonderful this is! Today there is a *Man* in the realms of glory—He knows exactly how you feel, and He knows exactly how I feel. And in that position He is interceding for us. How wonderful to know that we have Someone there for us. Things have changed for us sinners.

> Seeing then that we have a great high priest, that is passed into the heavens, Jesus the Son of God, let us hold fast our profession. For we have not an high priest which cannot be touched with the feeling of our infirmities; but was in all points tempted like as we are, yet without sin. Let us therefore come boldly unto the throne of grace, that we may obtain mercy, and find grace to help in time of need (Heb. 4:14–16).

Go back with me now to some little unknown village in one of the 127 provinces of the Persian empire. Possibly way out in the hinterland there was a community in which there were a few Jews. When they saw the decree, they looked at it and said, "We don't believe it," and paid no attention to the second decree of the king at all. I'm of the opinion that all of them perished. All they needed to do was to believe the king and act upon that belief in faith, and God would have delivered them.

Today God saves all sinners who will *act* upon the marvelous new decree of grace that He has sent out into the world: "Believe on the Lord Jesus Christ, and thou shalt be saved . . ." (Acts 16:31).

Let's look again at the theme of the Book of Esther: the providence of God. Although God's people in the days of Queen Esther had rejected Him, and He had withdrawn His name from them, they were not out of the reach of His providence. God preserved His people, and by His providence He still was gracious to them.

If you are a child of God, do not be led by God's

providence. Do not be like the horse that must be led forcibly by a bridle. Being led by His providence is the method He uses with those who rebel at being led. If you are His child, He wants to lead you directly. He says, "I will instruct thee and teach thee in the way which thou shalt go: I will guide thee with mine eye" (Ps. 32:8). This requires a blessed nearness to God if we are to have the guidance of His eye. God wants to direct us and touch our lives in an intimate way. But how many Christians are sensitive to the leading of the Holy Spirit in this day? God will not bring much pressure to bear, but when He makes just a little suggestion to you at the crossroads of life, are you too far from Him to know that He is indicating a certain pathway? You and I as believers should not be guided by the providence of God; we ought to be guided directly by the Spirit of God.

Yet even if we slip out from under God's *direct* dealings, we have not slipped out from under His *providential* dealings. God ever stands in the shadows, keeping watch over His own.